Praise for Peg Streep's *Daug.*
from an Unloving Mother an

A rare gem in the self-help genre, a book that eschews simplistic feel-good advice and offers specific and invaluable guidance, extensively supported by the science and beautifully illustrated with personal anecdotes. A moving portrayal of the challenges that face unloved daughters, written by one herself, with a step-by-step guided journey through the stages of growth that will help readers detox from their childhoods and mourn the loving mothers they never had. Highly recommended.

–Joseph Burgo, Ph.D., author of
The Narcissist You Know and *Why Do I Do That?*

A gifted science writer, Streep deftly weaves together rigorous research, personal experiences, and compassionate advice to not only help readers recognize how a childhood of abuse or neglect has affected them, but—with the help of deeply thoughtful exercises—she truly helps them heal and grow. *Daughter Detox* is a wise, insightful, and fiercely empathic gift to anyone recovering from the kinds of emotional wounds that are often hard to see, let alone soothe.

–Craig Malkin, Ph.D., author of *Rethinking Narcissism*

Daughter Detox is not a feel-good book. It is a frank, clear, and sobering wake-up call to all daughters of unloving mothers. Reclaiming your life will not be easy, but with the right amount of work, it is possible.

–Claire Dorotik-Nana, LMFT, on *Psych Central*

VERBAL ABUSE

PEG STREEP

VERBAL ABUSE

RECOGNIZING, DEALING, REACTING *and* RECOVERING

Ile D'Espoir Press

New York, New York

ISBN: 979-8-9872155-0-0 *Paperback*
ISBN: 979-8-9872155-1-7 *Ebook*
ISBN: 979-8-9872155-2-4 *Hardback*

Cover design by Berge Design
Cover images sourced from dreamstime.com

This book is thankfully dedicated to my readers, all of you who follow me on Facebook, and the women and men who answered the call for interviews. Without your willingness to share your stories, your decision to discuss your pain and struggle, and your thoughtful participation in open dialogue, my understanding of complex issues such as verbal abuse in all of its forms wouldn't have continued to grow and evolve on the daily. Without all of you, this would be a very different book.

And of course, to the best daughter in the world, once again.

Contents

Introduction

This book is about emotional pain and the ensuing damage. Because it is about words and not about bricks or cudgels, it may seem counterintuitive at first. But it is real. Words are more like bricks and cudgels than you might think.

The words hang in the air like a blast of scalding steam. Cruel, demeaning, critical, goading, or simply hateful, they seem as ephemeral as soap bubbles, but they still burn and burrow into your brain. The speaker leaves the room and there's silence, and no trace of the words remains, yet you feel beaten up and hurt. There are no bruises to show. There's no blood. Yet the image of the person saying the words—his or her face and body language—stays with you and turns up the volume of the words themselves. Later, much later, you wonder whether it happened at all. Perhaps you are too sensitive, you think to yourself, or maybe you deserved the tirade.

Sometimes, there are no words—just a wall of silence that chills you to the bone and makes you feel small and afraid as someone you care about disappears you from sight and you feel invisible. You plead, but there's nothing in response but a derisive gesture—a smirk, a glare, an eye roll—that makes you feel as though you are nothing.

The power of both the words and the silence—the essence of verbal abuse—depends on relationship. The more deeply connected you are to the abuser, the greater the damage and the deeper the effect. An insult hurled by a stranger delivers a momentary sting, but your life continues uninterrupted. The dude on the corner who calls you "fatso" and laughs, or the woman who looks you up and down, a smirk on her face, and then turns to her friend, whispers, and bursts out laughing. Or maybe you're in a Facebook group and someone says your post shows how dumb you are; yes, you'll react, but no real harm has been done. You might recall the incident or tell it to a friend or intimate, but in the scheme of things, it's not important.

Verbal abuse affects us most deeply in intimate settings; the closer the connection, the more lasting the emotional and psychological damage done to us.

* * *

This book grew out of the many interactions I've had with readers via email and on Facebook on the subject of unloving mothers and toxic childhoods over the last decade; the interactions number in the many thousands by now. It's been informed by the readers' comments at PsychologyToday.com, where I've written a handful of pieces about verbal abuse that have been read by more than three million people. It's been shaped by the experiences of hundreds of readers who filled out questionnaires or left comments and by a trove of scientific research. Finally, it's been inspired by my recognition that we aren't engaging in the kind of dialogue we should be having about verbal abuse.

If there's one insight that has emerged from my work over the years, it is how slow most individuals are to recognize verbally abusive treatment by an intimate, which includes mothers, fathers, siblings, other relatives, spouses, lovers, and friends. In the case of mothers, the subject I've written about most extensively, the pace of recognition is downright glacial. This is all anecdotal—I'm neither a therapist nor a psychologist and I don't do statistical research—but very, very consistent. While a daughter (or son) may recognize her or his own unhappiness and unanswered need for support and love early in life, accepting it as undeniable fact usually takes more than two decades of *adult* life. Counterintuitively, most women are in their mid-forties, fifties, and even sixties when they finally stop normalizing their mothers' treatment and behavior and are able to see them as abusive in nature.

Recognition is slow because even as the adult child begins to confront the truth of her parent's treatment, she still needs and wants her parent's love and support, and she remains hopeful that, somehow, she will find a way of getting it. This is what I called *core conflict* in my book *Daughter Detox*. The hopefulness is also fed by a steady stream of normalization and denial and, even more important, a general cultural misunderstanding about what constitutes abuse. This, too, is a common theme, so I'll let Mariah's story illuminate the problem. She's well-educated and 48, in case you were wondering: "I honestly thought that abuse had to be physical, and I was dumbfounded when my therapist called my mother abusive. Can you believe that I actually tried to defend her? Now I can see the confusion." What caused the confusion were the material facts of Mariah's childhood—the nice clothes, the pretty house, the food on the table, the cars in the driveway—which blocked her view of what had gone on in the rooms of that spacious house. In therapy, the story came out, not in a rush but in a slow accretion of details: "But my mother never said a nice thing about me, not ever, and criticized me constantly. She'd tell me I was ugly and a big disappointment. She would compare me to my sister and tell me I was a loser. She would automatically blame me for anything that went wrong and withheld praise when I did something right."

Because we don't talk much about parental verbal abuse, we make assumptions about what a toxic or abusive household looks like, and our imaginings never include pretty houses with beautiful gardens on tree-lined streets or children who appear well-tended and cared for. But abuse, as Mariah makes clear, doesn't require either poverty or squalor to thrive.

Verbal abuse takes place not between equals but when there is an imbalance of power. It is unsettling to admit it, but parents, by definition, hold all the cards and have the ability not only to define a child's world but also to dictate how that the world is to be interpreted, as Deborah Tannen has observed. All children first glimpse themselves as they are reflected in their parents' eyes, and that was true for Mariah until the moment it wasn't. But she still believed what she had been told about herself for years: "When I started to push back as a teen, she'd deny what she'd said or tell me I was too 'sensitive.' And you know, I believed her. I apologized for being me for years, and then I married a man who treated me in the same way. It was my treatment for depression that got me into therapy, which gave me the strength to divorce my husband and mother at once. But honestly, she never yelled. She never hit me. But she beat the emotional hell out of me, every day. And so did he."

Mariah's experience comes close to typifying how daughters and sons recount the slow course of their understanding, especially when there's no physical abuse involved, and all the surface needs of life—food, shelter, clothing, education—are met. But that isn't all that impedes recognition of abusive treatment, as we will see.

Verbal abuse gets rationalized, excused, and denied in other contexts as well, especially ones that include physical violence, as Kathy, 58, recounted. Her father physically abused and threatened both her mother and brother, who was two years older, and she remembers having to call the police to intervene when she was as young as seven. The violence was sporadic and unpredictable, and her mother would move out with the kids from time to time but would always return; her parents didn't divorce until Kathy was 19. Kathy herself wasn't the object of her father's rages, a fact that filled her with terrible guilt. But as she says, she now realizes that "he needed me as an ally, something I didn't understand at the time."

Her childhood and adolescence were chaotic but enlivened by one thing: Kathy was an elite ice skater with seemingly limitless competitive possibilities and an exacting and tough coach, whom she would later label abusive as well. Her mother lived vicariously through her daughter's triumphs, though that did little to temper her mother's continuous belittling of her. As Kathy wrote: "I could never do anything right to her liking. I had to do everything exactly how she wanted it done or I would pay for it verbally and have to do it over until it was right. I had to clean the kitchen after she used all the pots and pans and until it was to her liking. What was held over my head was her taking me to the rink and paying for it all. Nothing I did was ever enough. If she did something for me, I had to do triple of that for her." Her mother's criticism and control kept Kathy in place: "Nothing was unconditional. You didn't dare show anger, upset, pouting. My feelings didn't matter. I was a robot at home and at the rink. A good little robot! I was so easy to raise for her. I was fearful of everything. Just where she wanted me."

And then, suddenly, there was a turning point: Kathy suffered an injury and had to stop skating. Her mother turned the injury into a mark of shame, literally not speaking to her directly for two years and making her call her coach to say she was quitting without giving a reason; she forbade her to mention the injury. Her coach vilified her for being a quitter, and in the moment, Kathy understood that what she'd always excused as her coach's strict discipline had been abuse as well. (It turns out that this wasn't a unique experience either; coaches and teachers in highly competitive disciplines, such as sports and dance, have been shown to cross the line horrifyingly often. This is a subject we'll return to later in the book.)

Even though she first went into therapy at the age of 14, Kathy continued not to see her mother's constant criticism as abusive until she was in her late forties when, suddenly, the light went on. She attempted to set boundaries with her mother in terms of what her mother could and couldn't say and was rebuffed. She went no-contact with her mother when she was 57 and maintains low phone contact with her father. She absolutely believes that, while witnessing physical abuse was damaging, it was her mother's relentless gaslighting, belittling, and criticizing that affected her most, even though her mother never raised a hand to her: "I keep thinking of the fear I lived in. Growing up, there was always a distraction. A fight or flight response automatically in gear. It was exhausting."

If one parent is abusive, a child may often misread or not register the other parent's inaction for years; that, too, testifies to the slow pace of recognition. Women wrote me of their emotional confusion when they realized that their beloved fathers had effectively teamed up with their mothers, basically gaslighting their daughters without ever saying a word. Cindy is 52 but has only come to terms with what really happened in her family of origin in the last five years. Even though she has been working with a therapist, it has come as a shock to her. This is her story: "When people talk about my dad, they always mention his decency and kindness first. Or they say something like Jimmy Stewart would have played him in the movies back then or Tom Hanks would now." She and her brother looked up to him because, in her words, "he took good care of us." He was a bank officer who made time to coach his son's Little League team and to drive Cindy to Girl Scouts;

he was active in their church. Even though the world saw her parents as well-matched, Cindy had another view: "Dad was a quiet man who never raised his voice. Mom was like that in the outside world, but inside our house, she was someone else. Quick to anger if things weren't done right. A perfectionist who blamed me and my brother, especially him, for any failing or slight." Cindy's brother, Tim, was four years older, shy, easily upset, and overweight. Cindy recalls how her mother mocked him endlessly: "She called him stupid, a flop, a loser, and 'lard boy'; when he got upset, his lower lip would start to tremble and he'd sweat and she'd laugh at him and throw him a dish towel to 'dry off' so as to shame him more. I was the supposed troublemaker because she really wanted a daughter who would 'shine like a penny' and I didn't. I wasn't blond or appealing like her sister's daughter, but brunette and quiet. She never missed an opportunity to put me down, and, you know, I believed it."

As Cindy tells it, her brother floundered as a teen, lonely and isolated. He started acting out, which only served to unite his parents against him. He moved out when he was 18 and stopped contacting the family; his parents made no effort to get in touch either. At 14, Cindy became the only child in the home, and her mother ratcheted up the criticism and her dissatisfaction. There was nothing for Cindy to do except to duck under the radar and hope that her father would keep his promise about sending her away to college. That set her mother into high gear: "With my brother out of the house, I was the lone dumping ground. And it frustrated her because, by now, I didn't bother talking back or resisting; all I wanted was the college ticket out. So she focused on how that wasn't going to happen unless I changed; why would she spend good money on such an embarrassment? A daughter no one would want? I would go to my dad and he'd say 'Don't mind her' as if I were talking about some minor annoyance. But there would be no words of reassurance. None. I walked on eggshells for four years."

Cindy graduated from college and moved to another city but maintained her contact with both parents. Her brother stayed away from his parents, but he and Cindy maintained contact, as he bounced from place to place and job to job. She married and had two children; then, when she was 40, her brother died in a car accident. His funeral was the beginning of her coming to terms with both of her parents and *their* treatment: "My parents portrayed themselves as my brother's victims and talked about how ungrateful he was; they milked the community's sympathy, and it was clear to me that they'd been smearing him for years to anyone who would listen. Then a number of people came up to me and admonished me, saying that I wasn't doing enough for my mother and how unhappy she was with me. I couldn't believe it. Afterwards, with my husband present, I asked her about that, and she said, 'What do you expect? You've been a disappointment to me since the day you were born.' She went on and on, berating me for being a terrible person, a lousy daughter, and how both of her children were nothing but spoiled ingrates. She didn't shed a tear the day my brother was buried, and she attacked me. My dad stood there, silent, patting her on the back from time to time. My husband was shocked, and I was crushed."

Cindy had trouble recovering from the experience, suffering severe insomnia and agitation, and her doctor advised her to begin intensive therapy. It was during those sessions that she finally began to fathom the level of verbal abuse she and her brother had grown up with, and not simply at her mother's hands. Her recognition was deeply painful: "My father watched her berate me for years and never said a word, although one-on-one, he was always kind to me, and I took that as a sign that he loved me. For years, I couldn't face the fact that he flat-out refused to protect me or my brother. My brother clearly never was able to thrive, and when he left, I was forced into the role of the dutiful scapegoat who offered herself up for Mom's abuse and power plays. But Dad never said a word. Not once. He didn't defend us as kids or as adults; he is still Mom's biggest fan. You know? I think the damage he caused is somehow worse because of the weight of his betrayal."

The question she ends with is powerful and poignant: "How can a man who portrays himself as decent and a pillar of the community watch a woman tear down his kids and think it's okay?" It is an important question, one that will come up again, a variation on a persistent and painful theme.

And while these first stories are those told by women, boys and men are no less vulnerable to verbal abuse in childhood, as the heart-rending story of Cindy's brother makes clear. In fact, an argument can be made that boys are actually more vulnerable to and devastated by verbal abuse than are their female counterparts, even though it may not appear so on the surface; that was certainly true for Patch, age 52, who is the youngest of five boys. He is six years younger than the brother closest in age and fifteen years younger than the eldest; he is married with no children by choice. The family of origin he describes was chaotic, filled with physical threats and a constant stream of verbal abuse: "My parents had explosive tempers, and you never knew what was going to cause them to slap us or throw a dinner plate at the light fixture over our heads during dinner, or chase and beat us for not showing proper silence and respect to whatever was said to us or not doing what was demanded of us. Not one of us was taught that feelings were okay or manageable. No, it was 'Look out! I'm going to blow and there's nothing you can do about it.'"

Still, he is careful to distinguish between the kind of abuse each parent meted out: "Dad would do the silent treatment but not for long and it wasn't his go-to move; he was more overtly violent and abusive to us all. Mom switched between joining him in the screaming or trying to protect us, the kids, which only happened if they were in the same room when abuse happened. But she had to be careful because otherwise she'd become one of us. But both parents could be abusive on their own and Mom was just the lesser of two evils. You could try to talk her down, but there was no reasoning with Dad." Patch was also the family's appointed scapegoat because of the circumstances of his birth—his parents separated several times, and he was conceived as a result of make-up sex after a big fight—a well-known fact shared with many and incorporated not just into family lore but repeated and repeated again, which, in and of itself, was another form of verbal abuse. Yet he was told by everyone—his parents, siblings, and other relatives—that the problems in the family stemmed from his birth.

The story was straightforward: "My parents were not equipped to add another mouth to the already unstable mix and taught my siblings to see me as a burden."

Not surprisingly, he believed what was said about him, as most children do, especially when the narrative is consistent and voiced by not just his parents but everyone else as well; the effects on him were great and long-lasting, which isn't surprising either. Goaded for being babyish and made fun of for being too sensitive, he took on the role of peacekeeper as a small boy. He was mocked for that, too.

Luckily, he did have moments of respite as the youngest child— summers and holidays at his grandmother's and with his aunt and uncle and their two kids—when he was, in his words, "treated like a whole person and allowed to have my own thoughts and feelings." Still, his thinking was shaped by the rationalizations that his family offered up, such as "Other kids have it worse. We're not perfect, but family will always love you as no one else does." He now calls these family narratives "myths that were more like gaslighting than anything else" and, as an adult, he wryly notes that "it turns out I am thankful no one 'loves me' as they did."

He went into therapy at 13, and has spent his adult years actively recovering; he went no-contact with his family at the age of 35. Still, he sees himself as a work in progress, still having difficulties with boundaries, still struggling with feelings of inadequacy and self-loathing as well as depression. He summed up it: "Being called shy and a crybaby hurt but it wasn't the worst; the worst was really being unable to speak because of fear of being ridiculed. It's still in my mind all these years later, though I am less afraid now. I still worry when I post a comment online or send an email to someone I know or even speak to someone that I'll say the wrong thing and that they're going to tear me to shreds."

As we will see, even with therapy, the way verbal abuse is internalized, especially during childhood, can leave a lasting impression on adult development.

Of course, insecurity, self-doubt, and fearfulness aren't the only legacies of verbal abuse; Tim, 72, struggled instead with intense anger.

He, too, was part of a large family—five children in all—but he and his brother, two years younger, were the first wave. The first of the next three children was born when Tim was ten. He, too, dealt with the disparity of how the family looked from the outside and what it felt like to be a member of the clan; the family was well off, lived in a beautiful house, and the children seemed to enjoy every privilege available to them. But the dynamic within the household belied the view from the neighbors' yards: "My father was a tyrant. Forget 'my way or the highway.' There was no highway. Only his vision of what we each should be. Who each of us was was of no concern to him, or to my mother, who ducked the question. Love? Earned. How much love? How well you did. I failed because I didn't want what he wanted and that was enough for him to toss me overboard. My Ph.D. was meaningless because it wasn't the M.D. he wanted. He played favorites, too, depending on how closely you honed to what he wanted, but going after his love and support—if you can call what he was capable of by those names—was both a thankless and potentially ruinous task. My father didn't really know any of his five children. That's the truth."

Of course, Tim's remarks have the benefit of more than 40 years of hindsight, as a boy, an adolescent, and even as a young adult. Tim's desire to belong and to get his father's approval remained unabated, and his anger at being marginalized and criticized grew. It was his wife who demanded that he deal with his anger, for which he remains thankful; he spent a decade in therapy. It took him a long time to see past his father as the only villain of the drama that was his and his siblings' childhood: "My dad was almost always the chief verbal abuser, although my mother was always his chief supporter and enabler—always agreeing with his assessment about our failures and never stepping in to mitigate the abuse that the old man was dishing out. In some ways, my mother, a bit of a tyrant in her own right, was less the partner of my father in the pressure campaign (although she often was that) than something like the sixth child in the family, subject to the verbal pressure and intimidation of my father. She wasn't able, because of her dependent circumstances vis-à-vis my father as the main family breadwinner, to push back against his tyranny, or even to mitigate or soften his abuse of any of his kids."

This is another theme we'll explore in these pages: the role of the other parent in the face of verbal abuse. It's noteworthy but not surprising that, as sons who perceived their mothers in danger of being abused themselves, both Patch and Tim end up defending them even as they hold them accountable, in part because of financial dependency. This contrasts sharply with Cindy's painful assessment of her father as a silent partner. Recognizing the role of the other parent isn't just emotionally confusing but it can also effectively act as a blind spot since, sometimes, one parent seems to be "better" or "less hurtful" than the other.

Can Verbal Abuse Be Outweighed by the Other Parent's Treatment?

Let's start with the word "outweigh" here because it betrays a common misconception about the impact of events and circumstances on psychological development, especially in the case of verbal abuse. We like to think of the good outweighing the bad, that the presence of one reasonably loving, attentive, or even vaguely supportive parent will countermand the effect of a toxic one, or that something good happening in our lives at an otherwise difficult time will "balance" things out. Alas, that's simply not true in psychological terms. As researchers Roy F. Baumeister, Ellen Bratslavsky, and colleagues put it in the title of their article "Bad Is Stronger than Good," we are, thanks to evolution, hardwired to pay more attention to bad things, which we store in an easily retrievable part of memory. Yes, the same place our forebears stored the helpful observations that undercooked pork can kill you or that standing under a tree during a thunderstorm is dangerous is where we unconsciously park our mother's dressing us down for no reason or playing favorites with our brother. It is a psychological truism that bad events and experiences affect us more and leave more of a mental impression than good ones.

Similarly, even though we like to think that the affection of one parent can somehow buffer us from the abuse of the other, that turns out not to be true either. According to the work of Ann Polcari, Karen Rabin, and others, the abuse leaves its mark nonetheless, untouched and unmitigated by the affection offered by the other parent. So, strictly speaking, the experience of a father's love coexists with the damage done by the unloving and verbally abusive mother, and vice versa. If you visualize two train tracks running parallel, you've got it.

All of this contributes to the damage done, often unseen and unarticulated for decades.

Of course, our family of origin isn't the only place verbal abuse can flourish; it can root and grow in the parched soil of any close relationship, provided certain conditions are met. Two of the primary goals of this book are to shine a bright light on these and the other circumstances that permit verbal abuse to gain a foothold in someone's life and to define verbal abuse in such a way that facilitates recognition.

The stories of women and men fill the pages of this book and provide a firsthand look at what it's like to experience sustained verbal abuse and its effects, supported by the latest research. My hope is that, by sharing in this way, it will be easier for people to walk the path of recognition and abandon feelings of self-blame, fear, and hopelessness. With luck, they will adopt a zero-tolerance policy and stop excusing abusers. That is devoutly to be wished.

Verbal abuse is *never* okay. It is *never* justified. It is *never* a means to an end. See the word "never"?

* * *

I know firsthand what it's like to be verbally abused as a child; I spent years trying to get my mother to acknowledge that her justification of beating me with words instead of her hands was nothing more than rationalization, but she never did. I, too, had the outside appearance problem since my mother was beautiful, charming, and chic and I was smart, pretty, and accomplished; the face my family presented to the outside world might even have been seen as enviable. We weren't rich but we appeared to want for nothing material, and I looked as if I were well taken care of. That was emotionally confusing to me, growing up, since I knew that how I was being treated wasn't right.

The early photographs of my mother and me—from the past century, they are black-and-white—reveal much. I am usually dressed to the nines and facing the camera; after I could stand up alone, the photos never showed her touching or holding me. If you were to photoshop these old black-and-whites and substitute a really great-looking dog—say a regal standard poodle or an elegant borzoi or some dog that won best in show—in the space that little Peg occupies, it would be even clearer that I am an accessory. As it happens, I was born on the anniversary of the founding of the Girl Scouts and my mother was photographed for one of New York City's tabloids and appeared on the front page; I was supposedly the first baby girl born in the city on the anniversary. Mind you, this is highly dubious since I was born at 5 a.m. and it's way more likely that I had the prettiest mother who gave birth to a girl on March 12 in 1949. She appears in the photograph wearing a lacy bed jacket, a ribbon in her coiffed hair, and full makeup. She smiles directly and confidently into the camera, with the bundle of joy in the crook of her arm. She is proud of the photo, and I am told that when I was small, she told the story of that photo often.

I was a pretty child with a mop of blond curls, the kind of little girl people ooh and ah over, and, as the creator of said prettiness, I think she initially took pride in me. But it was also clear to me, by the time I was three or four, that her mood would darken when people complimented or paid attention to me; she would become irritated with me for any reason and no reason at all. I tried desperately to tiptoe around her, but I also knew she didn't love me. I saw how her eyes narrowed and her full mouth got taut when she looked at me, which was something the people who loved me—my grandfather, my great aunt, my father—didn't do.

In the confines of our home, my mother was highly combative and critical of me, always denying what she'd said or done. I was a fearful child—scared of spiders, jellyfish, dark rooms, polio, bees, lightning, drowning—but one thing terrified me most of all: being crazy. Just the thought of it made my stomach lurch and my throat tighten because I knew with the kind of certainty only a small child can muster that if

I were crazy, then no one would ever like or love me. No one. What if everything my mother said I was—difficult, too sensitive, unlovable—was true?

I was probably around six or seven when the crazy thing really worried me because I knew that either my mother was right and I was the crazy one or I was right and she was the crazy one—and the first thought was much easier to consider as a possibility than the second. Research shows that children whose emotional needs aren't being met or are actively being disparaged or ignored are more likely to blame themselves than to admit the truth of how they are being treated by the very people who are charged with taking care of them. For a child, the admission that your parents are the villains of the piece is simply too frightening to bear; it's way less scary to blame yourself.

Worrying about being crazy kept me up at night. I sucked my thumb and had a comfort blanket. I could read by the age of three, went to school early, and distinguished myself academically. I skipped a grade and bit my nails to the quick. My accomplishments and bright façade coexisted with a sweltering, blanketing fear. When my father—my source of comfort—died when I was 15, I started smoking cigarettes.

This all took place in my childhood bedroom in the Riverdale section of the Bronx when Dwight Eisenhower was President. It continued through the Kennedy years and then those presided over by Lyndon Johnson and Richard Nixon. When I was 22, I was partly rescued by a wise therapist, who, sitting behind the couch I was lying on, intoned, "Peg, has it ever occurred to you that your mother is wrong about you? That she's crazy? Or that she's trying to make you feel crazy?" That was a beginning, but since I still wanted to win my mother's love, I remained stuck. Like many women and men, I chose boyfriends and lovers who were manipulative in one way or another and definitely emotionally withholding; now, as a writer, I call that a comfort zone that is familiar but offers no comfort. Not one of those boyfriends disparaged me or put me down, but they all played mind games, and that, too, is verbal abuse. On the rebound from someone who was supremely manipulative, I married someone else who was nice in some ways but totally wrong for me; I knew it when I stood at the altar with a splitting headache and an intense desire to run but didn't have the guts. It was over in nine months and my divorce took longer than the marriage lasted. I was in therapy, but how I had been affected by verbal abuse had never really been addressed because why would it have? From the outside, it looked as if I had it all and all the answers.

And then fate stepped in.

I was 29 and met someone new through a friend; as it happened, she barely knew him, but I didn't know that at the time. At 37, Joshua was handsome, self-made, and sexy. Born on a hardscrabble farm, he'd been raised by his father when his mother decamped when he was five for reasons unknown and he'd grown up poor and knew what it was like to go to bed hungry, as I didn't. But he was smart and determined that he wouldn't end up like his father, who he said was "an old man before his time." He earned his degree at the University of Michigan with honors, getting through on a football scholarship, and then went on to get an MBA at Columbia. He drove a Porsche, wore custom suits from Brooks Brothers, and had a pretty apartment, but he was emotionally volatile. He'd been married and, as he told the story, devastated when his wife left him for no reason. He could be sweet and loving, but then would withdraw emotionally by turns. When he was angry, he could be nasty. I pushed back against his habit of stonewalling, walked out when he called me names or disparaged me, but I didn't break up with him. I spent way too much time either trying to catch him in his lies or trying to understand them. I didn't know what to make of him, but I was sure that, somehow, I could turn things around so that he'd be loving all the time. The relationship lasted more than a year with its drama and lots of make-up gestures.

Then, one night, as we argued in my apartment about something, he lunged at me and grabbed the gold chain I wore around my neck. He was six foot, two to my five foot, eight and in shape and probably 80 pounds heavier. I screamed and flailed to get his hands away from my neck. My cocker spaniel was barking like crazy, nipping at Josh's legs, and I was as terrified as I'd ever been in my whole life. The necklace was a little Elsa Peretti heart from Tiffany on a fragile chain, but it cut into my neck as it tightened. I kept trying to push him off, and then he pulled the chain hard and it snapped. He lost his grip on me and stood there, momentarily distracted, staring at the broken necklace in his hand. Maybe he understood what he'd done in the moment, but it didn't matter. I ran out the door and into the hall, screaming. I fled into the elevator, down to the lobby, and told the doorman to call the police. He was dialing when Joshua ran past him and out into the night.

The police said there was nothing to be done because I hadn't been hurt and, besides, I had let him into my apartment willingly. I remember the older cop said something like, "People just lose it sometimes, you know. That doesn't make him a criminal." In the following weeks, Joshua left dozens and dozens of messages with my secretary at work and on my answering machine at home. He sent flowers to my office that were returned to the florist. He sent bouquets to my apartment that I tossed down the garbage chute. He sent letters and cards that I marked "Return to Sender." He sent gifts that I gave to charity without opening them.

I never saw or spoke to him again. Sometime later, I heard he'd gotten the next girl pregnant and married her. I always fully expected to see his name in the newspapers or hear it mentioned on television in a story about domestic violence, but—to my knowledge, at least—it never happened.

But it was a turning point. I saw the connection between verbal abuse and physical violence in a single moment when I was 29 and a man tried to do me harm, and I consider myself blessed. I knew that I had to change what I wanted from men and the kind of person I wanted to be with because it was dangerous *not* to change. What would have happened if the chain had been heavier and not so fragile? Would he have stopped? I can't answer, but I do know that 40 years ago, I got lucky because Joshua was my wake-up call. I fired my therapist and hired a new one and started work anew.

This book is about the kind of abuse that breaks down your psyche and sense of self and not your bones; that said, verbal abuse is every bit as violent and damaging as the physical kind and is very difficult to recover from. It has the capacity to shape the developing brain of a child in literal ways and can absolutely affect the arc of his or her adult life. Is that surprising?

If you are surprised, you're not alone.

Verbal abuse is about power, and it takes place in the context of relationship. Paradoxically, it is easiest to see when the relationship is tenuous or even nonexistent; verbal abuse coming from someone you hardly know and don't need or want anything from is a snap to recognize. Unfortunately, it's in the context of relationships, especially very intimate ones, that our ability to identify abuse gets impaired both by our own needs and the manipulations of the person wielding the power.

That's why I've written this book. As someone who studied English literature on both the undergraduate and graduate levels, I have long known that words have great power. They can lift us up, expand our thoughts and horizons, and literally change our minds in positive ways. Did you know that just reading these words is changing pathways in your brain in a literal fashion, making new synaptic connections?

But here's the thing about words: Used destructively, they are rapier swift. You may not even see the wounds until, one day, you find yourself surrounded by blood, both dried and fresh. Hopefully, for most people, that will remain a metaphor, but, for some, it will be literal.

Chapter One

The Face of Abuse: Myths and Facts

Even in the Information Age, it's a truism that cultural myths have enormous staying power in the collective imagination. The word "rape" is still likely to summon up an image of a dark street and a menacing stranger, even though it's a sad reality that most victims know their attackers. Try to picture a kidnapper or pedophile and your mind will deliver up the creepy and unknown person sitting in an idling car, eyeing the playground, while the fact is that, according to the nonprofit Rape, Abuse & Incest National Network (RAINN), 93 percent of sexually abused children (and their families) know their attackers. And when it comes to murder, almost half of all female victims will have had an intimate involvement with their killers. Cultural myths die hard.

In a similar way, when we think about verbal abuse, we're likely to envision a burly guy in a wife-beater shirt who's always yelling and has an everpresent beer in hand, someone we immediately register as scary or threatening or misogynistic, or the screaming and slap-happy woman who's drunk or high on drugs. We don't envision the handsome and well-dressed investment banker who gets out of his BMW and dazzles you with his smile or the churchgoing mother of three who's famous for her beautiful garden and her generosity to the neighbors' kids at Halloween. All of us are more comfortable thinking that people who behave badly wear their behaviors publicly out in the world, obvious and evident, like the bad guys in black hats in old-style Westerns. But those who use words to cow and intimidate, subjugate or control, or wield the power of silent manipulation come in all sizes and shapes and usually don't dress the part.

Verbal abuse isn't limited to a single social class or ethnicity; being well educated or, for that matter, relatively uneducated is neither a determinant nor a risk factor. Abuse takes place in mansions as well as in trailer parks, in tenements and classic Park Avenue apartments. As we'll see, people who have grown up around verbal abuse may be more likely to become abusive themselves but not always; counterintuitively, those who have grown up around verbal abuse and suffered the pain of it often normalize it, to their detriment, and may find themselves with verbally abusive lovers, partners, or spouses, as Mariah's story in the Introduction makes clear. They may be drawn to friends who treat them as they have been treated in childhood; they may tolerate abusive behaviors from co-workers, colleagues, and bosses. They may doubt whether what they are experiencing is, in fact, abuse, for both cultural and personal reasons, a subject we've touched upon and will turn to in depth.

Verbal abuse is a behavior, not a character trait. Verbally abusive behavior is an active choice, and it is highly motivated, as we'll see. While the expression of anger can, in the moment, incorporate aspects of verbal abuse—calling someone names, mocking or shaming him or her, and the like—verbal abuse is sustained and, in its own way, consistent. Alas, the fact that people who aren't really abusive can display angry behaviors that cross the line makes it even harder for the culture to sort things out because excuses are so easy to find; after all, who doesn't lose his or her temper now and again? (Remember what the cop said to me after Joshua tried to choke me? "People lose it sometimes.") Who hasn't said nasty words or spewed out insults in a heated moment? Who hasn't behaved badly, lashed out, and crossed the line into abuse at least once? Nobody's perfect, right?

It's important to recognize that the tendency to normalize abuse can be seen in bystanders and witnesses as well as the victimizers and victims themselves. When you consider that the gold standard for abuse in our courts is deep bruising or physical injury, the fact that decent and well-meaning people can be abusive in the moment makes it even harder for the culture (yes, judges and all) to take verbal abuse seriously.

But verbal abuse is motivated. It is consistent. It is a strategy. That is what makes it different from my calling you stupid or an asshole in an angry moment when we're arguing; that is a one-off, and while, yes, it crosses the line into abusive behavior, it doesn't accurately characterize our relationship in the main or in the day-to-day. Momentary bad behavior has to be distinguished from verbal abuse in multiple and important ways because context matters. And true verbal abuse has identifiable patterns that establish the context for the labeling; wrongly, we use the context to think about abuse, but we need to focus on the pattern instead.

Abusers have goals and an agenda that have to do with power; verbal abuse is meant to subjugate, marginalize, and disenfranchise the person being abused, rendering her or him powerless, afraid, and insecure. Verbal abuse is meant to tear down our sense of self and to trigger us into apology and begging because we care about the person who is abusing us. Read that sentence again and try to wrap your head around it, but it is true. Let the sentence change your mind.

The bottom line? Abusers do not misspeak. They may also be angry in the moment, but the abuse is cold and calculated. There is an enormous difference.

Verbal Abuse Versus Emotional Abuse

Throughout this book, I'll be using the term "verbal abuse" because, as a layperson, I find it more focused and defined than the relatively fuzzy term "emotional abuse," which I believe only muddies the waters. Let me explain: If we identify verbal abuse and the various forms it takes, we just need to look at the behavior exhibited by the abuser without taking the effects on the intended victim into account. Whatever difficulty people have with defining verbal abuse gets magnified when you use the term "emotional abuse" because the word "emotional" in this context is confusing. Criticism can make you feel bad about yourself, so does that mean that criticism is always emotionally abusive? Being broken up with or divorced usually causes great emotional pain, so is ending a relationship or partnership always an emotionally abusive act? It is not.

Even skilled psychologists have wrestled with the term "emotional abuse." Marital expert and psychologist John Gottman has developed two "Emotional Questionnaires," which are meant to be used to assess domestic violence; one was developed with psychologist Neil Jacobson and the other with psychologist Julie Schwartz Gottman. The Jacobson/Gottman questionnaire is composed of 27 items to which you must answer "Never" (1 point), "Rarely" (2 points), "Occasionally" (4 points), and "Often" (5 points). Of the 26 items, 21 clearly denote verbal abuse, but five cross the line into physical abuse: "Makes me do degrading things," "Forces me to do things against my will," "Intentionally does things to scare me," "Threatens me physically during arguments," "Warns me that if I keep doing something, physical violence will follow," and "Drives recklessly or too fast when he is angry." But while verbal abuse can escalate into physical violence (and, as we will see, is always its foundation), if you answered "never" to all of these questions, you'd be unlikely to be classified as a victim of emotional abuse.

The second emotional abuse questionnaire, this one by Gottman and his professional partner and wife, has a true-or-false format and is composed of 26 questions; of these, 16 actually involve physical threats or actions meant to constrain the victim, and definitely cross the line into physical abuse. In addition to stated threats of violence, they include the following statements: "My partner forcibly tries to restrict my movements," "My partner makes me do degrading things," and "My partner makes me engage in sexual activities I consider perverse," and ends with four questions about a partner threatening to hurt someone you care about, doing cruel things to pets and animals, and threatening to hurt your children. This is clearly domestic violence territory, and the culture does have some clarity about identifying that behavior.

The problem with the term "emotional abuse" is that, absent a definition that includes constraints and physical threats or physical violence, it can only be ascertained by its effects, and we can only tell if someone has been emotionally abused if he or she shows deleterious effects or changes that are obvious and easy to identify. If there are no bruises or threats to harm, lawyers and other advocates end up trying to prove emotional abuse by pointing to drastic shifts in the alleged victim's behavior or mental health. For example, in a school-age child, that might include going from doing well in school to failing, radical changes in eating or sleep patterns, or going from being an easygoing or laid-back kid to one who lashes out in anger at everyone or shuts down when spoken to. In an adolescent, it might be a sudden indifference to a previous passion, an unwillingness to talk to anyone including friends, or going from being a sociable person to someone who deliberately self-isolates. In an adult, there might be changes in emotional volatility, the inability to focus and be productive, or significant variations in behavior and coping.

But labeling abuse by its effects requires that we know what the child, adolescent, or adult was like before and inserts another layer of uncertainty. How can you assume that emotional abuse is the root cause of a child's performance in school or a change in her sleep patterns? How do you know that an adolescent's shift in behavior isn't due to the stress of adolescence, or some other problem he or she is struggling with, rather than emotional abuse? How do you know that an adult isn't dealing with overwhelming financial issues or something else that is eating him or her alive? The problem with using this term is that it introduces real uncertainty, and that uncertainty pervades the thinking and actions of many figures of authority, including judges, police officers, teachers, social workers, and others in a position to make life-changing decisions. Since an accusation of abuse is a serious one, there should be a need for proof, but not the kind of uncertainty the term "emotional abuse" evokes.

Talking about verbal abuse, rather than emotional abuse, cuts to the chase. We can look at highly discernible patterns of behavior.

If we begin by defining verbal abuse and the forms it takes, we don't have to mess around with ascertaining the effects as we do when we call something emotional abuse; we can just identify the behavior as toxic in and of itself without needing to account for a victim's scar tissue to prove our case. Just as we don't need the proof of flattened buildings to ascertain that a tornado has passed through, using the term "verbal abuse" allows us to discuss it as one topic and its effects as another. That may seem like intellectual parsing or nitpicking but it's actually not.

Needing Proof: The Cultural Attitude Toward Abusive Behavior

Even now, if you claim that you are a victim of abuse, society as well as courts of law will demand that you be able to show your bruises to prove it. Of course, there *is* a reason for that: There is a legal difference between being physically pummeled and rendered verbally down for the count. People don't go to jail for verbally flaying their spouses, kids, colleagues, or neighbors, but they are rightly charged and imprisoned for taking a knife to their skin. I took that analogy as far as I did to make a point: The gold standard when it comes to judging abuse is physical harm. And that is a huge problem for you, me, our neighbors, our children, their friends, our children's children, and everyone else. Science knows better, but judges and their decisions make it clear that there's still a real and very dangerous cultural confusion. This stance also feeds the confusion of those who are being verbally abused: Does it count as abuse when you're not physically hurt? This is a question that resurfaces again and again in discussions of verbal abuse, and it really shouldn't.

That said, the cultural distinctions between physical and psychological damage are scientifically shaky. While you can't literally die from verbal abuse, the damage done is grievous and, in some ways, can inflict more lasting emotional and psychological damage than a beating. That's counterintuitive but true, and there's a great deal of science to back it up. Researchers continue to puzzle out the connection between emotional pain and physical pain and how the brain processes each; they may, in the end, not be as different as we've been led to believe. (Yes, when you say, "You're heartbroken," the word "heartbroken" may be literal in ways that you never suspected.) These are subjects that we'll examine in great detail over the course of these pages. The question here is this: What happens to the gold standard of the bruise if the psychological effects of verbal abuse and physical abuse are one and the same? How do we shift gears into greater understanding and stop undermining the kind of abuse that doesn't leave the body marked?

That said, there are known patterns that clarify and that we must pay attention to. While verbal abuse may not always spin off into physical abuse or domestic violence, verbal abuse *always* provides the foundation for what Rachel Louise Snyder has called "domestic terrorism" in her brilliant book *No Visible Bruises.* Her title, of course, evokes what I am calling the "gold standard" of ascertaining whether abuse has taken place, which is physical evidence. But as Snyder brilliantly makes clear, many victims of domestic violence have none except the invisible bruises of verbal abuse until their abusers finally succeed at fully subjugating and killing them.

Because verbal abuse is about asserting power and controlling someone, it provides the psychological foundation for physical abuse; it enables the mental and emotional confusion that keeps a victim stuck. That confusion is often aided and abetted by other abusive tactics such as isolating the person socially by disparaging his or her friends and intimates or testing the person's loyalty by having her or him choose among friends, relatives, and the abuser. Making the person doubt his or her perceptions—or gaslighting—is also on the abuser's menu.

Defining Verbal Abuse

Verbal abuse is highly motivated and intentional; it's the result of one person trying to control or exert power over another person, or part of a larger goal of intimidation or marginalization. Additionally, the abuser may be motivated by feeling better about him- or herself by marginalizing or leveling another person, but again, the abuser's motivation isn't what we are looking at to enlarge our understanding in this book. I know that there's a real fascination with what motivates an abuser—the wellspring of so many *Lifetime* movies and articles and books about the psychopath-next-door and the ever-present narcissist— but this book will focus on identifying verbal abuse and its effects on the child or adult who is the target, not the abuser him- or herself. (That said, it's doubtless true, as Dr. Joseph Burgo points out, that "the abuser uses the abusive relationship to regulate his or her own sense of self-worth and get rid of a personal sense of shame and helplessness.")

By focusing on the use of words—or the refusal to speak, as is the case with stonewalling, ignoring what someone has said, dismissing them, or maintaining a manipulative silence—we pay attention to specifics: the intent behind the words, the specific words themselves, and the techniques the abuser employs, because all verbal abuse is ultimately about power and the effort of one person to rise above or subjugate another. We are less likely to need to gauge the severity of the abuse by the effects it causes—which is a good thing, as we're not spending time looking for bruises— but instead to focus on the weaponry. Science has a very good bead on what that weaponry does to children, adolescents, and adults. That is, in my view, a necessary corrective to the cultural stance echoed by the old rhyme: "Sticks and stones may break my bones, but words will never harm me."

I happen to hate platitudes generally and would consign all of them to a hell made up of discarded tea cozies and refrigerator magnets, including "When the going gets tough, the tough get going," "Everything happens for a reason," and "What doesn't kill you makes you stronger," but the sticks and stones thing is in a class by itself because it is a lie, plain and simple. The other platitudes floating around aren't mainly true either, but this one is just flat-out wrong. Period and end of story. What makes it even worse is that just about everyone in the English-speaking world was told this as a child, supposedly to build up their resilience and strength against the bullies of this world, by every figure of authority they might encounter, including well-meaning parents, grandparents, neighbors, teachers, coaches, and clergy. The platitude is a double whammy: Not only does it not work, but it also implies that if you are hurt by words, it's your problem and fault and you're nothing but a weakling or an overly sensitive bundle of nerves. It's akin to sending someone into a battle zone armed only with a flyswatter, but blaming the child for the fact that the flyswatter isn't much of a defensive weapon.

Bullying and Relational Aggression

How long a shadow the cultural view of insults and verbal degradation as being annoying but benign casts can be seen in the tolerance of bullying at school, which was long considered pretty much a normal middle and high school rite of passage in American life and elsewhere. For generations, dealing with the bully in the schoolyard was a trial you had to get through, especially if you were a boy. I remember Joey, the bully in my fourth-grade class, who was big and as dumb as a post and picked on all the smart kids, especially my friend Raymond, who was the best artist in the school. Everyone knew the kids who were bullies, but their bullying was just a fact of life and got filed under "The Way Things Are" and that was that. It took the 1999 massacre at Columbine High School to change things, though—once again—for the wrong reasons. Even the story of Columbine is a testament to how our culture frames stories, and how verbal abuse figures in.

In an effort to understand how two Caucasian teenagers, 17 and 18 at the time, from well-to-do families and who wanted for nothing could unleash such carnage, the constant media coverage framed the horror as a revenge perpetrated by two bullied boys against their oppressors. The bones of the story were that the jocks and popular boys in the high school picked on these two Goth-leaning boys who were given to wearing trench coats. Precisely because bullying was such a common experience and because we love myths that make sense of senseless acts, the story rang true to journalists, the people reading the story, and those watching it on television, even though it was pure fiction. As we came to learn years later, the killers were neither bullied nor were they intent on exacting revenge on specific people. Eric Harris had planned the attack for a year, and had aimed at maximizing carnage and body count so that it would rival the 1995 Oklahoma City bombing, in which 168 people were killed and more than 680 injured; he and his partner, Dylan Klebold, only resorted to shooting when the propane bombs they'd planted in the cafeteria and in their cars failed to go off. In fact, the two perpetrators had totally different motives and very different psychological profiles; one was a leader and the other a follower.

But the bullying narrative sounded plausible and was repeated over and over until it had a momentum of its own. It served to galvanize most of the nation into looking at the allied tactics of bullies who sought to marginalize and exclude people deemed socially weaker or vulnerable. In 1999, there were no bullying laws, but by 2015, every state along with the District of Columbia had anti-bullying laws on the books, even though they varied widely in terms of remedies and punishments. Of course, laws only give you recourse when someone commits an act, and not surprisingly, bullying hasn't disappeared from our schools. But a corner had been turned nonetheless.

The ripple effect from Columbine pushed the narrative and focus to expand past male bullying behaviors, which tend to be physical in nature even if they include verbal abuse; experts began to look carefully at the verbal and social aggression practiced by girls and women, which was largely nonviolent on the surface but equally toxic and psychologically damaging. This was an important shift in cultural thinking and gave the discussion of bullying an expanded vocabulary beyond the male model of overt physical and verbal antagonism.

Girls and Relational Aggression

In 2002, girl bullying became part of the national dialogue with the publication of two big bestsellers, *Queen Bees and Wannabees* by Rosalind Wiseman and *Odd Girl Out* by Rachel Simmons. Even though Wiseman's book became the basis for the hugely popular movie *Mean Girls,* which effectively turned girl bullying into a cultural trope of its own and spawned dozens of other movies on the same theme and even a Broadway musical, it was Simmons's book, which drew on interviews and psychological research, that affected the popular understanding of verbal abuse among girls and women.

Simmons's argument is very much a part of its time, influenced by a feminist overview of a culture that sees anger and open conflict as still off limits for girls and women and thus, in her words, "forces their aggression into nonphysical, indirect, and covert forms." This is an especially apt observation since, just a few years before, in 1998, William Pollack in his important book *Real Boys* had effectively argued that the only emotion permissible in what he called "The Boy Code"—the traditional American cultural definition of what it means to be masculine and a man—was, in fact, anger. I don't think it's an accident that *Real Boys* became a huge bestseller as part of the need to make sense of Columbine.

Understanding how girls bully expanded the sense of how words and gestures can be weaponized in the absence of physical violence, even though it didn't do much to change the gold standard for proving damage. Drawing on interviews with girls (and some mothers), Simmons laid out a case for how girls "use backbiting, exclusion, rumors and name-calling, and manipulation to inflict psychological pain on targeted victims." Perhaps most tellingly, she showed how friendship gets weaponized by threats of exclusion and is central to girls' relational aggression. The term "relational aggression" had been coined by two psychologists, the late Nicki R. Crick and Jennifer K. Grotpeter, in 1995, and was the engine for Simmons's argument, and pivoted psychological understanding. Without their work, this view of another kind of abuse—sneaky, manipulative, and way harder to see—would simply not have been possible. Anyone interested in verbal abuse owes the late Dr. Crick a great debt, in fact.

What sets girl bullying apart from that of boys—which typically includes physical aggression, verbal threats, and intimidation—is that it is played out in the context of relationship and uses the threatened loss of relationship and belonging as a way of exerting power. That includes behaviors that are meant to damage existing friendships or the feeling of inclusion in a peer group such as "angrily retaliating against a child by excluding her from one's play group, purposefully withdrawing friendship or acceptance in order to hurt or control the child, or spreading rumors about the child so that peers will reject her." Keep in mind that Crick and Grotpeter's original research used a sample of 491 third- through sixth-grade children, roughly between the ages of eight and twelve. Indeed, they found that girls were more likely to participate in relational aggression than boys, and that of the 121 children who were identified as aggressive, 72.7 percent exhibited either relational or overt aggression, but not both. Interestingly, since the study used peer reporting, it found that relationally aggressive girls were more disliked by their peers but the connection of that dislike to the girls' aggressive behavior was unclear. The researchers wondered out loud even as they reported: Is being disliked a function of relational aggression or does rejection provide the motive for the aggression? It is a variation on the chicken and the egg problem.

Bullying and relational aggression, their effects, and their prevention moved from the fringes of the culture to center stage. Bullying gained a tight CDC definition: an aggressive behavior that is repeated or has the potential to be repeated and reflects an imbalance of power between the aggressor and the victim. According to the National Bullying Prevention Center one out of every five students experienced bullying in 2019. Interestingly, verbal abuse and relational aggression were the most common forms of bullying: While 5 percent of students surveyed reported being pushed, shoved, tripped, or spat on, 13 percent said they were made fun of, called names, and insulted, and 13 percent said they were the subject of rumors. An additional 5 percent reported being deliberately excluded from activities. Not surprisingly, a slightly higher percentage of males than females reported physical bullying (6 vs. 4 percent), while twice as many females reported being the subject of rumors (18 vs. 9 percent) and deliberate exclusion (7 vs. 4 percent) as males.

Yet the larger question remained: Were boys and girls born to bully or to be relationally aggressive, or did they learn to? Yes, another variation on which came first, the chicken or the egg, but focused on the roots of abusive behavior.

Tracing the Roots of Bullying and Relational Aggression

Everyone wants an answer to the question of what makes a bully, but disappointment lies ahead: There is no one-size-fits-all definitive answer. But taking a look at the theories that have been advanced gives us insight into the dynamics of abuse and the results of research studies, some of which have yielded contradictory results. Clearly, since very small children physically bully and, later, display relational aggression, the first place to look is at the familial environment and parental behaviors.

There's a body of research that promotes the idea of the direct learning model, meaning that children duplicate the bullying they receive from their parents and apply it in peer contexts. It's been proposed that coercive and hostile strategies are modeled by parents and that a child may actually be rewarded for his peer behavior by his parents. (For example, a parent being proud of a child for showing that he can hang tough and be dominant, rather than identifying the behavior as bullying.) Other researchers have suggested that children whose parents model coercive behaviors and who lack a positive model of conflict resolution adopt those models and take those behaviors out into the world of peers; it's thought that witnessing negative behaviors desensitizes a child to their impact.

Another approach, which we will also discuss in the next chapter, is to focus on deficiencies in emotional regulation as a result of parenting styles or coercive tactics. This segues into attachment theory, which posits that early childhood experiences produce relatively distinct styles of attachment in children and adults that are either secure or insecure in nature. We will delve into attachment theory in greater depth in the next chapter, *What Science Knows*, but for the moment, let's simply focus on two consequences of an insecure attachment style. The first and most important is the inability to regulate negative emotions and the subsequent maladaptive coping mechanisms each of the three types of insecure attachment adopt; the second is the mental model of relationships each type unconsciously internalizes. Generally, an inability to regulate emotion leads to impaired peer relationships, and Yoshihiro Kawabata and the coauthors of a meta-analysis published in 2011 suggested that "when provoked, relationally aggressive children may not be able to regulate their emotions effectively, and may use relational aggression as a means of dealing with their heightened distress." One Swedish study, for example, found the adolescent children of parents who mocked and derided them were more likely to lapse into dysregulated anger, which, in turn, led to problems with their peers and both made them more likely to be victims of bullies and to become bullies themselves.

Parenting styles have also been implicated by research in producing not just bullies but also children who are likely to bully their siblings, the subject to which we'll turn next. Again, the answers are less cut and dried and precise than we'd like. For example, you'd expect that an attuned, warm, nurturing, and authoritative parenting style would consistently be negatively associated with relational aggression, right? Well, as reported in the chapter by David A. Nelson and Craig H. Hart in *The Development of Relational Aggression*, the research delivered very mixed results: The protective aspects of positive parenting are nowhere as consistent as you'd think. Authoritative parents do appear to put the brakes on physical bullying but not on relational aggression. Nelson and Hart offer up two possible reasons for the findings. First, it may be that some children are more influenced by peers when it comes to social learning. Because they're the beneficiaries of good parenting, the authors opine that they're likely to be popular and they may well learn that relational aggression is necessary to maintain social standing. (I personally think this sounds like a script for a television show about mean girls, but that's just my opinion. Not everyone is willing to be nasty to stay popular.) The second possibility that they raise is that some authoritative parents are also too permissive and that their kids don't end up observing or understanding behavior boundaries.

But the connection between relational aggression and negative parenting styles appears to be pretty robust. (Yes, here we are in "bad is stronger than good" territory again. Remember that the brain stores away negative experiences in an easy-to-recall and -retrieve location.) According to Nelson and Hart's review, coercive parenting, harshness, maternal control, and maternal expression of negative affect were positively associated with relational aggression at basically every stage of development; paternal authoritarian parenting predicted physical aggression, but not relational aggression, in preschoolers. Permissive parenting has also been implicated in numerous studies as well.

In their review, Yamamoto and his colleagues also single out psychologically controlling parenting, which includes inducing guilt, withholding love, shaming, and the like; you will note that these are all forms of verbal abuse so, not surprisingly, children of psychologically controlling parents may demonstrate relational aggression. Interestingly, the authors point out that research shows that this is a robust association across all age groups and cultures; it is as true in China as it is in Belgium and the United States. Finally, another source for relationally aggressive behavior may be an inability to read social cues except in negative terms, especially when they are ambiguous. The researchers write that parents "may directly or indirectly 'teach' their children to interpret social information in a hostile, relationally aggressive manner." Basically, they are teaching or tacitly modeling "tit for tat" reactions, such as reinforcing a child's mistrust of someone else's motives ("There's no need to invite him to your party because he's really not your friend") or encouraging a child to retaliate for a slight. Insecure attachment, as we'll see, plays a role, too.

In the end, though, it would appear we learn these behaviors. We're not, as Lady Gaga would have it, born this way.

The Abuser Down the Hall: Siblings

Abusive behavior doesn't just sprout and take hold in public settings such as the hallways and playing fields of schools; in fact, there's evidence that peer bullying in school has its roots in sibling bullying and abuse.

Once again, a cultural trope—in this case, sibling rivalry—rolls off the tongue as a universal truth and normalizes all manner of behavior, as if the Old Testament didn't point out the real dangers of that particular rivalry in the story of Cain and Abel. Alas, the cultural acceptance of sibling rivalry as normal, expected, and benign effectively allows us to turn a blind eye to domestic bullying, which, not surprisingly, is connected to bullying outside the home.

In his book *Sibling Aggression*, Dr. Jonathan Caspi notes that this normalization isn't just limited to laypeople but to professionals as well. He writes that, despite a growing body of research that shows otherwise, "the mistaken belief that sibling violence is not harmful normalizes it. Statements such as 'My brother beat on me and I am fine' and 'Boys will be boys' minimize honest appraisals of possible effects and validate its continued use." He notes that practitioners, too, grew up with the same social context—thinking that sibling aggression is normal—and so their judgments about family dynamics are often clouded by their own internalized views. He surmises that this point of view limits research as well.

First published in 2012, Caspi's book was a response to the paucity of information on sibling aggression and the absence of strategies for professionals to identify and treat it. He uses sibling aggression as an umbrella term that encompasses four categories that he arranges in order of effect, going from most mild to severe; in order, they are competition, conflict, violence, and abuse. I think that his approach illuminates our discussion of verbal abuse in meaningful ways, especially when it comes to normalizing it. I have omitted his discussion of sexual violence and abuse because it is beyond the scope of this book.

• Competition

This isn't necessarily a bad thing since healthy competition can motivate and challenge siblings to develop their skills and talents. Famous siblings in sports—the Williams sisters or the Manning brothers—immediately come to mind. That said, when a parent or parents initiates the competition and its aim is to highlight one sibling's flaws or inadequacies, competition moves from being inspirational to hurtful and damaging. (Think about the Jackson Five, their siblings, and their horribly abusive father, for example.) Caspi notes that most of the time, one sibling's advanced skills don't damage the other's self-esteem.

• Conflict

Every family experiences some amount of conflict and, as Caspi notes, constructive sibling conflict promotes social and emotional competence, teaches problem solving, and helps a child hone his or her emotional regulation. (As a side note, my own thought is that for this to happen, parents have to have modeled and implemented cooperative ways of dealing with disagreements and conflict.) On the other hand, it's clear that constant negative conflict between siblings can alter the dynamic of a family in myriad unhealthy ways. As we will see in the next section of this chapter, verbally abusive parents often have a hand in sustaining or amping up this kind of sibling conflict.

• Violence

Dr. Caspi notes that the terms "sibling violence" and "sibling abuse" are often used interchangeably because they both entail physical and verbal acts that intend to do harm. However, he distinguishes violence from abuse, adding another level of understanding to our inquiry. He writes that "Violence reflects mutual or bidirectional aggression in which both siblings aim to harm each other in a concert of perceived egalitarian relationship." Sibling physical violence—hitting, biting, pinching, kicking—is astonishingly prevalent; some researchers' estimate its prevalence to be as high as 96 percent of all families, while others put it at 80 percent. But, as Dr. Caspi points out, physical violence is very difficult to distinguish from animated roughhousing or even rough-and-tumble play so these numbers may be greatly inflated or understated because of parental confusion about what's "normal" between siblings and what's not. Most importantly, research supports Dr. Caspi's contention that this kind of mutual sibling violence doesn't damage self-esteem.

Some readers will share my initial confusion, reading that this "even-steven" and mutual mano-a-mano type of violence isn't necessarily harmful or damaging, but that is what research shows. Let's consider rough-and-tumble play, for example. Joseph L. Flanders, Vanessa Leo, and their colleagues cite research that shows that physically aggressive behaviors are observable as early as 18 months but begin to taper off in most children by the age of two to three; their study looked at father-child rough-and-tumble play (RTP) to determine whether the father's behavior influenced a higher incidence of continuing physical aggression in children. It's widely recognized that fathers play with children differently than mothers do, regardless of gender, and that kids prefer dads' style of play over moms'.

RTP is characterized by aggressive behaviors such as "wrestling, grappling, jumping, and chasing in a play context." Fathers often socialize both sons and daughters through this kind of physical play, which is associated positively with emotional regulation, self-control, the ability to read emotional cues, and even sensitivity to others; these are important skills for self-development and permit children to negotiate social rules in peer settings with more ease. What Flanders and his team found was that when fathers controlled and set limits during RTP, their children demonstrated lower levels of physical aggression in daily life; in contrast, the children of fathers who didn't set limits and shucked off dominance were more likely to be more physically aggressive in later life.

So mutual physical aggression actually has its benefits, as counterintuitive as that may seem. To put it all in context, I turned to Dr. Joseph Burgo, an expert on narcissism, shame, and masculinity, and author of *The Narcissist You Know*. In his words, "Physically violent interactions between siblings that are bi-directional serve two purposes. First, they teach boys how to manage their own aggressive tendencies as well as those of other boys; and second, they help them to feel they can hold their own in rivalry or competition with other males (their brothers), thereby making them feel more confident in their own abilities and raising their self-esteem."

Abuse is another matter entirely.

• Abuse

The distinction that Caspi makes between violence and abuse largely rests on power; if he considers the first to be "bidirectional" or "mutual," then sibling abuse is "unidirectional hostility where one sibling seeks to overpower the other via a reign of terror and intimidation and reflects an asymmetrical power arrangement." The abusive sibling not only wants to humiliate and render the other powerless but he or she is also intent on aggrandizing him- or herself through the act; there are absolutely no psychological benefits to abuse. Caspi notes four kinds of sibling abuse—physical, sexual, psychological or verbal, and relational—but verbal abuse is by far the most prevalent.

Among siblings, verbal abuse includes insults and name-calling, as well as threats to property. Again, because siblings do chivy for attention in the household, it may be difficult for the parents to distinguish among vying for attention, expressing frustration, and true verbal abuse, which is about dominance.

We will explore what science knows about the effect of verbal abuse on young children in the next chapter but will mention here the research specifically pertinent to sibling abuse in childhood, which has been associated with misconduct at school, peer bullying, and poor peer relationships, as well as anxiety and depression. Research by R. C. Kessler and J. W. Magee in 1994 found that children victimized by a sibling or other family members were six times more likely to experience a major depressive disorder in adulthood.

A 2012 article by Dieter Wolke and Alexandra J. Skew reviewed four quantitative studies of sibling bullying from the United State, Israel, Italy, and the United Kingdom, both to look at trends and to see whether sibling bullying predicted bullying in school settings. They found that bullying was widespread, with nearly 50 percent involved in bullying every month (either as a perpetrator or victim) and some 16 to 20 percent reporting bullying at home. And indeed, they found that sibling bullying predicted school bullying, either as a victim or a perpetrator.

The Familial Context for Sibling Abuse

Parental tolerance of what is actually sibling abuse may be a function of ignorance and misunderstanding of its severity and impact, as well as a failure to distinguish between abusive treatment and "normal" sibling rivalry; when this happens, it is misguided but not intentional. Alas, that is not always the case, and in some dysfunctional families, parents actively help drive sibling abuse.

Parents who are combative by inclination, controlling, high in narcissistic traits, and who are verbally abusive themselves often weaponize whatever competition and conflict already exist among the children in the household, both by favoritism and by scapegoating.

Cultural myths tell us that parents love each child equally. But for reasons that are both complicated and simple at once, what experts call Parental Differential Treatment—yes, that would be playing favorites—is so common that it has an acronym, PDT. The truth about PDT is complicated, and yes, it happens in families where there is no verbal abuse at all as well as in those where abusive behaviors are rife. Let's begin with the benign because that will give us insight into how PDT gets normalized and overlooked.

Some of favoritism has to do with what experts call "goodness of fit," which refers to the way a mother's or father's personality "fits" with that of the infant; it's really shorthand for describing how one child is simply easier to parent than another because of similarity and likeness to the parent. The example I always use is that of a mother who needs a fair amount of quiet in her life and is more introverted than not; imagine her first with a child who is more like her than not—an infant or toddler who's relatively low-key and prefers quiet stimulation to physical play—and then imagine her with a child bursting with energy who is quick to explore and needs guidance and boundaries. The quiet child will be easier for her to mother than the one who requires her to be on active duty 24/7; she may love both children, but she may inadvertently play favorites with the easier child. The same thing applies to a father who may find it easier to parent a son or daughter who mirrors his temperament and personality more closely. The task of the loving parent is to stay conscious and aware and make sure that she or he doesn't differentiate treatment in this way.

Do keep in mind that this unintentional differential treatment nonetheless has deleterious effects on the individual growth and development of every child in the family that, research shows, last long into the lifespan, whether the child is the favorite or not. Judy Dunn and Robert Plomin, experts on siblings, famously asserted that seeing a sibling being treated differently outweighed whatever love the child was actually shown by the parent. Even the so-called benign version of PDT, which sometimes has a real-life rationale—a child needs more support and attention because of some sort of disability, for example, or has experienced some kind of developmental lag, has real and untoward influence on family dynamics.

But this isn't the kind of favoritism we are focusing on in this section. We're looking at the kind that tends to be conscious and is often rationalized, on the one hand, and denied, on the other. Mothers and fathers high in control or narcissistic traits, those who are combative by nature or hew to an authoritarian style of parenting, deliberately use favoritism and scapegoating to manipulate sibling relationships and dynamics. In some families, the favorite and the scapegoat are rotating roles—reflecting how well or badly a given child is playing by the parent's rules—or they can be fixed and stable. Either way, verbal abuse is used to manage behavior. Favoritism heats up whatever competition and conflict already exist and makes them even more toxic. A mother or father adds fuel to the fire by comparing siblings and uses personal attacks and name-calling—"Why can't you be like your brother instead of being lazy and dumb?" or "Why can't you make me proud like your sister does instead of embarrassing me and the rest of the family?"—not just to solidify the parent's power (and the rush that comes with exercising it) but also to motivate all the children in the family to fall into line. There are numerous studies that link parental favoritism and sibling aggression, as Neil Tippett and Dieter Wolke note.

The shadowy flip side of favoritism is scapegoating, which is also a form of verbal abuse.

In ancient tribal societies, a goat—yes, that's where the term comes from—was chosen to represent the group's collective sins to appease an angry deity; it's mentioned in the Old Testament in the Book of Leviticus. By casting the animal out, the tribe symbolically guaranteed itself a clean slate going forward. Scapegoating appears in most, if not all, groups—from entire nations to towns to organizations—in times of turmoil. Naming a scapegoat and blaming him/her/them for the crisis at hand facilitates not just a sense of unity (us versus them), but also, in authoritarian societies, provides a go-to explanation for societal problems.

In an interesting article, Gary Gemmill, an expert in organizational behavior, points out that assigning a child the role of the scapegoat allows all the other members of the family to think of themselves as emotionally healthier and more stable than they actually are since they're not required to take responsibility for their behaviors or actions. The one thorn in the family's side (so the mother or father maintains) is the presence of the scapegoat, and if he or she could be "fixed" or "made to act better" or perhaps gotten rid of, then family life would be perfect. Needless to say, this is part and parcel of the verbal abuser's power play because it pins blame on one person for a grab bag of ills.

The presence of a scapegoat provides a ready explanation when things don't go as planned or as the parent imagined them taking place and also provides a person to blame the mistake or disaster on; sometimes, scapegoating and blame-shifting, another form of verbal abuse, are indistinguishable. Blame trumps responsibility, and of course, blaming makes everyone left standing eager to belong to the blameless team; needless to say, the parent is *never* to blame. So when the dog gets out and digs up the neighbor's garden, it's going to be Aidan or Leann who takes the fall for not latching the door, and that will prompt either or both children to tattle on each other. Controlling people want there to be a reason bad things happen and someone to pin them on. In the household that includes verbal abuse, knowing that someone is going to have to bear the blame, regardless of the circumstances, pits siblings against each other, and those siblings work hard to stay in a parent's or the parents' good graces. As part of their strategy to duck and cover, many will participate in the blame game; in this way, verbal abuse often has generational roots.

The pattern is much more scarring to individual development when being the scapegoat is permanent. The permanent scapegoat permits the parent to make sense of family dynamics and the things that displease her or him without taking personal responsibility or feeling the need for any introspection or action. Scapegoating delivers a ready-made explanation for fractiousness or any other deviation from what a parent expects the family to look like. Similarly, the attention of the other children in the family is directed away from how the parent acts and, instead, is focused on the one person who's "messing it all up," and effectively, blame becomes a team sport. In that way, sibling rivalry gets weaponized and normalized.

A large-scale study by Neil Tippett and Dieter Wolke showed that lack of parental warmth and support, poor parent-child relationships, and use of physical punishment were all associated with sibling aggression, confirming the findings of other research. It will surprise no one that sibling aggression is also predictive of peer bullying, either as the bully or victim.

Surveying the Landscape of Verbal Abuse

Because these behaviors take place in the context of emotional connection, the person being abused may have difficulty identifying them as toxic and abusive for many different reasons, including a fear of losing the relationship, a tendency to placate even at the cost of being abused, being insecure about the validity of one's own perceptions; and other considerations such as financial dependence, shared assets, or dependent children. Remember that verbal abuse *always* depends on an imbalance of power in the relationship.

I've divided the behaviors into *overt* verbal abuse—the kind that is articulated and spoken—and what I call *covert* or *quiet* verbal abuse, which actually may not involve words at all. On the overt list, I have included *contempt*, which is not a behavior but an emotion. It deserves singling out because when it's added to other kinds of verbal abuse, it turns up the heat.

Looking for Clarity

Because there's confusion about what is and isn't abusive, let's lay out some distinctions that may help you navigate the landscape; this section is adapted from *The Daughter Detox Question & Answer Book*.

• Arguing per se is not abusive

Marital expert John Gottman is very clear on this: It's not whether you argue but how you argue that matters. People in intimate or close settings are bound to have all manner of differences of opinion, and being able to express those differences openly, being able to compromise and find middle ground or, occasionally, cede to your partner's wishes are the working parts of a healthy relationship. Someone losing his or her temper or getting angry isn't automatically abusive either. It depends on how often it happens. But you can reasonably expect everyone, including you, to lose control once in a while.

But arguing is abusive when the other person demeans you, marginalizes you, silences you, stonewalls, and/or gets personal. Abuse includes calling you names, mocking you, telling you to shut up, refusing to answer you, or using the argument as an opportunity to name and list all of your flaws. The goal of this behavior is to shut down dialogue, put you down, and keep you in place.

• Criticism is not abusive

Again, in an ongoing relationship—whether it's intimate or professional—taking issue with someone's actions or attitude isn't off limits. Suggesting to someone that there might have been a better way to handle something or to respond to someone isn't abusive, nor is it abusive to suggest that someone cool down because they're overreacting to a situation that isn't, by its nature, emotionally charged. Many rejection-sensitive people are quick to label any kind of criticism, no matter how mild, as abusive. Hearing the truth about our missteps or failures can sting, but if it's done with care, it's not abuse.

But making criticism a litany of your character failings or flaws *is* abusive. John Gottman calls this "kitchen sinking"—as in throwing everything but the kitchen sink at the other person—and if every time he or she criticizes you, the person begins with the words "You always" or "You never," he or she has crossed over from constructive criticism to abuse. The person will usually mention every misstep and mistake you've ever made with the intention of making you feel utterly worthless; the intention is to demean, not enlighten, you.

• Complimenting or admiring other people is not abusive

Pointing out good qualities in other people—from their looks or charm to their success or ability to do something well—and talking about them as appealing may be annoying to a spouse, partner, or friend but it's not abusive. It's perfectly fine to admire other people even if you're in a committed relationship or a friendship. It's normal to think that an actor or actress is hot or to comment on your neighbor's cool. You are allowed to look and admire, but it's wise to keep your spouse, partner, or friend's insecurities in mind.

This is a very tender area for children so, as a parent, you should absolutely make sure that you are *not* making a comparison between your child and another. If your parent did this—constantly compared you negatively to your siblings, cousins, neighbors, or anyone else— in terms of behavior, looks, achievement, temperament, or anything else you were verbally abused.

But complimenting others to make someone feel small, ugly, or less than *is* abusive. Drawing comparisons between how you look and act and how utterly fabulous someone else is is mean-spirited and nasty at best and, if a habit, downright abusive. There's a big difference between commenting on how good Joe looks now that's he working out and saying "Boy, if you took care of yourself the way Joe does, I'd be so much more turned on" or admiring the décor in a neighbor's home and saying "If you were as talented at homemaking as Leslie, I'd be spending more time at home." This is an area where many rejection-sensitive people, especially those who are deeply insecure, often get tripped up. How the thought is expressed and the intention behind the thought both matter.

• Ending a relationship is not abusive

Yes, that's right. Relationships from marriages to friendships to business partnerships end for lots of reasons and deciding that the connection is no longer right for you is completely legitimate and not abusive at all. Yes, people may be hurt by your decision, but it's within your rights to make it.

But threatening to end a relationship if you don't do X or Y is abusive. Capitalizing on knowledge about you and your fears and insecurities is the modus operandi here. This kind of brinkmanship— especially if it happens often—is verbal abuse, highly manipulative, and meant to make you capitulate, along with feeling inadequate and guilty.

If a relationship has been serious or has lasted a significant length of time, ghosting, or disappearing without a trace—being unreachable by phone or text or any other way—is not the same as ending a relationship thoughtfully and consciously. This behavior is meant to punish you and make you feel powerless; it is abusive.

The Tactics of Verbal Abuse

There is some overlap among and between these—for example, blame-shifting and guilt-tripping are kissing cousins in a way, as are ignoring and the silent treatment—but the point here is to provide an adequate survey for those of us who live in a culture that doesn't quite believe in the power of words to subdue, subjugate, and manipulate and that questions whether something that leaves no visible bruises (once again to echo the title of Rachel Louise Snyder's brilliant book) is actually real. The point is that whatever self-doubt we may have gets magnified by that cultural lens. Most people will ask themselves the same questions over and over: Is it really abusive? Am I exaggerating? Am I too sensitive? These are also the default positions of a person who is in a relationship he or she is not willing to lose but in which there is continued verbal abuse.

If there is a common thread among those who were verbally abused, it is this statement: "I wish I had been hit instead. That way, I would have had bruises to show." The second-guessing and insecurity about verbal abuse, the wondering whether the behavior was deliberate or really abusive, that dogs so many who were targeted is one major reason we must bring the subject out of the shadows and into the light so we can see the invisible wounds.

Over the course of many pages, we will discover that verbal abuse plays dress-up in our culture. It masquerades as strength, directness, discipline, good intentioned correction, tough love, and other supposed forms of "improvement." It is time to draw back the curtain on all of that.

Overt and Fully Expressed Verbal Abuse

These behaviors employ words but may also be reinforced by physical gestures (eye rolling, laughter, headshaking, for example). Since all verbal abuse is meant to be threatening, I have not made "threats" a category, but I have categorized it as "brinkmanship," which is at the end of the threat spectrum, just before physical harm.

Note that I haven't included sexual harassment, which does have a verbal component and always involves an imbalance of power. That said, it is a highly directed form of abuse that intends a specific kind of exploitation and takes place in a tightly defined arena and is thus different from these other forms of verbal abuse.

Belittling

Parents who are high in narcissistic traits, combative by nature, or high in control exercise their power over family dynamics by a system of reward and punishment. Those children who are deserving of reward for hewing to the rules and standards are complimented and allowed to feel good about themselves; this teaches children that praise and what passes for love come with strings attached and must always be earned. Those who are punished are labeled losers, in contrast, and are belittled and made to feel small, insignificant, and unworthy.

Belittling is deliberate and highly motivated; its intent is to chip away at the target's self-esteem and resilience and make him or her more malleable. It may be very hard for a child to see belittling as abusive and calculated behavior because it doesn't require a raised voice, and sometimes, in addition to the parent's home court advantage of having the power, there's enough of a factual basis in what's said that the child just absorbs it as truth. Here are some random examples: "What makes you think you'll make the team since you didn't last year?" or "If you got an A on the test, it must not have been very hard" or "Boy, they must have had some bottom-of-the-barrel applicants if you got it." All of these are relatively subtle ways of diminishing a person's present while reminding him or her of past failures.

Adults can be belittled, too, and again, the abuser will often mix in just enough of a reminder of a past failure or misstep to make the put-down more effective. Again, belittling someone is a way of keeping the imbalance of power sturdy.

Blame-Shifting

First and foremost, blame-shifting exploits the imbalance of power associated with verbal abuse to the max. It is a "Get of Jail" card, as in the Monopoly game, that reassures the abuser by offering up an excuse for behavior and entraps the abused in a single swoop.

The imbalance of power in the parent-child relationship makes it easy to blame-shift; other forms of verbal abuse, such as belittling, shaming, and the like, are easily mixed into blame-shifting. Basically, the parent uses justification of her or his behavior as another verbally abusive tool: "If you weren't bad so often, I wouldn't have to yell at you" or "If you acted more like your sister, you'd get treats, too" or "I wouldn't have to punish you if you listened to begin with."

With an adult, this particular form of verbal abuse and manipulation depends on the abuser really knowing your insecurities and typical responses to arguments or disagreements, which might include your steadfast avoidance of conflict or your proclivity to play the peacemaker, your tendency to backtrack on your positions, your desire to please or your tendency to question the validity of your thoughts and feelings, or a combination of some or all of these behaviors. Most of the people caught in this web grew up in households where their emotional needs weren't met and were unloved, unsupported, or downright picked on in their families of origin. This is also true of the abuser, but he or she has learned to cope differently.

Mind you, most of the time the abuser doesn't look you in the face and say, "This is all your fault because . . . ," although he or she might from time to time; it's usually stealthier than that. Let's say you complain about his or her behavior and the argument escalates until suddenly the abuser says, "I wouldn't have acted that way if you weren't always nagging me" or "If you didn't always start in when I am dead tired from work, I wouldn't lose my temper" or "If you weren't always focused on you and your needs, we wouldn't be fighting." The chances are good that the blame-shifting works because you want this relationship to thrive and suddenly you feel awful, and you hear yourself apologize. Since your goal is to have things work out between the abuser and you, you don't even see you've been played.

Blame-shifting is also motivated by the need to strip the target of a sense of agency; what's likely to happen is that, under attack, the target will resort to old default positions such as apologizing to or trying to placate the abuser. Inevitably, she or he will revert to another old, learned behavior, which is self-blame. That is, of course, what the narcissist or controller wants.

Body-Shaming

Body-shaming is a specific kind of bullying that can take place in every setting you can imagine, including inside the family of origin or in a family of your own making, in any relationship you can name from acquaintances to friends to spouses, in school, the office, and, yes, on the Internet. While it's often thought of as a problem that just girls and women face, boys and men are body-shamed as well. This kind of verbal abuse is given a boost by the backdrop of cultural standards of female beauty and definitions of masculinity.

Not surprisingly, body-shaming in childhood, especially by a parent, doesn't just affect self-esteem but can also skew a son's or daughter's ability to see his or her physical self clearly. I hear this from daughters all the time, and I will admit this was a problem for me for years. My mother told me I was fat from the time I was little, and I believed her because, in truth, my body looked nothing like hers. She was naturally thin—she never dieted—and had a boyish build; I was a slightly chubby child who grew up to be a busty and curvy teen who was always on a diet. I wasn't overweight by any stretch of the imagination, but between my mother's carping and the ideal body image of the 1960s and 1970s—boyish, small breasted, with a concave belly—I looked in the mirror and saw a fat girl. Old photographs tell me something else entirely and make me sad for that young woman, me, who fretted so about being fat and was always trying to starve herself.

Body-shaming is often used by parents to humiliate, demean, and marginalize their daughters or sons—again, it's a form of bullying—

and can be overt or covert, focused on looks or physical ability. It can make a short and unathletic son fill with shame and self-loathing when his lack of prowess on the ski slope and tennis court is considered a deficit of character, especially when it's pointed out that his taller siblings are aces. One theme that comes up with frequency is looking like someone disliked or hated and having that person's looks and flaws projected onto you. It might be an ex-husband and father ("No wonder you are so difficult and awful. You look exactly like your father!"), as it was for one daughter, but it could easily be some other relative, such as an overbearing grandparent. All of it is projection and none of it has anything to do with the person who is the target of this kind of verbal abuse.

The end goal of all verbal abuse is to make one person feel powerful and the other humiliated and powerless, and body-shaming is no different. Body-shaming packs a wallop because it's echoed by society at large, with its image of the skinny and perfect girl who seems to subsist on air and the guy who's the captain of the team. Body-shaming can be overt (telling someone she's fat or calling someone a runt or mocking how he or she looks) or covert, as in telling someone that "you are brave to wear that piece of clothing" (translation: you are actually too fat to wear that) or "I'm not sure that prints suit you" (translation: you look like a walking couch) or "I know you love your chocolate, but I try not to eat too many carbs" (translation: maybe you should try my approach and then maybe you wouldn't be so fat) or "It's amazing how different a jumpsuit looks on Denise than it does on you" (translation: Denise looks hot and you don't).

Body-shaming finds fertile ground almost everywhere, but it remains verbal abuse. It's never a joke.

Brinkmanship

Of all the types of verbal abuse, none relies more on the imbalance of both power and commitment than this one, which is a close cousin of stonewalling because they both effectively halt any dialogue or discussion. While stonewalling involves a refusal to speak, brinkmanship relies on a few carefully chosen words and a not-so-veiled threat. As the term suggests, this tactic pushes the dialogue to its furthest point, most usually a point of no return, so that the target of the abuse is forced to back down. Brinkmanship is also closely aligned with dismissing, once again pushing dismissal to its ultimate conclusion.

Adults report being shut down during childhood by parents who used brinkmanship to have them toe the line. An example of brinkmanship from parent to child might be the following or a variation on this theme: "Well, if you're so unhappy here, maybe you should just move to a friend's place. Or maybe you want me to contact social services and have you placed somewhere." As outlandish as this sounds, you would be surprised how many daughters and sons reported being threatened in this way. It happens even more frequently to children of divorce who are either splitting their time between parents' homes or live permanently with one. Kit, 47, wrote that, "The threat of being sent to live with my dad and his new wife, who lived in another state, was constant during my childhood; it was her go-to tool when I displeased her or questioned her. And of course, it worked until I was about 13, when I suddenly realized that she was bluffing because she still resented my father's leaving enough and had fought so hard for full custody that she'd never let him 'win' in that way. She still used brinkmanship, but the threats were different, like grounding me for life, not paying for college, and stuff like that. But I didn't realize until I was married that I had no clue how to argue or talk things through without resorting to brinkmanship myself. It was a skill I'd never learned and, thank God, my husband called me out on it. I was lucky because the realization came early on in the marriage and the counseling I received allowed me to learn how to argue constructively without threats. My mother continued to do it to me and then tried doing it to my daughter and son, and I went no-contact with my mother about a decade ago." It should be said that not everyone is as lucky as Kit in terms of realizing what exposure to brinkmanship does to you.

Brinkmanship in adult-on-adult relationships happens all the time, alas. Again, what's being manipulated here is the target's desire to have the relationship work, so the words "If you're so unhappy, why don't you just leave?" are likely to end in a flood of apologies or placating or retreat. It is all about the imbalance of power.

Contempt and Disdain

There's probably no need to discuss what happens when a mother or father—in the flush of power—dismisses a child with contempt. Since children look to their mothers and their fathers for love, validation, and support, we know that contempt—which strips you to the bone and makes you feel worthless—is highly damaging. If the person or people who put you on the planet think you're not worth their time of day, who will?

When seen in the context of adult relationships, contempt is the second of John Gottman's "Four Horsemen of the Apocalypse," his predictors of marital failure. (Criticism, defensiveness, and stonewalling are the other three.) Criticism, when combined with contempt, is a specific form of verbal abuse, when your supposed habits of mind and character traits become the focal point for the attack. But even though contempt is the fuel that can burn a relationship to the ground, it may also be used as a cudgel or threat.

An interesting paper by researchers Agneta H. Fischer and Ira Roseman published in 2007 specifically looked at the differences between anger and contempt, and their observations are of use to us as we puzzle out what is and isn't verbal abuse, especially since we've already seen how the fact that angry people can, in the moment, be verbally abusive seems to sow confusion. Their tack was to focus on the motivational and relational components of anger and contempt, which, they posited, were indeed very different. From their perspective, they categorized anger as an *attack-oriented emotion*; anger, they argue, is aimed at attacking another person in order to get a better outcome. Put another way, the angry person's motive is to have the target change his or her behavior and anger is an effort to get that done; so while anger is a negative emotion, it can actually play a role in problem-solving and reconciliation. (I have to say, as someone who's not a psychologist, that I think this happens some of the time but not always. Anger can also be an abusive tool.) But what's more interesting is the contrast to contempt, which they identify as part of the *exclusive-emotion family.* By the time you have begun to feel contempt for the person you are targeting, you have already crossed the Rubicon, appraising the person as inferior and not even worthy of reconciliation. Their three studies confirmed their observations.

But remember that the expression of contempt can be an abusive tool, basically threatening the target with exclusion if she or he doesn't toe the line or do the abuser's bidding, plus it lobs grenades into the target's neediness and self-esteem. Since verbal abuse is about an imbalance of power, we can't ignore the fact that the abuser may well enjoy the show.

Controlling by Stealth

I've literally taken a page out of Dr. Craig Malkin's book, *Rethinking Narcissism*, by including stealth control; in the book, he flags it as a warning sign that you are dealing with a narcissist. I happen to think it's a hugely useful term because when we think of controlling or manipulative people, we tend to imagine overt control, such as insisting on being the only one to make important decisions (about finances, spending, vacations, etc.) or being adamant that there is only one right way of doing things. The stereotype of this kind of abuser is the guy or gal wearing a T-shirt that reads "It's my way or the highway."

But there are others, including those high in narcissistic traits, who prefer playing the puppeteer and pulling the strings out of sight. Stealth control gives the narcissist and the manipulator a far less obvious strategy—it looks nothing like "my way or the highway"—which permits him or her to maintain independence, on the one hand, and take over fully without the target being any the wiser, on the other. Stealth control starts small and may be quite charming at first blush: for example, insisting that the restaurant you both decided on isn't "good enough" and changing it up, or telling you that the clothes you bought don't do you justice and steering you in another direction. These gestures may come across as thoughtful caring or concern, but they are often the starting points of a pattern of stealth control, which will escalate. The bigger game plan here is to have you forget your own wants and needs and to conflate them with what the controller wants; keep in mind that verbal abuse is always about power. Eventually, you might find that the laid-back weekend with old college friends you had planned has been upended by "way better" tickets or a trip to another city, or, if you are married, that the monies you had allocated to something you had both agreed on were switched to something "better."

The goal of this kind of verbal abuse is forgetfulness, as in forgetting you are you and that you once had needs and wants that were yours. It exploits insecurities and neediness, and it works because, at the beginning at least, it looks like solicitousness and caring until it devolves into overt control. The victim ends up drinking from the river of forgetfulness that the Greeks called Lethe and becomes a pawn in someone else's game. Not good.

Dismissing

While this may, at a glance, seem akin to ignoring—when a person simply pretends that he or she isn't seeing or hearing you—or even belittling, it's actually different and more akin to gaslighting in its effects. Dismissive mothers and fathers specifically marginalize their children's thoughts and feelings, as well as their expressions of need, by undercutting those expressions. This can happen in a very literal way with the mother asking the child what she'd like to eat or what color she'd like her room painted, getting an answer, and then serving up a different meal or choosing another color as if the child had never spoken; done often enough, it's an effective way of teaching a child how very unimportant she is. Dismissing emotions and thoughts often follows a set script, too. For example, a daughter confides that she's been excluded from a group at school and tells her mother that it's painful; her mother keeps doing what she's doing until, finally, the daughter asks her if she's listening. The mother responds by saying, "I am but you really have to stop being such a whiner and crybaby. You'll get over it. It's not that big a deal."

This smack-down happens on a number of levels, crushing self-esteem and making the son or daughter feel unimportant and insignificant. The chances are good, though, that he or she will normalize the behavior— "it's just how Mom is"—unless the mother treats a sibling differently.

This kind of verbal abuse follows the same pattern in adult-on-adult relationships; dismissing someone's feelings or thoughts as irrelevant or insignificant consistently increases the abuser's sense of power and increases the target's insecurities while decreasing her or his sense of agency. It is often hard to recognize and easy to rationalize.

Gaslighting

What is gaslighting, precisely? It takes its name from a 1938 play, Gas Light, and then a 1944 movie, *Gaslight,* the latter starring Charles Boyer and Ingrid Bergman. In it, Boyer manipulates Bergman and distracts her from his criminality by trying to convince her that she is going insane. And that's what gaslighters do: They make the target believe that his or her grip on reality is tenuous at best and nonexistent at worst. The most common tactics are insisting that something that happened didn't, dismissing a claim by saying it was simply imagined, telling the person flat out that she or he is losing it or crazy or that their perceptions aren't to be relied on. Gaslighters exploit their target's fears, insecurities, vulnerabilities, and neediness to their own ends.

While it takes some concerted effort to gaslight another adult— even a needy or insecure one—gaslighting a child is remarkably easy because of the enormous power and authority a parent has, by definition. What child can stand up to the words "You're imagining it because it never happened" when uttered by her or his mother or father, each of whom is the ruler of the very small universe in which the child lives?

The successful use of gaslighting very much depends on the exploitation of your vulnerabilities as an adult. Among them are:

- Your own normalization of gaslighting as you experienced it in your family of origin. If you don't recognize the pattern in its past setting, you aren't likely to recognize it in the present.

- Your inclination to self-doubt. If second-guessing yourself is something you do all the time because you don't trust your own perceptions, you're an easy target for gaslighting. The person who's trying to control you will manipulate you by telling you that you're overreacting or too sensitive or any other criticism that will get you thinking it must be your fault or that you misread the situation.

• Your avoidance of conflict. The gaslighter knows this about you and uses it to his or her advantage. One way to disarm a gaslighter is to challenge him or her with straightforward facts and not to duck and run for cover. He or she is counting on your avoidance.

• Your tendency to appease and please. This is also learned in childhood, especially if you had a hypercritical or combative mother or father or one who scapegoated you or anyone else who didn't go along to get along. While peacemaking is a good thing, appeasement isn't, and the gaslighter knows that threatening to or withdrawing affection makes you feel vulnerable and anxious and uses that to his or her advantage. Rather than brook outright anger, you may see buying into his or her version of things as the path of least resistance; this, too, is something the gaslighter knows about you.

Guilting and Guilt-Tripping

Some of the most confusing and hardest to see types of verbal abuse are connected to guilt; I've used the words "guilting" and "guilt-tripping" to try to distinguish these from the positive and prosocial role feeling guilty can play in close relationships. Guilting and guilt-tripping are strategies aimed at making you feel bad about yourself and to exert control over you, first and foremost. Even though people often use "guilt" and "shame" interchangeably, it's important to know that, according to psychologists, they are different in meaningful ways. Feeling guilty is *not* the equivalent of feeling ashamed, although both are unpleasant and negative emotions.

Guilt pertains to a single action, inaction, or intention; it's a form of emotional distress, as social psychologist Roy Baumeister and his coauthors point out, "based on the possibility that one may be in the wrong or that others may have that perception." Shame, on the other hand, involves the self, as we will see in detail under the entry on shaming.

While early theorists such as Freud and others believed that guilt was an emotion that resided within the self, according to Baumeister, it's now seen as an emotion that is distinctly interpersonal and that emanates from close connection and relatedness. Guilt can actually strengthen emotional bonds because guilt is triggered by commitment and caring, and when you feel guilty about having hurt someone you care about or having transgressed in a meaningful way, guilt can facilitate personal change. Feeling guilty can lead to apologies and amends, as well as real changes in behavior. If you substitute the word "guilt" with "remorse," the difference is easier to see.

In contrast, guilting and guilt-tripping are meant to deliberately manipulate a person and make him or her bend to the abuser's will by inducing guilt; these strategies often induce shame as well, involving the whole self and not just a single action, as true guilt does. Studies confirm that the children of controlling and coercive parents who use induced guilt in this way suffer psychological wounds that are in line with other kinds of verbal abuse. Let's use the example of the child who is served a dinner he or she doesn't like and the mother says, "You really are an ungrateful and awful person. I get home from work, cook for you, and you can't even be bothered to eat the food." While the mother's words may be rationalized as a way to get the child to eat dinner, the real main course is coercion and control, with side dishes of marginalization and shame. Parents who guilt-trip may often frame things in terms of loyalty and love ("If you really loved me and this family, you wouldn't be fighting me to go to that sleepover"), especially when adolescents begin to voice their own needs and wants.

Adult-on-adult guilting needs an imbalance of power and commitment to thrive; it's the weaker partner—and the one who is desperate for the relationship to work—who can be played in this way. This kind of control is more overt than stealth control, but the target may not recognize it as control if he or she feels guilty.

Hypercriticizing

In many households, verbal abuse is rationalized by parents as addressing the need to correct perceived flaws in the child's character or behavior. Hypercriticality—nitpicking and then magnifying every misstep or mistake—may be "justified" or "explained" by having to make sure the child "isn't too full of himself," "doesn't let his successes go to his head," "learns humility," "knows who's boss," "toughens up," and other self-serving statements that are just excuses. No shouting is necessary because even when delivered in a quiet tone, this barrage of criticism is overwhelming, impossible to process, and internalized as "truths" by the child about his or her essential character. It also makes a child believe she's unworthy of attention and support because she's worthless.

In adult relationships, the abuser may also rely on justification, but criticism shifts from being about an action—overspending, lateness, unwillingness to share chores equally, or anything else—to being highly personal. John Gottman calls this *criticism*, the first of the Four Horsemen, or signs that a relationship is on the brink, and contrasts it to *complaint*. When you complain about someone's action, you are focused on why the complaint is valid—the budget you mutually agreed to didn't include new golf clubs, he/she agreed to walk the dog after work and doesn't, etc.—and you ask him or her to remedy the situation. Criticality focuses on the personal—using words like "You always" or "You never"—and brings up a litany of character flaws. As I mentioned, Gottman calls this "kitchen sinking"—as in throwing everything but the kitchen sink at the person you're criticizing.

Hypercriticality forces the target to walk on eggshells in a perpetual defensive crouch for fear of making a mistake and drawing attention to his or her flaws. It is very psychologically damaging.

Mocking

Almost every one of us has experienced being made fun of—most usually about a physical attribute or habit we cannot change or some aspect of our identity—and the hot flush of shame that accompanies it; being the target of mean laughter hurts whether you are a 45-year-old standing in your living room or a 6-year-old in his mother's kitchen. It is especially devastating when a mother or father—the very person on earth who is supposed to love you unconditionally—treats you with derision.

Although mockery was reported by many who answered my questionnaire for this book, it was often not a stand-alone form of verbal abuse but connected to belittling, ignoring, stonewalling, shaming, and other behaviors. Both men and women reported being mocked for showing emotion—crying, for example—in households that were run largely on the basis of control or combativeness. A finding in the Swedish study I've already mentioned about derisive parenting—that something confided in a parent was not only made public to siblings and others but then weaponized and mocked—was echoed by a surprising number of respondents, many of whom saw it as a breach of trust and/or disloyalty. As one reader wrote," I told my mom about something in strictest confidence that was so upsetting to me. Two days later, my brothers, father, and mother were laughing at me for being 'so sensitive.' It has been 40 years and I cannot tell you how angry that moment makes me. When I finally set boundaries as an adult, my mother and father said everything I said was a fantasy. I now know that's called gaslighting."

Mockery in adult relationships is part of contempt. The abuser deflects the abuse by a litany of defenses—as in "You can't take a joke" or "You are too sensitive"—but they are deflections. Mockery intends to humiliate, is very different from a joke, and is *never* acceptable.

Name-Calling

Here is where the "sticks and stones" trope really enables abuse and also prevents targets from calling the abuser out; thinking that "they're only words" provides children who can't leave a situation a comfort blanket and offers some shade to adults who are sitting under the harsh light of abuse and can't or won't make the hard choices. Name-calling is the most common form of bullying on the planet—children as young as two or three can be relatively adept at it—and is often given a pass with a nod to the "sticks and stones" thing. There isn't a person on the planet who hasn't found him- or herself on the receiving end, and if each of us was honest, we'd cop to being on the giving end too. It is damaging to children and, yes, hurtful to adults, especially in the context of an intimate relationship.

Between and among adults, name-calling is meant to shame you and strip you of power. Using derogatory language again and again—using the b**** or the c*** words to a woman you're in a relationship with or denigrating a man by calling him a useless f**k—can only serve one purpose.

Scapegoating

We've already seen how scapegoating permits a parent or parents to believe that the family is healthier than it is and how it reinforces control over all the family's members, who do what they can to not become a scapegoat. Scapegoating impacts sibling relationships in many ways, some of which last long into adulthood and become part of the family narrative as the scapegoat becomes the black sheep.

A study by Zachary K. Rothschild and others posited and then showed that scapegoating allows a perpetrator to minimize guilt or responsibility for a negative outcome and gives him or her a sense of enhanced control because there's always a reason for a bad outcome. The example I often use is the family car that is vandalized at night—the sides keyed and a tire slashed—while parked in the driveway. If this happened to you, you might be concerned or even call the police, but you're likely to consider it a random incident. But the parent who habitually scapegoats won't approach it that way; instead, he or she will focus on the fact that Jack drove the car last and he didn't lock it, which made it so much easier to vandalize, as if locking it would have protected the paint or the tire. Moreover, Jack didn't turn on the lights that illuminate the driveway and entrance, which gave the vandals the cover of darkness. Voila! In the family's curated narrative, Jack is actually to blame for the car's being vandalized. That is how scapegoating works.

In some families, like Tim's, the scapegoat role was rotating, one that permitted his father to drive his message across with force: "Failure was unacceptable. Talking back was treason. You did what he said, you took the abuse he meted out, or you were ignored and scapegoated. The son who didn't listen up then became the scapegoat until he reformed and 'got the message,' and then the next slacker would become the target. This went on from childhood to the first decade or so of adulthood, until I finally set sail."

In many families, the scapegoat is a permanent role, as it was in Alisha's: "My middle brother, Tom, was the scapegoat because he talked back and resisted my mother's manipulations. It was ironic because, of the four of us, he was the highest achiever—he was athletic and got good grades—but my mother couldn't deal with the fact that she couldn't contain him the way she could me and my two younger siblings. She blamed everything that went wrong on Tom and that, in turn, set off my father, who believed every single lie she told about Tom. The rest of us made ourselves scarce and said as little as possible, trying to stay as neutral as we could so she wouldn't turn on us. Tom left home at 18, put himself through college and then law school, and stopped speaking to our parents ten years ago. He's got to be the most successful black sheep in history. I still see him, but my sister and brother are too scared, even as adults, of pissing my mother off. Even though I wasn't scapegoated, I have tons of issues that I am dealing with in therapy. I spent my whole childhood curled up in a defensive ball."

Counterintuitively, you don't need a herd to become a scapegoat; only children can be scapegoated, too. This is what Dora recounted: "In my mother's telling of the story, everything that has gone wrong in her life can be traced back to me. It was my birth that alienated my father from her and ended up in his seeking a divorce. That isn't the story my dad tells, of course, and I was seven when he left. She never remarried because no one wanted a woman with baggage, the baggage being me. This could be funny since Dad married a woman with two kids, but she didn't mean it as a joke. Ditto her job and why she never rose up the ranks: yes, the Dora factor. At 30, I walked into a therapist's office and ended up confronting my mom, who denied ever doing it. As my therapist pointed out, she shifted from scapegoating to gaslighting. I maintain low contact these days, but I am moving toward estrangement because her inability to own her actions or words makes me nuts."

Not taking responsibility is the home court advantage of scapegoating.

While science illuminates what motivates the abuser to scapegoat, there's no research on how the target gets chosen, so I've culled from the hundreds of stories shared with me for this project and *Daughter Detox* some thoroughly unscientific patterns, which may, nonetheless, be of interest. Some of them are more obvious than others.

• The resister or rebel

Since all verbal abuse is about control and an imbalance of power, it's not surprising that the kid who won't go with the program—whatever that program may be—will be singled out and marginalized for it. This pattern echoes the story Alisha told about her brother, Tom, and may also be the impetus for the rotating scapegoat role in other families.

• The sensitive one

Scapegoating and bullying have similar intentions, and each gives the abuser a rush of power; that's going to be much more satisfying if the kid you pick on really responds and reacts. Additionally, this permits the parent to rationalize the scapegoating as being necessary to "toughen the kid up" or "to stop him or her from being too sensitive." This happens to both sons and daughters and shows up as a strong pattern in many families, unfortunately. The other children do what they can to repress all their emotional reactions, which gives them cover but causes a different kind of damage.

• The outlier

I've come to see that, especially with mothers who scapegoat, thinking a child is an outlier is usually a function of the mother's own goodness of fit; the child is sufficiently different from both herself and her other children that whatever parenting skills she does have are completely overwhelmed and she reacts by shifting the blame onto the child. In the family narrative, this child usually bears the burden of responsibility for the household being hard to run or any other problem the mother might be experiencing.

• **The reminder**

This comes up most frequently with children of divorce who either look like or supposedly "take after" or act like a parent's ex-spouse, but it also comes up with those from intact households in which the child supposedly resembles a family relative who is disliked or hated or is a black sheep or some combination of the three. It can be overtly expressed— "You are just like your dad, irresponsible and lazy"—or covert, as was the case for Dina, who happens to be a psychologist: "As a kid, I couldn't understand why I was always to blame and my sister was always fabulous. I was a straight-A student, high achiever, and my sister was none of those things. But there was history. My father committed the sin of leaving my mother and remarrying happily. I committed the sin of looking like him—tall, thin, brunette, and intellectual. My sister is my mother's physical—blond and petite—and not-too-serious clone. It took the therapy which was part of my training to see the pachyderm in the living room."

Of course, while scapegoating a child is easy for the parent, who holds the reins of power, it can and does happen in adult-on-adult relationships and in larger settings. In the adult intimate relationship, scapegoating does a shadow dance with blame-shifting. Like all verbal abuse, scapegoating is a form of manipulation and the abuser wants the target not just to step into the role but also to believe it is deserved.

Shaming

In the world of popular psychology, no other negative emotion has been explored more than shame, beginning in the 1980s with John Bradshaw's *Healing the Shame That Binds You*, which introduced the term "toxic shame" to millions of people. The damage done by shaming a child has been widely explored in studies specifying effects as various as depression, suicidal thoughts, addiction, and more; internalized and hidden shame is believed to be at the center of narcissistic personality disorder. While guilt focuses on what you've done or haven't done, shame is about who you are, and to be filled with shame is to feel worthless, inadequate, loathsome, unlovable, and more. Shame makes us want to disappear and disconnect, especially from the feeling itself, which Dr. Joseph Burgo calls "a painful awareness of self." Controlling, narcissistic, and combative parents use shaming as a tool of control and manipulation and rationalize it as discipline, which it absolutely isn't. In the culture and some homes, it's regularly used to "toughen" boys up by shaming them for crying, showing emotion, and being "a momma's boy." As one woman, now in her sixties, wrote, "My mom could shame me with a look on her face, sometimes just a flash of a look. The feelings of unworthiness, guilt, and knowing I was bad/defective/too needy were reflexive. It colored all of my relationships."

In his book *Real Boys*, Dr. William Pollack specifically singles out the culturally broad use of shame to control boys, enforcing the code of masculinity through what he calls a "shame-hardening process." Indeed, he suggests that while girls may be shame-sensitive, boys are shame-phobic: "they are exquisitely yet unconsciously attuned to any signal of 'loss of face' and will do just about whatever it takes to avoid shame." The behaviors he notes "range from avoidance of dependency to impulsive action, from bravado and rage-filled outbursts to intense violence." Shaming by a parent is never positive; it is verbal abuse, pure and simple.

In an adult-on-adult relationship, shaming is meant to further weaken the person lacking in power and fill his or her mind with self-loathing. Again, in an intimate relationship, the abuser uses his or her knowledge of you to manipulate you.

Undermining

The goal of this particular form of verbal abuse is to rob the other person of a sense of authority and to invalidate their thoughts or feelings. With small children, who by definition have neither power nor authority, undermining is indistinguishable from dismissing or gaslighting. It can become a form of abuse with older children, especially tweens and adolescents, who are trying to assert themselves or a specific point of view. One caveat, though: While undermining can be deliberate, it can also be unintentional and the result of unattuned or just flat-footed efforts at parenting. Let's distinguish between the two. Let's start with the unintentional undermining first. The girl bursts into tears because she overshot the goal and her soccer team lost. Her mother or father says," Come on. It's only a game. You have to learn to be tougher than that. There's no reason to cry." It's entirely possible that this parent is, indeed, attempting to comfort his or her daughter, but what's actually happening is that the validity of her emotional response is being undercut; again, this isn't deliberately abusive but it is very unhelpful to the child. On the other hand, undermining can be deliberate. Let's say that the older child is having an argument with her mother about politics and the mother responds, "You're just a kid. You don't know anything. Wait until you're older and then you'll see it from my point of view." Bam!

Undermining between adults is usually very deliberate and can be both overt and covert. Parents who undermine each other's authority with regularity—one taking on the disciplinarian role with the other being the "soft" touch—and do so in front of their children model behaviors that, research shows, eventually get aped by their children. Undermining can be mixed with hypercriticality as well as contempt—"Sure, we'll do it your way because your last plan was so successful that it cost us a fortune" or "You're telling me I should listen to you because you once took a psychology course and got a C"—or any other statement that puts the person down and makes them feel small or incompetent.

No Loud Voice Needed: Seeing the "Quiet" or Covert Forms of Verbal Abuse

As hard as it can be to recognize verbal abuse that is articulated for all the reasons I've already noted, quiet abuse is even harder to see because it's so easy for the abuser to deflect any pushback. The charge that "you are too sensitive" or that "you can't take a joke" is used with such frequency by abusers that almost everyone who has been a target mentions it. Yet when people recall the physical gestures or meaningful silences that often comprise quiet abuse, they often say that this kind of abuse packs more of a punch. Remember that the abuser uses her or his knowledge of you—what rattles you, the depth of your emotional neediness, what frightens you—to manage the relationship and maintain power. When a gesture is involved, it's easy to gaslight and simply insist that it never happened, or that you're always reading in, overanalyzing, or just plain making things up. On the receiving end, the voice of self-doubt often pipes up because it all seems so vague. Did he or she really mock you with that eye roll? Did you overreact? And should you make a big deal out of it when nothing was said?

Self-doubt is about your insecurity and doesn't change what happened. The truth? *All* of the above are abusive behaviors.

Expressing Contempt in Gestures

Eye rolling, raised eyebrows, looking down at someone, smirking or laughing, shaking your head with a smile on your face all communicate contempt. This is extraordinarily easy to do to a child given the height advantage an adult has. Yes, it cuts an adult down to size as well. You can abuse someone without saying a word.

Ignoring

A very famous experiment elucidates how ignoring an infant, toddler, or child affects development. Much of the information children have about the world and relationships, as well as about themselves, comes to them secondhand. With a caring and attuned mother who responds to his or her cues, a child begins to fathom that he or she matters and is worthy of attention; these are the seeds that yield healthy self-esteem. The attentive mother communicates the message that "You're fine just as you are," giving the child the courage and confidence to explore the world. But the child with a mother who ignores her learns instead that her place in the world is precarious, even though she doesn't know why.

Thanks to the work of Edward Tronick, his colleagues, and the "Still Face" experiments conducted almost 40 years ago, we actually know how being ignored affects infants and toddlers. (At the time, it was widely believed that infants as young as four or five months didn't actually interact with their mothers.) Tronick videotaped mothers interacting with infants who cooed, pointed, vocalized, and waved their arms in response to their mothers' words, gestures, and smiling faces. (Keep in mind that using videotape in this way in 1978 was new and innovative.) Then Tronick had the mothers simply stop and present a still, expressionless face to their babies. Initially, the babies continued to vocalize and gesture, but when the mothers' faces remained emotionless, the babies looked away and then began to wail. The tapes show the infants literally collapsing in their chairs, overwhelmed by feeling.

Studies done with toddlers capable of speech showed precisely the same pattern when their mothers stopped interacting and presented the still face. They began by trying to reengage their mothers—doing all the cute things that usually worked—but when those failed, they turned their backs on their mothers. Avoidance was preferable to feeling the pain of being ignored, excluded, and loveless.

Of course, in the experiment, the mother's smiling face returned, and the babies recovered, though not quickly or completely. But the effects of being regularly ignored on a child's development are complex and profound. The coping mechanisms she adapts—an anxious or avoidant attachment style—affect her long past childhood and into adulthood and, without therapy or some other earned attachment, for life.

Adults who were ignored in childhood report feeling as though they were "disappeared" by their mother or father; what they internalized was their own lack of worth and importance, as well as the unimportance of their thoughts and feelings. Many of those who answered my questionnaire remarked on how being ignored made them frantic—much like the babies and toddlers in Tronick's "Still Face" experiment. It's impossible not to register the terrific cruelty in deliberately shutting a child down and out in this way.

For ignoring between adults, please look at the next two categories, the silent treatment and stonewalling.

The Silent Treatment

This is what I received from one woman, now 50: "I remember how incredibly scared I got in the moments before—when I had done something wrong—and I saw her eyes narrow and her mouth tighten and she looked at me as though I was something beyond disgusting. I knew that she wouldn't talk to me now, maybe not for days, and I would just start to weep and wail but she'd pretend she didn't see or hear me. My dad and sister would follow her lead, too. Honestly, it would have been less painful if she'd beaten me."

The silent treatment when used on either children or adults is specifically punitive and meant to "teach a lesson" to the offending party by effectively ostracizing them, literally ignoring them, and rendering them powerless to fix or change the situation. The power lies with the person keeping the silence. Like scapegoating, the silent treatment derives its firepower from our human hardwired need to belong and our unconscious fears of being abandoned and cast out. Again, keep in mind that verbal abuse takes place in the context of a close relationship and it's not hard to see why the silent treatment would hurt like hell. That's why the silent treatment works so well as a fulcrum in relational aggression.

Stonewalling

When a person stonewalls you, he or she simply refuses to respond to whatever statement or question came before. Stonewalling among adults can include words and physical gestures as well—folded arms, frowning, and the like—but this abuse is largely defined by the refusal to continue dialogue. Stonewalling is very predatory, and if a child is involved, it's as easy as shooting fish in a barrel, as the saying has it. Being stonewalled is absolutely devastating to a child because she or he lacks developed and effective defense mechanisms. That's exactly what Israeli researchers Ricky Finzi-Dottan and Toby Karu homed in on when they examined the long-term effects of childhood emotional abuse. They concluded that the damage done to individuals' self-esteem had to do with their inability to protect and defend themselves and internalizing the thought that they weren't good enough to warrant their parents' attention when parents were uncaring or harshly controlling. From a child's perspective, being stonewalled may seem very much like being ignored, but it has different emotional consequences, especially as he or she matures; intense anger and frustration, directed at the person stonewalling him or her, may become par for the course.

For adults, stonewalling is built into the relational pattern experts call demand/withdraw and identify as the most toxic and destructive mode of connection; it has been singled out by marital expert John Gottman as the most reliable sign that the union of two people is doomed to fail. The pattern has been studied so often that it even has its own acronym (DM/W). Understanding this pattern and why stonewalling is so toxic gives us special insight into verbal abuse. A meta-analysis review by Paul Schrodt, Paul L. Witt, and Jenna R. Shimkowski revealed that women are most often in the demand position and men in the withdraw slot, although there are exceptions. Theorists have proposed that the differences in how women and men are socialized may account for the skew; in this scenario, women seek out affiliation, are more expressive, and fear abandonment, while men are more autonomous and worry more about engulfment in relationships. While this may be true in some cases, this socialization argument, explored in the late 1980s and 1990s, seems to echo the cultural tropes of the times, epitomized by the enormous success of John Gray's *Men Are from Mars, Women Are from Venus.*

Here, though, is where we need to pay close attention. Other research has investigated how power and the nature of the issue at the center of the conflict contribute to this particular pattern with its two polarized roles. In a relationship characterized by an imbalance of power—with one person more dependent on the other, either monetarily or emotionally, or with one partner making the lion's share of decisions—the less powerful member of the couple is likely to find her or himself in the demanding role. It's the person in the withdrawing position who holds the power. As to conflict, if one person wants change and the other is perfectly happy with the status quo—whether that's the division of labor in the household, the level of intimacy and sharing, the frequency of sex, or anything else—the person seeking change will make the demands. Needless to say, the more a partner is invested in either holding on to the power he or she has or keeping things the way they are, the more he or she will withdraw from the discussion.

Securely attached people who are emotionally confident, accustomed to being both loved and valued, and who believe in their own worthiness tend not to engage in the pattern. Alas, that is not true of the avoidantly attached—individuals who, by virtue of their childhood and life experiences, are uncomfortable with intimacy and are disinclined to pursue it—especially if they are men. A study by Robin A. Barry and Erika Lawrence found that avoidantly attached husbands withdrew in direct proportion to the amount of negative affect expressed by wives in demand situations. This was true both in conflict situations and in those that required the husband to support and take care of his spouse. Similarly, avoidantly attached husbands who perceived discussions about solving problems in marriage as potentially destructive were much more likely to withdraw and disengage.

Regardless of one's original intention—let's assume it was to have a quiet, reasonable, and civilized talk about a relationship—escalation is built into the DM/W pattern, and the pattern itself effectively straps each member of the couple into a reserved seat on an ever-spinning merry-go-round. Withdrawal is likely to spark an increase in demand—a voice that grows louder with every moment of frustration at not being heard. It's at that moment that the dynamic will likely change, with the person in the withdraw position turning toward blame-shifting.

Between adults, the success of stonewalling very much depends on how badly the person being stonewalled wants or needs the relationship to continue. That is always true of verbal abuse.

Withholding

This may seem a counterintuitive inclusion, but I believe that deliberately withholding support and love is verbal abuse in the most important sense. This is absolutely true in the case of a child; the power of what isn't said (and given) cannot be overstated because the void it leaves in a child's psyche and emotional heart is enormous. Children are hardwired to need all the things that the verbally abusive parent neither voices nor demonstrates in order to thrive and develop normally. In truth, words that articulate why a child is worthy of love and attention are as essential as food, water, clothing, and shelter. The next chapter will detail the specifics so you don't need to take it on faith.

In my informed opinion, mothers and fathers who verbally abuse their children absolutely see the effects their words have on their sons and daughters—children weep, tremble, and have no defense mechanisms—and they also see the effects of what is withheld. This was my experience and that of countless others, some of which are recounted in memoirs. When mothers whose children have estranged themselves contact me, which happens often, it takes minutes to see who's who. Since abusive parents tend not to sign up for research that shows them to be abusive, we will have to rely on the reports of professionals in the field.

In adult-on-adult relationships, the abuser also sees the pain inflicted by that which is not given or acknowledged, but the knowledge becomes part of the gamesmanship that keeps the relationship going. Children can't leave a family, but theoretically, an adult can leave a relationship, so there's often a pattern where withholding is momentarily disrupted—giving the target hope that a corner has been turned and ramping up positive emotions fueled by intermittent reinforcement—only to return after a time. Since withholding is a way of keeping the power and control, you need to change the pattern up to keep your partner in thrall. (This is similar to the cycle of domestic violence psychologist Lenore E. Walker brilliantly and famously adduced: tension-building followed by a violent episode followed by a remorseful, or honeymoon, stage.)

Moving Forward

Over the course of these pages, we've seen that verbal abuse takes on many shapes, but its goal remains singular in focus: to maintain control and power over the targeted individual. Our simplistic vision of verbal abuse as being about yelling or calling someone names belies the confusion sown by the covert forms of verbal abuse, especially coming from an intimate. The cultural mantra that "they're only words" adds to the confusion targets of abuse often experience. We'll be looking at why and how we normalize verbal abuse later in these pages, but the important thing to remember is that the abuser is relying on you to default to self-blame or to believe that, somehow, you brought the abuse upon yourself. Sometimes, that will be articulated, but not always. Making you somehow responsible holds you in place and makes it hard for you to assign responsibility where it belongs. This is especially true for the children of a verbally abusive parent, but it can also be true for adults, especially if the relationship is one they're not ready to give up on or leave.

In the next chapter, we'll explore what research, and especially brain science, have discovered about the effects of verbal abuse. It is, in a word, sobering.

Chapter Two

What Science Knows

For all that the culture hesitates to classify verbal abuse as truly damaging and life altering, it's noteworthy that the very opposite is true of physical abuse and violence. Yes, we are back to the gold standard of bruises that show. Everyone—and there are no naysayers in this case unlike other issues that face us—knows that it's not just experiencing physical abuse or violence but even witnessing it can induce trauma and have extreme psychological consequences. Many different streams have fed into this certainty, including the experiences of veterans returning from war with PTSD, years of movies such as *The Deer Hunter* and *American Sniper*, studies of mass killers, research on children who witness domestic violence, stories about how community violence affects children who are simply bystanders, the experiences of survivors of traumatic events such as 9/11 or school shootings, and much more. The robust nature of this train of thought is demonstrated by the extensive inquiries and research that have gone into studying the effects of *simulated* violence contained in video games and movies on children, adolescents, and young adults.

So it is ironic that the culture still adds a question mark when it comes to verbal abuse, especially since Bessel van der Kolk, M.D.—the man who brought awareness of trauma into America's living rooms with his bestselling blockbuster book, *The Body Keeps the Score*—wrote that "over the years our research team has repeatedly found that chronic emotional abuse and neglect can be just as devastating as physical abuse and sexual molestation." It is also ironic that sometimes the bias is evident even in the research community because of the difficulty of separating out verbal and physical abuse. As has been discussed in the Introduction, while verbal abuse doesn't necessarily or automatically lead to physical abuse, verbal abuse is *always* a foundation for domestic violence. Since the effects of physical abuse are so widely known and accepted, it's easy to think that verbal abuse is more like a benign cousin or a steppingstone instead of a force of emotional and psychological destruction on its own. Some of that has to do with the fact that most studies emphasize or focus on the presence of physical abuse because, yes, it can either kill you or turn you into a killer. But the bias is there, as a study by Shalon M. Irving and Kenneth F. Ferraro showed.

The aim of their study was to see the long-term effects of adverse childhood experiences—of physical and verbal abuse—on adult health; they had over 4,200 respondents, roughly half male and half female, who answered questions about abuse and self-reported their health issues (such as smoking, drinking heavily, cancer, diabetes, obesity, heart problems, etc.). The questionnaire participants filled out separated verbal abuse (such as being insulted, sworn at, ignored, threatened with violence) from milder forms of physical abuse (being pushed, grabbed, shoved, slapped) and more violent forms of physical abuse (being beaten up, choked, burned, etc.). The respondents had to identify the abuser (mother, father, sister, brother, general other) and frequency for each item of abuse (never, rarely, sometimes, often). Not surprisingly, the effect of abuse on adult health was robust, confirming other studies, but as the authors note, what *was* surprising was that "the parental physical abuse measures were not significant. When the abuse items were originally separated, it was anticipated that childhood physical abuse would be more consequential." Instead, it was verbal or emotional abuse that was the more salient experience in the sample. There's the cultural bias at work; after all, researchers live in the culture, too.

The goal in this chapter is to pull back the curtain and reveal what science knows about verbal abuse; each of us needs to know it, too. If everyone knew what science knows about verbal abuse, the cultural hesitation would disappear in a nanosecond. Even if the science isn't categorical (and it often isn't), it is convincing enough to reform someone still murmuring, "sticks and stones." We'll begin by looking at the behavioral effects of verbal abuse and then move on to the effect it has on the developing brain.

Verbal Abuse, Attachment, and Mental Models

When daughters and sons answered my questionnaire, the descriptions of how they felt as children growing up in an atmosphere permeated by parental verbal abuse were almost universally in physical, not emotional, terms. Almost everyone noted that they weren't able to identify their feelings at the time because they had, by and large, normalized the abuse, a subject we will turn to in detail in the next chapter. Additionally, one of the legacies of verbal abuse is deficits in emotional regulation and emotional intelligence. The culture expects dialogue worthy of a Lifetime movie or a confessional when adults reflect on being verbally abused as children—I was so sad, I was so scared, I was so nervous—but that isn't what respondents to my questionnaire reported. Kids do what they can to shut down and cope, in patterns that turn out to be predictable. It is, of course, worse when parental verbal abuse gets amplified by a sibling chorus.

Respondents described being coiled, crouched, tightly wound, or almost paralyzed when they moved into a conflict zone in the house, went downstairs, or came home from school. They recalled feeling small, shrinking, sinking, or disappearing from view when the verbal assault began. They imagined themselves floating above the fray, watching it happen to some other little girl or boy, or being somewhere deep in their imagination. They wrote that their throats tightened, their stomachs ached, their mouths went dry, their heads pounded, the world turned blurry, or that they threw up. They said they froze, went numb, or turned to stone. They wept hysterically or dried up on the spot because they feared being mocked. They shook, quaked, trembled, or recoiled as if they'd been hit. They bit their lips, dug their nails into their palms, desperate not to cry because crying would just restart the hailstorm of name-calling and shaming. The childhood selves they described were almost always between the ages of five and eight, when a child is old enough to see the pattern but powerless to stop it. The only defense is to push off from feelings, and once that is learned, it is remarkably difficult to unlearn.

The problem is evolution. Evolution has you adapt to where you find yourself in the moment; if a child finds him- or herself in a verbally bullying environment, he or she will adapt to it both physiologically and behaviorally, finding ways of lowering stress so as to feel fewer painful emotions, which is basically turning off feelings and needs. It goes without saying that these ways of adapting are detrimental to long-term emotional and psychological health because they involve shutting down emotionally and staving off feelings. Since emotional intelligence is defined as being able to use your feelings to guide your thoughts, this is definitely not a healthy move.

Attachment theory, first developed by John Bowlby and then significantly expanded by Mary Ainsworth and others, provides us with a specific lens through which to see the effects of childhood treatment, including verbal abuse, on our development, specifically on what are called our "mental models" of relationships, and our ability to manage emotions. For most of us laypeople, the words "mental model" may seem very abstract, but the truth is that the way they function is more literal than not. These are unconscious assumptions about people and relationships that are learned in childhood and that may never even be consciously articulated; they have the power, nonetheless, to inform our thinking, our behaviors, and our thoughts long into adulthood. They basically act as filters on our experiences, coloring how we see the world, people, and relationships. Studies show that attachment styles stay consistent through the lifespan, absent therapy or concrete efforts to change unconscious assumptions.

Verbal abuse doesn't exist in a vacuum, of course, and parents who weaponize words behave in other ways that contribute to a child's developing an insecure style of attachment. Most important, the child's emotional needs aren't being met; keep in mind that in addition to overt verbal abuse—shaming, name-calling, gaslighting, for example—withholding praise and support is also verbally abusive. We'll see that brain science pulls back the curtain on the attachment and reveals what goes on beneath the surface.

While John Bowlby had posited that it was attachment to a primary caretaker, most usually the mother, that determined the emotional health of a child and his or her ability to make meaningful connections, it was Mary Ainsworth who actually showed the world how it affected a child. Mind you, Bowlby also believed the mother and child were both equally hardwired to care for each other and that the mother would provide a "secure base" from which the child could both explore the outer world and his or her feelings.

Working from that premise, Mary Ainsworth would find otherwise through a series of experiments.

Mary Ainsworth and the "Strange Situation"

This was laboratory research, but it turned out to be remarkably reliable, though not in the way Ainsworth expected. The setup was simple: A mother brings her infant into a room the child has never seen before and that contains toys and other objects to explore. The focus throughout is on how the child reacts to the changes in scenario, which has eight steps: 1) the mother and child enter the room with the researcher; 2) the mother and baby are alone in the room together; 3) they are joined by a stranger; 4) the mother exits, leaving the baby alone with the stranger; 5) the mother returns and the stranger leaves; 6) the mother exits, leaving the baby alone in the room; 7) the stranger returns; 8) the stranger leaves and the mother returns.

What Ainsworth expected was that, with the mother present, the child would explore the toys and would be unperturbed by the stranger, would be distressed when the mother left and would be wary of the stranger, and would be happy and calm when the mother returned. And that's what happened with a bit more than half of the babies. But surprisingly, there were other consistent patterns that didn't fit into the notion of a secure base. Some of the babies didn't try to explore when the mother was present, didn't react when left alone with the stranger, and didn't show affect when the mother returned. Some were distressed when their mothers left but ignored or pushed their mothers away when they came back. Some cried and wailed when their mothers came back, even though they were clinging to them.

Why did these babies behave differently? Was it a function of temperament? Or did their behaviors reflect the nature of the mother-child relationship?

That is where attachment theory comes in.

Attachment and Filters on Experience

Infants extrapolate from their earliest experiences, forming impressions of how the world works; all of this happens unconsciously but nonetheless has long-lasting effects. There are three styles of adult attachment, and we'll begin with the optimal one first, which is called *secure*.

The Secure Attachment Style

The child whose primary caretaker responds reliably and consistently to his or her cues, who is comforted when stressed, who experiences support and validation rather than verbal abuse, and who is taught to manage her or his emotions develops a secure style of attachment. This child's working models of relationship are positive, and the emerging vision of the world of relationship is one in which people can be trusted and depended on and seen as sources of joy and caring. This secure base allows the child to develop into an individual who seeks out emotional connection, has a strong sense of self, and is capable of dealing with negative emotions. This isn't to say that the adult with a secure attachment won't experience heartbreak or pain, of course, but it does mean that he or she has the coping mechanisms to deal with them.

The Styles of Insecurity: Anxious and Avoidant

And then there are those who grow up not having their emotional needs met, or met unreliably and inconsistently, each of which yields a different style of insecure attachment, in contrast to the secure attachment already described. Do keep in mind that verbal abuse is one part of an overall experience; it is not the only damaging element, but the others are cognate.

Anxious-Preoccupied Style

Adults who exhibit this attachment style, largely the result of inconsistent attention and attunement, had mothers who sometimes showed up and sometimes didn't, sometimes listened and sometimes ignored them. They may have weaponized their words some of the time but not always. Once the grown children of these mothers leave home, they are highly driven to get validation and support, but at the same time, they are also super-sensitive to slights and rejection. This makes them emotionally very volatile because when they sense rejection, they strike back. Their vision of the world is highly colored as a result, and they're likely to misread cues and overreact under many different circumstances and in all manner of relationships.

What are the mental models and assumptions that affect the anxious-preoccupied style?

- Assuming that you must always be watchful because relationships aren't stable

- Never completely trusting anyone's motives or statements

- Needing constant validation and reassurance from friends and romantic partners

- Believing that you are never safe, no matter what

- Having trouble reading cues and overreacting, which also means mislabeling things as verbally abusive when they aren't and missing the behaviors and statements that are

Avoidants: Dismissive and Fearful

These are adults whose emotional needs weren't met in childhood, or who were actively marginalized, criticized, scapegoated, or ignored. The first is the *dismissive-avoidant*; people with this style of attachment have a high opinion of themselves and a low opinion of others. They pride themselves on being more independent than other people and are more comfortable with superficial relationships than ones that involve real intimacy. This isn't to say that they don't like being in relationships; they do, but only on their terms and if they can call the shots. They don't worry about their relationships too much, and they are quick to rebound when a relationship ends. This is the style of attachment most closely associated with those high in narcissistic traits.

What are the mental models that affect the dismissive-avoidant style?

• Believing that emotional needs are a sign of weakness in yourself and others.

• Dealing with negative emotions by pushing off from them or exiting the situation.

• Disdain for others and reduced empathy or lack of it.

• Disconnection from those you are supposed to be close to.

• Disinclination to pay attention to other people's cues or to plumb others' motivations.

• Needing to control the course of relationships in all aspects.

• Having a high opinion of the self and a low opinion of others.

Second up is the *fearful-avoidant* adult. While this person was deprived of love, attention, and support in childhood, that deprivation did nothing to abate their need, unlike the dismissive-avoidant. If the dismissive-avoidant seems cool as a cucumber on the surface while hiding shame and other feelings below, the fearful-avoidant is in a very different place. He or she has a low opinion of self but a high opinion of others; this adult is always waiting for someone to finally pay attention. In some ways, this is the worst of all possible situations because this adult really wants connection but he or she is always fearful of rejection and holds back in situations that could yield real results.

What are the mental models that affect the fearful-avoidant style?

• A desire for relationship along with a paralyzing fear that it will result in emotional pain

• Extreme ambivalence in relationship and a pattern of getting close and moving away

- Behaviors that are triggered by emotional overload and appear impulsive

- Being on high alert for betrayal and other signs that his or her fears will be realized

- Extreme emotional reactivity followed by a shutdown of feelings

Keep in mind that not one of these styles, including secure, is absolute; when you consider your own style of attachment, focus on what you assume about people and relationships and how you react most of the time. Also remember that these mental models are unconscious and not articulated.

Attachment Styles and Verbally Abusive Relationships in Adulthood

The not-too-heartening truth is that when it comes to affairs of the heart, we are drawn to what we know and what we've experienced; that's one reason that children who grow up around verbal abuse often find themselves with partners who are, alas, deeply familiar. Discovering to your shock and horror, despite your intentions, that you've ended up with someone who treats you as your abusive mother or father did isn't unusual.

While there's no Star Wars-type force field to shield anyone from verbal abuse, the reality is that the securely attached person will be quick to spot it and exit the premises. Why? This person didn't experience it young so won't normalize the behavior and will be quick to label it as abusive. Additionally, she trusts her perceptions and has mental models of real connection. A securely attached person knows the difference between a well-meaning joke and a jab that's meant to hurt or demean. Her forcefield is composed of valuing real intimacy and true partnership.

The most vulnerable people are those looking for love and validation—yes, calling all those anxious-preoccupied folks—who are likely to be drawn in because they are generally lousy at reading cues, often mistake emotional *sturm-und-drang* with passion, and are very reactive themselves. Chances are good that there was verbal abuse in their family of origin, and because of their neediness, they're the most likely to end up stuck on a carousel controlled by a verbally abusive person.

Next in line is the fearful-avoidant, who may be swept in by someone's blandishments because of neediness but will find him- or herself in a familiar echo chamber when the verbal abuse starts and will reach for his or her running shoes.

Finally, there is the dismissive-avoidant, who is most likely to dish out verbal abuse him- or herself and is unlikely to stand for being the target. These people are often high in narcissistic traits or highly controlling, and verbal abuse is often part of their emotional toolkit. Yes, they often experienced it themselves in childhood, but the chances are good that the dismissive-avoidant just thinks this is how the world works.

What we will see, from largely anecdotal evidence and some research, is that it's the people with an anxious-preoccupied or a fearful-avoidant style of attachment who are most likely to normalize verbal abuse in adult relationships and will be most vulnerable to manipulation. While some of this has to do with their internalization of the messages conveyed about themselves and their characters in childhood, it also points to their willingness to participate in relationships in which they are the powerless partner; these tend to be relationships driven by unconscious needs. Alas, those needs make it very easy for them to mistake controlling and abusive behavior for strength and conviction. That does not ever happen to the dismissive-avoidant; if there is an imbalance of power, he or she is always holding the reins.

Verbal Abuse and Being Able to Manage Emotions

There is an important scientific thread that argues that mother-infant attachment is really about the regulation of emotion. Among others, the work of Allan Schore has been in the forefront, explaining how early attachment experiences "shape the early organization of the brain, the neurobiological core of the human unconscious." By responding to her infant's cues, by making eye contact, by giving him or her space when he or she is overstimulated, the mother begins to help the infant learn how to self-regulate in moments of stress. When this mother-infant dyadic dance doesn't happen with regularity or happens rarely, the infant doesn't learn to self-regulate.

Research confirms that all those with an insecure style—and that includes all three types—show deficits in both emotional intelligence and regulating negative emotion. The worst-case scenario, as sketched out in a paper research by Allan Schore called "Relational Trauma and the Developing Right Brain," is that the mother's actions actually exacerbate the infant's distress. This might happen because she's not accessible or rejecting in response to the baby's cries or acts aggressively or inappropriately; not surprisingly, the infant becomes, among other things, frightened. The infant reacts to the trauma in two stages, first becoming hyperaroused, which sets off a startle response in the right hemisphere of the brain, resulting in an elevation of heart rate, blood pressure, and respiration. The second stage involves what we might call an emergency shutdown or, in Schore's terms, "dissociation"; the infant "disengages from stimuli in the external world" and thus tamps down the hyperarousal. As an adult, this person deals with painful emotions by directing his or her attention away from internal emotional states; rather than managing emotions, these individuals learn to cut off from them. As we will see, this also happens on a physiological level.

What does it mean to manage emotion? And why does it matter? Research shows that the people who are able to maximize positive emotions—savoring experiences that evoke those feelings—are more resilient and both physically and psychologically healthier than those who can't. And that's also true of people who can use positive emotions to regulate negative emotions. While successful emotional management happens unconsciously and automatically for the securely attached, it does not for those who are insecurely attached.

Insecurely attached children adapt to stress in ways that won't serve them as adults, alas, unless there is an active intervention, such as therapy, that can actively boost emotional intelligence. Because parental verbal abuse is a power play, aimed at making the child feel terrible about him- or herself, many children learn that expressing emotion—crying or begging for the parent to stop—only adds fuel to the fire.

Jim, 50, described how his father thought showing emotion was a sign of weakness so he and his brother learned to steel themselves so as not to react. He wrote me that, "I got so good at it that by the time I left home, I felt practically nothing at all. My wife, bless her soul, pushed me to go into therapy. My brother wasn't so lucky; he ended up addicted to drugs." Another daughter, 32, now a therapist herself, wrote, "As a child I remember her going from zero to 100 with impressive speed. She would tense up and become so furious. The yelling felt like it could shake the walls, but the worst of it was how long it went on. The more she yelled, the angrier she became and the nastier and more painful her words would be. It was excruciatingly painful, but worst of all so isolating. I remember just feeling so alone and so misunderstood. I cried myself to sleep maybe half of my life and remember thinking the discomfort I felt (much therapy later, I would come to recognize this discomfort as anxiety and sadness) because I was just made to feel so out of place in my family. I felt like a loser and a misfit. I was so frequently criticized for what felt like any feeling or emotion. It was heartbreaking."

According to research by Mario Mikulincer and Phillip R. Shaver, when there's a threat or stress, vividly recalled negative or painful attachment-related experiences are likely to come to mind; that's the very opposite of what happens to a securely attached person, who is able to calm him- or herself down by pulling up experiences of support and help. Liam, 50, reported that "Every time something went wrong at work or my boss or colleagues criticized my handling of an issue, I'd freeze like the ten-year-old who cowered when my mother or father dressed me down. I'd stuttered as a kid when they yelled at me, and I was just as tongue-tied as a 36-year-old manager of a team of 20 people. If my boss criticized me, I'd hear my dad's stream of abuse start up in my head, telling me I was no good and worthless. It could be touched off by something small, like a report needing editing, or something bigger. It didn't matter." Liam's boss finally sat him down and talked to him about being so thin-skinned and reactive, and that prompted him to go into counseling. It was a game-changer because Liam became conscious of the old default triggers and was able to control them.

And while securely attached people turn to others in times of need, insecurely attached people do not. While the avoidantly attached adopt a model of self-reliance—they don't think much of other people, after all—the anxiously attached will voice their needs and fears to anyone who will listen, usually exaggerating their distress. Neither throwing up a wall nor creating a flood plain is a healthy response to managing negative feelings.

Of course, failures in emotional regulation don't just end up with emotional shutdowns or flooding. Being this unemotionally prepared for the inevitable setbacks and hurtful episodes in life means that even a light rain can turn into a storm with hail the size of golf balls. Adults who grew up with verbal abuse continue to have real problems navigating the world, unless they go into therapy and actively start to heal.

Verbal Abuse and the Sense of Self

I don't think it will surprise anyone that every adult who experienced consistent and sustained verbal abuse in childhood, accepting it as a mental model of how relationships work in the world, has also internalized the messages conveyed by the abuse. Some children do have access to other adults—teachers, ministers, neighbors, relatives—who contradict those internalized messages, but given what we know about the effect of parental abuse, they hardly get off scot-free. What may be surprising to many is that those internalized messages can absolutely coexist with real-life success and accomplishment. Yes, the messages are loudest for those who are afraid of failure first and foremost, have trouble setting goals, and prefer to skirt challenges, but they can be a steady hum even for those who are high-achieving and appear confident, which results in their feeling like a fraud or an imposter, (For more on this, see the section on "Revisiting Bad is Stronger than Good," page 92.)

That feeling as if you're posing as someone you're not actually has a name, the Imposter Phenomenon, coined by psychologists Pauline

Rose Clance and Suzanne Imes over 40 years ago. Childhood verbal abuse primes you for feeling that, no matter what you've achieved, you are bound to be found out sooner or later. Growing up with verbal abuse endows you with a default setting of real self-doubt, which persists despite, and perhaps because of, your real-world achievements. Clance and Imes' original work, published in 1978, focused on professional women and noted anecdotally that men seemed to suffer from less from the phenomenon. (I personally think this is more a reflection of the times, when women in the workforce wore suits and shirts modeled after menswear and the secret code was pretty much "don't act like a girl.") Clance and Imes attributed the Imposter Phenomenon to early childhood experiences, stemming from seeing a sibling designated as being superior or being told constantly that that sibling was perfect or a star. As the authors saw it, in the first case, a girl may set out to disprove she's inferior (and be plagued by self-doubt) or, in the second, be hobbled by her inability to deal with setbacks. Clance revisited the issue in 1993 with coauthor Joe Langford and linked feeling like an imposter with anxiety, introversion, a belief that the self is defined only by achievement, and growing up in a family high in conflict and lacking in support. There's no question that verbal abuse fits right in.

More recent research has revealed that men also suffer from feeling like imposters, as a study by Sonja Rohrmann and her colleagues showed; they found no association between the imposter phenomenon and gender. Unlike samples used in other studies, theirs was of working managers, not students, which may explain the different findings. Not surprisingly, they also noted a link between anxiety and the imposter phenomenon. Counterintuitively, they also found that people who felt like imposters were both perfectionists and procrastinators, two working styles that seem, on the surface at least, to be contradictory. They explained their findings by suggesting that people who feel like imposters tend to over-prepare and work to impress others—showing their perfectionism—while also procrastinating, which tends to bolster their vision of themselves as fraudulent.

An even newer study by Rebecca L. Badawy and her colleagues specifically looked at gender differences and came up with some really interesting findings, limited only by the use of student participants, not adults in real-life workplace situations. They point out that, theoretically, someone who already feels like an imposter will have their feelings validated by negative feedback and will consequently decrease their efforts. While it was true that more women identified themselves as feeling like imposters, the men who did had greater anxiety in the wake of negative feedback, and their subsequent work was more affected than that of women who felt like imposters. The women didn't just show more resilience, but their subsequent efforts were also less affected by the feedback.

I think it's clear how these feelings of fraudulence are fed by the older stream of internalized verbal abuse and, of course, the anxiety it instilled.

What's Left Behind: Shame and Undeveloped Self-esteem

Of course, verbal abuse doesn't just affect a child through internalization of its messages; it also thwarts the growth of healthy self-esteem and self-knowledge. The child in this case is a garden tended to by a cruel and insouciant caretaker who deprives seedlings of light and water while mulching invasive weeds. Shame and self-blame flourish in the spots where self-worth and learning from mistakes ought to reside.

In the next chapter, we'll be looking carefully at the effects of normalizing verbal aggression.

Verbal Abuse and the Unborn Child

You are probably stunned by the heading above, but a Japanese research study by Kaori Komori, Masahiro Komori, Masamitsu Eitoku, and others published in 2019 suggested strongly that verbal abuse actually affects the hearing of unborn children! This was actually a very large study, composed of just under 80,000 mother-child pairs, and the authors wanted to build on the research already showing the effects of verbal abuse. Specifically, the authors wanted to further explore the earlier research that strongly suggested that emotional abuse and verbal abuse (their terms) have an even greater impact on the incidence of postnatal depression and abusive maternal behavior than physical and sexual abuse. Since they were aware that maternal stress from prenatal depression had been associated with fetal and newborn anomalies and that verbal abuse against the mother affected the development of the newborn's brain, their intent was to find out if verbal abuse affected the auditory functioning of the newborn. And the answer was, indeed, yes; that was proven by the results of their study of those mother-child pairs.

Their theoretical explanations of why—which are tentative since their study showed correlation, not causation—are still of interest to us. They began by looking at three factors that could explain the negative impact on newborn hearing. First, maternal stress in the wake of verbal abuse can trigger vasoconstrictors—nerve fibers that can decrease blood flow to the uterus, which, in turn, affects fetal development. Second, they point out that the fetal auditory system is anatomically mature by 20 weeks, and by week 27 through week 35, the fetus has begun to respond to low, middle, and high frequency sounds, as well as loud noises. By week 36, the fetus is able to respond to the maternal spoken voice and to hear and react to the loud voices of both parents. The researchers underscore that the mother's increased heart rate in reaction to verbal abuse—which also increases the fetus' heartrate, since the two are synchronized—combined with loud noises creates an environment that is uncomfortable and may negatively impact auditory development. Since loud sounds in occupational settings have been shown to be associated with newborn hearing loss, they suggest that shouting by both parents may be a factor, too. As I said, the research is stunning in the real sense of the word. The evidence of the direct damage inflicted by verbal abuse is undeniable.

Below the Surface: Verbal Abuse and the Developing Brain

Comparatively speaking, brain science is relatively new, thanks to the development of the Magnetic Resonance Imaging (MRI) machine over the last 20-plus years; because the MRI machine doesn't emit ionizing radiation like a conventional X ray and is noninvasive, it's considered safe for nearly every age group, as noted by physicist Charles A. Nelson. The MRI has permitted researchers not just to study typical brain development across the first two decades of life but has also allowed them to see which parts of the brain are activated during a specific task, such as memorization or identifying a happy or sad face. This field of research has debunked long-held beliefs about the brain and its development, such as brain maturity taking place at the same time as the skull reaching adult size; in fact, the fully adult brain matures long after skeletal growth ends, sometime between the ages of 25 and 30.

Most pertinent to our inquiry is what the field has been able to ascertain about the effects of verbal abuse on not just the physical brain itself but also its functioning. Perhaps the most surprising thing about the human brain is its malleability, which represents both the good news and bad news at once. Because it is malleable, it can be shaped in both positive and negative ways in childhood; at the same time, its malleability also suggests that it can continue to change in adulthood.

Let's begin with the developing brain. Most important, the brain develops from the bottom up. Human infants are born with the most primitive parts of the brain fully developed; these are the areas that control autonomic functions such as breathing. But the development of the higher brain—the parts that govern emotion, language, and abstract thinking—develop slowly over the course of the first three years of a child's life. By the time a child is three, his or her brain is almost 90 percent of its adult size but the parts themselves and how they function together are still a work in progress. In fact, the synapses—the transmitter cells that send signals—are overproduced during this period, creating more connections than are actually needed. They get "pruned back" in later childhood.

MRI studies have permitted researchers to study the neurobiological effects of various kinds of maltreatment on the developing brain. A review of broad findings published by Martin H. Teicher and Jacqueline A. Samson in 2016 specifically singled out three factors—parental verbal abuse, witnessing domestic violence, and sexual abuse—that appear to actively change the physical structures of certain parts of the brain as well as their functioning. So much for the "words will never harm me" thing; changes to the physical structure of the brain and how it works sound as real as it gets, don't you think? We'll see how the brain science helps us better understand the behavioral changes that result from verbal abuse in the next sections of the book. In essence, these findings are the unseen backstory that can help enlarge our understanding of the behavioral effects of verbal abuse. As Teicher and Samson write, "these alterations are adaptations to an anticipated stress-filled malevolent world." That is also true of the behaviors adopted to cope with that stress-filled world of childhood, as we'll see later in this chapter.

In their review of the research, Teicher and Samson point out that studies not surprisingly began with investigating physical and sexual abuse and its effect on the brain—there's what I call the gold standard in this book—but as studies expanded, the effects of emotional abuse, verbal abuse, and emotional maltreatment were looked at separately from physical maltreatment. From my point of view, this is a true sea change that gives us a good barometer of the distance between what science knows and what the culture believes.

Let's look at the most important findings, plumbed from the research, pertaining to verbal abuse and the other neglectful or toxic parental behaviors that usually accompany it, insecure attachment, and the effects on the brains and behaviors of those who have experienced them.

We've already seen that the development of the right hemisphere is seriously impacted by both attuned and neglectful parenting according to the extensive research done by Allan Schore and supported by other studies on which he draws. What are called "mental models" of how relationships work are the unconscious filters through which human experience is poured *and* neurologically encoded on the circuit wiring of the orbital prefrontal cortex. For we who find the science sophisticated and dense, the key takeaway is that the effect on the brain's development is direct and affects its functioning and is detrimental to healthy development.

Other research has pinpointed effects on the development of other parts of the brain as well. The hippocampus stands out as one that is highly susceptible to stress; this happens on a detailed cellular level, but for this book, since neither the reader nor the writer is a scientist, we'll stick to the broad outlines. (The research, in all of its detail, is in the Reference section that begins on page 261 and is organized by chapter.) Part of the limbic system, the hippocampus is crucial to the formation and retrieval of memories and connects specific sensations and emotions to those memories.

It's the hippocampus that allows a scent—the smell of baking bread, lilacs, a salty ocean breeze—or a taste—a bite of apple pie, the sweetness of a cherry, the licorice you loved as a kid—to bring up a memory from the past. (We can thank the hippocampus for Proust's eating a morsel of the madeleine that evoked his instant recall and gave us *Remembrance of Things Past.*) "There's compelling evidence," as Teicher and Samson note, that those who were maltreated in childhood have smaller hippocampi; moreover, the effect is more evident in men who suffered emotional abuse than in women. It's thought that higher levels of estrogen may be a mitigating factor. Interestingly, there appear to be times in life that the hippocampus is more vulnerable to the effects of verbal abuse and neglect; the period between ages 7 and 14 seems to be one. Another study, conducted in Korea, shows that parental verbal abuse also affects the volume of the hippocampus; that will be discussed in the next section.

The amygdala is yet another susceptible area. Popular science knows the amygdala as the key respondent to potential threats, including the fight-or-flight response; while it's true that the amygdala does the heavy lifting for us when it comes to fear—it gears us up to deal with the snake before we've consciously registered that it *is* a snake—the characterization is also an oversimplification. There are actually two amygdalae, one in each hemisphere of the brain. The amygdala is key to processing information, and it's the integrative center for emotions, emotional behavior, and motivation. It turns out that maltreatment affects the amygdala by both increasing and decreasing its volume, and by making it hyperactive. While studies on the relationship between anxiety and decreased volume in the amygdala have had inconclusive and sometimes contradictory results, a study by Katherine Rice Warnell and her coauthors published in 2017 suggests that perhaps there is one; they point out that understanding the structural brain bases of anxiety is key to unraveling why some people suffer and others don't. What made this study different was that the researchers depended on children's self-reports of their anxiety instead of their parents' as other studies had done, and they indeed found a correlation between reported anxiety and a decrease in the volume of the amygdala, with boys showing greater linkage between anxiety and brain changes as well as the effects weakening with age. The participants were between the ages of six and thirteen.

Other studies point to the fact that the amygdala plays an important role in processing social emotions—being able to read facial expressions such as happiness, surprise, disgust, and sadness—because individuals who've sustained damage to their amygdalae are unable to recognize and label in this way, as was demonstrated by research by Ralph Adolphs, Simon Baron-Cohen, and Daniel Tranel. Another study, this one on healthy adults, conducted by Birgit Derntl, Ute Habel, and others, and using MRIs, detected bilateral activation when it came to recognizing facial expressions of emotions. It would appear that changes to the amygdala underlie many of the problems individuals who were subjected to verbal abuse at young ages experience.

Finally, the structure of the cerebral cortex—the outermost layer of the brain—is also susceptible to stress. This is the part of the brain that is responsible for higher thinking and processing information from the five senses; it is divided into four lobes, which are the frontal, parietal, temporal, and occipital. This is the part of the brain that allowed Descartes to say, "I think, therefore I am." (*Je pense, donc je suis.*) Teicher and Samson's review of studies states that there are two periods of susceptibility for the cerebral cortex, which isn't surprising given the long maturation of the thinking parts of the brain; they are, respectively, infancy to early childhood and late adolescence through early adulthood. It won't surprise you that most studies focus on physical or sexual abuse for all the reasons we know about—yes, what I call "the gold standard"—but there are a number that actually focus on verbal abuse alone, and we'll turn to them.

Even so, I am guessing you are letting go of that "sticks and stones" thing.

Homing in on the Target

Parental verbal abuse (PVA) has also been the subject of numerous studies that add significantly to our understanding of the impact on both the child's brain and subsequent behaviors in adolescence, young adulthood, and even later. In a study published in 2009, conducted by Jeewook Choi, Bumseok Jeong, and others, including Martin Teicher, the researchers went to extraordinary lengths to limit their findings to PVA alone; they started with more than 1,200 respondents and whittled them down to 32 because of their exacting standards. The study focused on respondents 18 to 25 with self-reported PVA but no other forms of trauma or stress; the researchers specifically excluded those who had experienced parental loss, childhood sexual abuse, or other forms of trauma, including motor vehicle accidents, fires, gang violence, and the like. They also didn't include those who were born prematurely, had any neurological health issues, suffered maternal substance abuse during pregnancy, or other similar problems; they tested for alcohol and drugs before each visit.

What the researchers found was that exposure to parental verbal abuse was "associated with alteration in the integrity of the neural pathways." While the study relied on a small sample, the researchers concluded that its results raised "the possibility that parental criticism, condemnation [sic] and ridicule can exert deleterious effects on the developing brain." This is important to keep in mind when we discuss coping mechanisms, normalizing, and internalizing the messages delivered by verbal abuse. In a similar vein, a study of Korean adolescents in their first year of high school who'd experienced verbal abuse showed decreased volume in the hippocampus compared with those who had low or no experiences with verbal abuse.

Another small study—which, again, screened for PVA in the absence of other abusive behaviors or traumatic events—by Akemi Tomoda and other observed changes to the gray matter of the brain in 21 subjects, ages 18 to 25. The results echoed those of other studies:

Tomoda and his colleagues not only found structural changes but also suggested that "the development of the auditory association cortex involved in language processing may be affected by early stress and/ or emotionally abusive language." One of the more interesting observations made in this paper is that, drawing from other studies, the researchers suggest that "the sensory systems involved with processing and relaying the aversive sensory input may be specifically altered." Keep in mind that these findings are correlational, not causal, but the researchers do note that longitudinal studies might show causality. So in a nutshell, hurtful words do harm to our ability to process what we hear.

So shall we forget about reciting "words will never harm me"? I should hope so.

Revisiting "Bad Is Stronger Than Good"

You may remember that in the Introduction, I mentioned that, thanks to evolution and its skew toward survival, humans store memories of bad experiences and potentially dangerous situations in a more accessible part of the brain than where the good ones are stored. Yes, that's the always accessible filing cabinet where our memories of verbal abuse are stored. You may also recall that I mentioned research by Ann Polcari, Keren Rabi, and others that explored whether the experience of verbal aggression by one parent could be mitigated by the verbal affection of the other parent or even the same parent at another time, thus warding off the depression, anxiety, and other effects known to be associated with PVA. Their thinking went like this: "On the one hand, it's plausible that such signs of affection delivered by the same person or by another parent may be a protective fact that softens the impact of verbal aggression. It is just as plausible that the combination of affectionate and abusive statements could create an uncertain and inconsistent environment that might do more harm than good." These are interesting possibilities, don't you think?

But what they found was that high exposure to parental verbal aggression "cannot be easily overcome, neither by the verbally affectionate ministrations of the offending parent nor the verbal affection of the non-offending parent." More tellingly, they found that the subjects' self-reported effects of exposure to verbal aggression, such as depression, anger, and other maladaptive behaviors, stayed just as strong whether there were high levels of verbal affection or none at all.

This is an important finding and underscores the whole principle of "bad is stronger than good." While in common parlance we talk about good experiences "balancing" the bad ones, that's not what happens psychologically. Every time we think about balancing or outweighing and we visualize a scale, we are simply kidding ourselves. The reality is that the impact of abuse and the impact of occasional affection run on two separate tracks.

It's worth noting, too, that the idea of "balancing" is used all the time to rationalize, minimize, deny, or normalize verbal abuse. An underage child, as we've seen, is a captive of her or his little world and adapts, but since she or he still wants a parent's love and approval, she or he will initially downplay the extent and depth of the verbal abuse as an adult, pointing to the parent's other "good" behaviors as "balancing" things out. To do so is to look away from the ways in which he or she has been wounded.

Alas, an adult in a verbally abusive relationship with another adult is also likely to draw on the idea of "balancing out" to justify staying in the relationship, pointing to the positive behaviors displayed by that friend, lover, partner, or spouse. This is a reflection of the imbalance of power that is an engine for verbal abuse; the victim rationalizes because she or he still wants something from the abuser. The train of thought goes like this: "Nobody's perfect, right? He [or she] has other qualities that make up for the meanness most of the time. Not always. But often."

But affection doesn't mitigate verbal abuse, which, like the cheese, stands alone.

What's Left Behind: Shame and Undeveloped Self-esteem

Of course, verbal abuse doesn't just affect a child through internalization of the messages; it thwarts the growth of healthy self-esteem and self-knowledge. The child is a garden tended to by a cruel and insouciant caretaker. Shame and self-blame flourish in the spots where self-worth and learning from mistakes ought to reside. In the next chapter, we'll be looking carefully at the effects of normalizing verbal aggression.

A Contrarian View Worth Considering

In article after article, the impact of verbal abuse and other forms of abusive behavior on an individual's mental health includes depression, anxiety, PTSD, and other disorders. But a contrarian view has been offered by two social anthropologists, which can help broaden our thinking and understanding. Kristen L. Syme and Edward H. Hagen argue that the reliance on DSM (Diagnostic and Statistical Manual of Mental Disorders) categories of "illnesses" and treating those illnesses with pharmaceuticals, which either don't work or don't work well enough, is misguided and that we should be looking at depression, anxiety, and PTSD as "being caused by adversity and involve symptoms that seem to be adaptive responses to adversity." Unlike other disorders, they do not involve heritability, yet combined, they are a significant fraction of the mental disorders that are treated. They go on to posit that "These may not be disorders at all, however, instead aversive yet adaptive responses to adversity."

As a layperson, I find that this makes perfect sense. It echoes the findings of brain science. It mirrors the behavioral adaptations that targets of verbal abuse adopt, which are all adaptations—unhealthy and self-denying—to the situation at hand. It encourages looking back at those moments of adversity and how they tie into the emotions of the present. It's worth pondering, don't you think?

Chapter Three

How (and Why) We Normalize Abusive Behavior

No, this chapter isn't about victim-blaming—the bugaboo adopted by social media groups and people supposedly triggered by the use of all caps in texts—but a straightforward look at why and how we often deliver ourselves into the hands of the enemy unwittingly. This is a complicated subject because the motivations involved are themselves complex and much of the behavior is either unconscious or unexamined, even by adults. Once again, I hearken back to the soil in which verbal abuse thrives: the relationship that is defined by imbalance.

Children who grow up in households in which healthy boundaries are maintained, whose parents act authoritatively without abusive tactics, and who feel worthy of good treatment become adults who want relationships to be dyadic and filled with mutual caring; they are relatively quick to discern relationships that are about power and the use of it. They don't normalize verbal abuse for very long, and if they tolerate it, that's usually a function of a misguided effort to understand where the other person is coming from. They aren't at risk for normalizing verbal abuse in the long term.

That's just not true of someone who has grown up around verbal abuse and who has had her or his mental models of relational behavior shaped by it. The tendency to normalize verbally abusive behavior is fed by many streams that overlap and energize each other; combined, they make recognition very difficult. The first stream has to do with the insularity of childhood; each of us grows up in a tiny world that we think reflects the larger, outside world we don't yet know as children. While this is a reliable belief for those who grow up without verbal abuse, it is a hobbling one for those who do. When the abuser is a parent or parents, children are much more likely to rationalize because they desperately need that person's love and attention; they will self-protect against such a painful—and frankly terrifying—truth, as research shows. These motivations coexist with the child's hardwired need to gain his or her parent's affection and support; any recognition of abuse is thwarted by that continuing need that results in what I call "the core conflict" in my work. The need to belong to your family of origin, your so-called "people," trumps calling out abusive treatment for a very long time, even into adulthood.

Remember that the messages conveyed by either fully articulated verbal abuse—that the child is dumb, worthless, an embarrassment—or the silent kind—demonstrating that the child isn't worth listening to or important enough to notice—are absorbed as supposed truths about his or her essential character. Remember, too, that they are uttered by an impeccable source: the larger adult, who rules the little world the child lives in. In turn, those "truths" support self-blame as a default position, which serves a number of purposes. First, blaming yourself for your parent's treatment and feeling it was somehow deserved are much easier to deal with than the truly terrifying thought that your parent won't protect you and is hurting you for absolutely no reason. As we'll see, researchers have, in fact, opined that avoiding that very scary conclusion is a major reason children normalize. The second thing self-blame does is create the possibility that, if you can just figure out how to fix yourself, the abuse will stop and, more important, your parent will relent and love you. Think about that for a moment because it applies to adult-on-adult verbal abuse, too. In this context, blaming yourself opens what seems to be a window of opportunity, while making the abuser responsible does precisely the opposite.

All of these largely unconscious behaviors are usually hand-carried out of childhood and into adulthood, where certain psychological processes aid and abet continuing to normalize verbal abuse; I will lay out that concept in full detail on the pages that follow. But as I have learned firsthand in hearing from readers from all over the world, the most powerful driver of normalizing verbal abuse is understanding what will happen when you stop and admit that someone you love or whom you need to love you is actively and consciously hurting you. Think about it. That fear of loss is why we tend to make sure the door is shut on truth, and not open.

If you call him or her out and hold that person responsible, what happens next?

The Little World of Childhood

"Children learn what they live," Dorothy Law Nolte famously wrote, and this observation has enormous resonance for those of us unlucky enough to grow up in families of origin where verbal abuse was standard fare, served up on the daily. Verbal abuse affects us in many ways, all of them damaging, but it's often our own denial or rationalization that stands in our way in adulthood. Understanding how that works is a key part of claiming a life that is abuse-free.

As children, we all assume that what goes on at our house goes on everywhere, and that our parents are no different from the strangers with children we see in the park or at the grocery store. Our first inkling that maybe our house is different comes later in childhood, usually when we're old enough to go on playdates or we visit with relatives or other adults and see that the children in the house are treated differently and that there are different ways of communicating than the ones we are used to. I was probably five when it happened to me, playing at Beth's apartment. We were finger painting in the kitchen when I accidentally knocked over a bowl and paint went flying everywhere. I started to cower, thinking of how to apologize, since I expected a barrage of screaming and recrimination. Instead, Beth's mom cleaned it up without complaint, murmured something like, "Accidents happen. Don't worry," and poured out some more paint for us to use. She actually patted me on the back to reassure me. I was literally stunned into silence. I remember thinking that maybe this was how born-in-America moms were because mine came from the Netherlands.

Of course, it had nothing to do with nationality, and what I didn't know until many years later was that, while there were mothers who forgave mistakes and hugged their children, there were other girls and boys growing up in families with mothers or fathers who yelled and screamed and constantly criticized, belittled, dismissed, or gaslighted them or called them names, laughed at them, or scapegoated them. Or just ignored them. Or gave them the silent treatment.

But that day at Beth's cemented my understanding that there were girls who had moms who were nothing like mine. That recognition—and the sense that the way my mother berated me and picked on me wasn't right or fair—kept growing year by year. I began noticing that other people could be disappointed or angry without resorting to name-calling or insult and that some people were open and affectionate with their children. And that there were daughters who didn't walk tiptoe around their mothers as I did. But my recognition—and my growing sense that I was more of a bystander to her fury than its cause—absolutely coexisted with a deep need for her to love me and be like the mommies I so envied that other girls had.

That uneasy coexistence gets its energy from the fact that, while you do see that you're being abused and you do care about that, you care more about getting what you want from the abuser. It is true when the victim is a child and the verbal abuser is a parent, but the dynamic stays the same in adult-on-adult relationships. Once again, one person has the power and the upper hand.

The Core Conflict and Verbal Abuse

What I am describing—the push-pull between my recognition that my mother was actively wounding me and my need for her to love and support me—is what I called "the core conflict" in my book *Daughter Detox,* as I mentioned in the Introduction. While that book was aimed at women, sons, too, get trapped in this conflict, either with a mother or a father. That conflict can go on for years, even decades, and as long as it's ongoing—and the adult child's eyes are still on that elusive prize, a parent's love and support and a sense of belonging—the chances are good that he or she will rationalize and normalize the ongoing verbal abuse.

Daughters and sons tell me that they spent years explaining away the put-downs and efforts to control by thinking their parents didn't know any better or meant well, deep down, which kept the core conflict going. That was the story George, 51, shared: "My father was a harsh taskmaster who saw the world divided into winners and losers and, if you failed at something, he'd treat you like the loser you were. I honestly didn't understand for years and years that this was abusive behavior—calling us names, shaming us, demeaning us—because I thought he was just trying to set the bar high. My wife was the first person to point out how ugly and cruel the things were that he said to me and about me. I'd gotten laid off from my job and we had my parents over for dinner and he kept saying how embarrassed he was to have me as his son and then he spent an hour talking about what a winner my brother was. When they left, Sarah turned to me and said, 'That was the worst display I've ever witnessed.' She had to explain what she meant. I was 30 and I didn't have a clue. I thought he acted this way because he loved me."

Take a moment and appreciate that last sentence: "I thought he acted this way because he loved me." It sounds almost unbelievable—how could George think that was what a loving parent did, you might ask yourself—but it's neither weird nor unusual. It's a theme that runs through many of the stories recounted in this book, beginning with Mariah's in the Introduction.

Our need to belong and be accepted in our families of origin often keeps us from seeing the real impact of verbal abuse. We want to be loved by our parents and we want to love them, so it's easier to say, "He doesn't mean the things he says" or "He's tough on me because he wants me to be better" than it is to acknowledge and take in the true import of a parent's behavior. Others continue to make excuses for their mothers or fathers by referring to their own less-than-perfect childhoods because it's so much less complicated and painful than facing the truth. Carole's story gets to the heart of the matter and has the benefit of hindsight and some 20 years of healing: "When I was a girl, I was simply scared of my mother and her anger. She'd yell and scream if I did anything that displeased or disappointed her, and I did what I could to be the person she wanted me to be. Any efforts I made to express myself were mocked—she would literally laugh at me and call me clueless and stupid— so I let her pick my clothes and my friends and participated in activities she thought worthy. My father made it clear that he thought she was doing a great job, so it was all on me to do mine. I wanted to act in the school play, but that wasn't what she wanted so I did sports instead. When I went to college, I had absolutely no idea who I was or what I wanted, and without her control, I floundered and then sank. I ended up in the college's counseling office, talking to a therapist, and I was terrified she'd find out I was talking about her."

But even as the therapist enumerated the ways in which her mother's control was stifling and damaging her, Carole continued to resist the idea: "I just wasn't ready to accept the fact that I couldn't be myself around my mother or that she was cruel so I latched on to the idea that she'd grown up with hardship and very controlling parents, so it really wasn't her fault. She just didn't know any better."

Not altogether surprisingly, Carole married someone more like her mother than not when she was 24: "I didn't realize I was repeating history, of course. I thought Charlie was just trying to take care of me, so I basically did whatever he wanted me to do, just as I always had with my mother." It was the birth of her first child, a son, when she was 28, that finally began to shift her perspective: "Charlie was immensely critical of everything I did as a mother, and when Tommy turned four, he started berating me for making him 'soft.' I could see that my boy was scared of his dad's screaming and yelling, and I finally began to grow a backbone. I went into therapy, despite Charlie's strenuous objections. He absolutely did not want me to be independent or have ideas of my own, and the relationship went downhill fast. His abuse became louder and louder and constant. I filed for divorce when I turned 34. Then there was another wrinkle: My mother took my husband's side, and tried to help him get custody! Birds of a feather. The only way I could begin to be myself was to get rid of them both."

Many adult children simply revert to self-questioning and doubt, questioning whether their childhood memories are accurate. It often takes years for the strategy to run out of gas, as Mathilda, age 47, wrote: "Seeing her was always painful, a trip down memory lane but in a bad way, when she'd attack me in those old familiar ways. 'Oh,' she'd say, 'that's so brave of you to wear that!' (a way of telling me I looked fat or lousy) or she'd comment that my sister's new job was wonderful and how it was a pity I'd never been as successful (a jab at my teaching job, which paid pennies to my sister's gig.) If I pushed back, she'd tell me that I was too sensitive or just being difficult. And for years, I just accepted her meanness, thinking that was just the way she was or that she didn't get how hurtful it was or that maybe I *was* a disappointment. I was still trying to find a way of pleasing her so that she'd fork over the love I wanted. Finally, I went into therapy because I had no choice; I couldn't take another emotional beating from her. But she didn't want to hear it, and she wouldn't allow me to set boundaries. She finally cut bait on me, and I simply let it go. I speak in a guarded way to my sister, but basically, my whole family of origin believed in my mother's version of the story. She swears she never abused me in any way."

Why Self-Blame "Works"

Yes, those quotation marks are meant to denote irony since, in the long run, blaming yourself for verbal abuse not only doesn't work but also destroys whatever shreds of self-esteem and trust in your perceptions you have left. That said, remember that a child under the age of majority who's a target of abuse doesn't have many choices at hand; life has served up a smorgasbord of coping mechanisms, none of them particularly healthy or productive. (Keep in mind the contrarian suggestion at the end of the last chapter that rather than labeling "disorders," we instead look at maladaptive responses to adversity.) As I mentioned at the beginning of this chapter, blaming yourself has a protective function—allowing you to look away from the awful truth of your vulnerability at your parent's hands—while also allowing you to fantasize about fixing those awful flaws in your character and, by doing that, stopping the abuse in its tracks and getting love instead. It's an avoidant strategy that lowers the risk of confrontation and things actually getting worse, though it has real risks of its own.

Research by Jennifer J. Freyd in the 1990s set forth betrayal trauma theory, which explained how children "may isolate abuse experiences from consciousness and memory in order to maintain a necessary relationship with a caregiver." In a study Freyd conducted with Rachel E. Goldsmith in 2005, she explored the links between emotional abuse (her term) and emotional awareness, which was defined as the ability to name and define what you are feeling, in a small sample of some 80 participants drawn from a college population. (The term for the inability to do so is alexithymia.) While the researchers found a clear connection between emotional abuse and lack of emotional awareness, they also noted that "strikingly few participants who indicated having had emotional abuse experiences had acknowledged having been abused." This echoes the anecdotal reports from men and women I've quoted in this book and in *Daughter Detox*.

Freyd and Goldsmith, along with Anne P. DePrince, plumbed the topic again in 2009, looking specifically at perceptions of abuse among college students with a follow-up one to two years later. The study included 185 participants and the questionnaire used the word "abused" for three questions (e.g., "Would you say that you were emotionally or psychologically abused as a child?") while three used the word "maltreated." They found that participants who self-reported themselves as "abused" had more psychological symptoms (depression, anxiety, and the like) at the two-year follow-up than those who didn't. The researchers opined that filling out the questionnaire itself may be like an intervention, prompting a reassessment of past experiences. As they noted, most of the participants in the study were in their first year of college when they participated, which might well have been their first time away from an abusive environment. Put in the terms I've used, either the questionnaire or a new independent environment may have helped to uproot the default position of normalizing or denying.

Even though self-blame makes you feel dreadful about yourself, in this context it is, counterintuitively, a posture of self-defense and protection, a way of avoiding the truth about both the abuse and the abuser.

Understanding the dynamic is sobering, especially since without specific intervention such as therapy, this unconscious but motivated behavior can be carried over into adulthood and used as a coping mechanism with a verbally abusive partner. Needless to say, the ten-

dency to self-blame can also be ruthlessly exploited by an abusive partner. The key thing to understand is how self-blame facilitates avoiding
the possible loss of the relationship, which is, whether you are a child
or an adult, even more frightening than the abuse itself or the psychological pain of self-blame. We'll be looking at the psychological mechanisms that empower this self-destructive coping mechanism in adult
relationships later in the chapter.

Family Narratives

Parents are the authors of the family narrative and its mythologies; since they are figures of real power and authority, younger children simply buy into the narrative presented, which rationalizes verbal
abuse. That narrative can be relatively simple: "I call you names because you don't listen when I'm nice"; "You are lazy, and that's why I
criticize you"; "Your sister makes me proud, and you disappoint me";
and similar statements that shift the blame for the abuse onto the child
and justify the parent's action. Silent verbal abuse is justified in the
same way.

Even when a child sees that the narrative is false, as I certainly did
by the time I was 11 or so, the core conflict and her or his essential
powerlessness keep the child on the treadmill of recognition followed
by self-blame, denial, or self-doubt until the age of majority. Faced
with verbal or other kinds of abuse, children don't have choices, and
there is always one other factor. Verbally abusive parents tend to cu-
rate their public personas very carefully, so even as the child gets older,
who will believe him or her? I will return to this question in the pages
that follow because it is an important one. In the meantime, let's look
at the tenacity of family narratives.

Sandra had bought into the narrative all of her life, especially her
mother's relentless badgering her about her weight and looks: "All my
mother cared about was that I reflected on her well. My brother and
I were public testaments, like the good cars in the driveway and the
expensive carpets on the floor. Who I was, what I was thinking, didn't
matter one lick. Good grades were for her bragging. My looking good
showed how my dad was a good provider and she was a great moth-

er. She'd belittle me and then mock me when I cried, so I stopped crying in front of her. I'd bite my tongue or cheek to distract myself. But I didn't push back. It was just what I thought I had to do." But when Sandra was 43, she could no longer keep silent or make excuses: "When my mother started shaming my nine-year-old for eating 'too much' and told her that fat girls never had friends or boyfriends, sirens went off in my head. I called her out on it, and she wouldn't back down. She did this to me, and she doesn't get to do it again. Not on my watch. I haven't seen or spoken to her since." It doesn't escape Sandra's attention that she was able to do for her daughter what she couldn't do for herself: extricate herself from an abusive relationship.

Because the use of verbal abuse is thoroughly rationalized by a parent, adult children often find it hard or nearly impossible to set boundaries. That was the case for Mary, 42, the mother of two children herself: "I have to admit that it was my husband who really pushed me hard to do something because he felt strongly that hearing my mother criticize me and tear me down was really bad for our kids. It finally reached a crisis when they were eight and ten. She'd always done this, of course, but now the kids were old enough to really hear her. She would go on and on about what a lousy housekeeper I was, how I was raising the kids to grow up to be failures, how I was a failure—all within earshot of the children. I tried talking to her calmly, but she blew a gasket, and she told me my problem was that I could never take constructive criticism and that she was only doing it for my own good. Who calls someone a fat slob for their own good, or thinks that calling her daughter's house a pigsty is constructive criticism?"

What happened next shook Mary to the core, but maybe it shouldn't have. Confronted, her mother stuck to her guns and refused to tone down her comments or stop making them altogether, and then took the next step and ended the relationship. She initiated a smear campaign against Mary, making it an "it's me or her" loyalty test. Mary was shocked and devastated when her entire family—her father, brother, aunts, and uncles—all sided with her mother and, despite her efforts to explain her side of the story, rebuked her.

As she tells it, it was a terrible experience and a rude awakening: "I don't know whether my father and brother think as little of me as my mother does, but it is clear that certainly my father has her back totally. My brother doesn't want to say much because our parents gift his kids with things they wouldn't get otherwise and babysit for him and his wife when they go on vacation. He does agree that Mom was very hard on me, but he'll only say that in private. In public, he's on her team."

It's actually common for siblings to lay claim to different versions of the family narrative. Some of this has to do with parental differential treatment, or PDT (turned into an acronym by psychologists because it's so common), which we discussed in the first chapter: One child may be the focus of a parent's abusive tactics while another escapes negative attention almost entirely, especially if there is a designated scapegoat. When the scapegoat role is a rotating one—someone always has to shoulder the blame for what went wrong, but it may not always be the same child—it's much more likely that the siblings will share similar, though not necessarily identical, views of the toxic environment. Temperament and personality are partly responsible for how an individual's family narrative differs from another's, as is the sibling's attachment style.

But a lack of consensus between and among adult siblings is yet another reason verbal abuse gets normalized for long periods of time. Because the default setting is usually self-blame, it's very difficult for a son or daughter to be the lone voice identifying a parent as abusive, especially if there's pressure for him or her not to. And even when the adult child ceases to normalize, his or her ability to act on the newfound knowledge is often stymied by feeling like an outlier. And then, too, there is real emotional confusion, as witnessed by these questions posed by two of my readers, Leslie (age 44) and Ted (age 41), several years ago. Here's the first: "How is it possible that my older sister's view of our mother is utterly different from mine? She is Mom's staunchest defender and advocate. Heaven forbid I say anything negative about her, or I absolutely get attacked. She says it's all in my head. Is it?" And the second: "The party line is that Dad is a great guy and that his way of talking—laced with contempt and put-downs—is just the way he is and that it's my problem that I'm too sensitive and that I need to man up. Mind you, I am the oldest of three sons and my father's namesake to boot, and his criticism of me is never-ending and withering, despite the fact that I am the most successful male in the family by far. He's not nearly as tough on my brothers, but I wouldn't call his treatment of them much better. It's created a terrific rift between us because I'm not taking the old man's garbage any longer."

The truth is that all the members of a family defend their own personal narratives fiercely, especially when a charge like verbal abuse is leveled against a parent or parents; it's not just personality but also beliefs about the meaning (or sanctity) of blood relatives and filial duty. Note the blame-shifting in Leslie's and Ted's stories: She's told "it's all in her head," and he's labeled "too sensitive." Another truth is that if there's scapegoating, your siblings are likely to normalize the verbal abuse you received since the parental narrative insisted that you were the troublemaker and they may well believe it themselves.

If you look at the complexity of the issue—the possibility of losing all family ties, the cultural onus of estrangement—is it any wonder that we revert to normalizing verbal abuse as a way of protecting ourselves from other painful truths?

Let's tackle that directly, shall we?

The Cost of Pushing Back: Another Motive for Normalizing and Denying

"It's not as though you don't know what will happen when you challenge an abusive parent," wrote Grant, 52. "My father demonstrated by example when anyone dared to challenge him; he literally didn't speak to my older brother, who was 13 at the time, for two whole months. My brother actually talked back and told Dad he was nasty for no reason and that was enough to send Joe into exile. He wasn't welcome in the kitchen or the living room. My mother left his meals in front of his bedroom door; she was fully on board with what Dad called 'discipline.' The only reason he didn't throw him out then was he couldn't legally. But Joe kept pushing back and Dad kept punishing, and he threw Joe out the first minute he could. Yes, on the day of his 18th birthday. It was clear to me and my sister that it was a winner-take-all thing and so we sucked it up."

Fear of loss of family ties also animates normalization for adult children. Since abusers are generally loath to own their behaviors and, instead, either gaslight or justify, adult children understandably worry about the cost of confrontation. Studies by Kristina Scharp and others show that recognition of abusive behavior is responsible for the initiation of estrangement from a parent by an adult child; both the overt and quiet kinds of verbal abuse, the latter being neglect, are cited as causes.

Similarly, in a study by Kristen Carr, Amanda Holman and others, the researchers specifically looked at the reasons parents and adult children chose estrangement and found real divergence. What was particularly interesting about this relatively large study—898 participants of which 546 were parents and 352 were adult children—is that they were mismatched pairs, meaning that the parents' children and the children's parents weren't in the survey. While parents cited objectionable relationships and entitlement as the deciding factors in estrangement, it was toxic parental behavior that was the spark for adult children. Additionally, while parents attributed the rupture to outside influences, adult children focused on their parents' self-centered or toxic behaviors that left little opportunity for change. The researchers also noted that, while parents seemed relatively lacking in confidence about why the estrangement had occurred, adult children were, in contrast, very sure indeed. And then there was this observation: "Overwhelmingly, parents discussed their children's perceptions of being unloved but were uncertain of their own roles in creating these feelings. Children, on the other hand, were explicit about the reasons for feeling unloved, and often attributed these causes to stable and internal characteristics of their parents."

In my own anecdotal research on adult child-parent estrangement, it becomes clear that many adult children spend decades considering the move before they make it; they are much more likely to continue to normalize verbal abuse than they are to rush into a decision. Again, that is because so much is at stake, most usually ties to their entire family. It tends to be, as my respondent Grant noted, a winner-take-all situation.

The Problem with Intention: Another Source

As we've seen, children subjected to verbal abuse bob and weave like fighters in the ring, trying to avoid a painful truth. But there's a reason this particular truth is so painful, which is pointed out in a paper by Kurt Gray and Daniel M. Wegner, "The Sting of Intentional Pain," exploring whether the psychological context of pain—accidental or intentional—actually affected the intensity of the pain itself. The experiment they conducted had participants grouped into pairs, one of whom would be administered tasks by the other, who was called the "confederate." There were four tasks, three of which were benign (color-matching, number estimation, and pitch judgment), but the fourth was the delivery of an electric shock, which the participant would have to rank on a scale from "not uncomfortable" to "extremely uncomfortable." In each trial, a computer showed two possible tasks and the participant was told that the confederate would determine which task was administered. In one group—the intentional condition—the confederate was told to choose the shock when it was a possible choice; in the other condition, the confederate was told to choose the pitch judgment, not the shock, when it appeared on the screen. But the participant was told that, unbeknownst to the confederate, the tasks had been switched so that the pitch judgment would yield to the shock being administered, albeit unintentionally. The experiment showed that intended pain was perceived as more painful, even though the literal amount of pain administered was the same. Attributing malice to something painful not only makes it hurt more but also makes it harder to recover from.

Let's keep that in mind when we step out of the lab and into the real world, we are talking about the people who are supposed to love us and instead *intentionally* hurt us. Yes, that is why children—even as adults—bob, weave, and normalize because acknowledging the truth of what is happening is both terrifying and painful.

Outliers and Other Rebels:
The Children Who Didn't Normalize

Not every child under the age of majority normalizes verbal abuse, but that doesn't guarantee a happy ending, and confrontation has its costs. Family dynamics are hugely complicated, as the story Melanie, now 57, tells makes clear.

Her father was verbally abusive, given to rages, and an absolute tyrant who ruled the household and cowed everyone, including his wife. It is ironic but true that her father was a hospital chaplain whose job was to offer solace to those in pain and grieving. Melanie and her older sister were born just 13 months apart, but it was clear to her by the age of four or so that it wasn't just that her father preferred her sister but that he also actively disliked Melanie. The story she tells is heartbreaking in the small details—how her father would come home from work and want to be the center of attention, and her mother would chime in, "Look, Daddy's home! Run and give him a hug and a kiss!" And Melanie would try to snuggle up to her father, but he'd tickle or push her away, and she'd be left standing there, watching her sister cuddle with their father on the couch, wondering what was wrong with her.

As she tells it, it was a long struggle made worse by the fact that her mother was equally cowed by her father's abuse: "He liked to point out everyone's faults and make fun of them and then laugh and say, 'I'm only teasing.' But he wasn't teasing, and it was constant. He would ask us how our day at school was, and anything we said was met with criticism. We learned very early on to say nothing. Each night, he'd walk in the door and ask, 'What's burning?' as my mother was cooking as a way of putting my mom down." In the end, it was Melanie, at age 14, who brought the house of cards down by running away and refusing to come back until the family went into counseling. It was in those counseling sessions that Melanie talked about hating her father and why. Her father looked up and said, "I feel as though Melanie gets angry at me for no reason," and she replied, "Really? You yell at my mother and make her cry. And I'm angry for no reason?" While her outbursts were a jolt of support for her mother, they were torture for her sister, who ended up walking out of the sessions.

It turned out that bringing things to a head both saved the family in one sense and doomed it as a unit in another; even though they'd long been in marital counseling, her parents divorced and Melanie cut her father out of her life. She wrote: "After he moved out, I wanted nothing to do with him. Again, he seemed completely mystified as to why. He would call and say, "But I'm your father, why don't you love me?" In hindsight, I wish I had written him a long letter itemizing everything he had said and done, because it never did sink in." Her mother continued to replay the tape of her marriage gone wrong for years, and Melanie notes that verbal abuse often surfaced in mutual conversations. The extended family has never forgiven her and has castigated her for the "lies" she told about her father.

This is, in many ways, a dispiriting story, but it testifies to the fact that verbal abuse is a deep-rooted invader when it's given the right soil, and affects each member of the family in different ways. Melanie herself is still trying to fully recover all these years later.

Sometimes, it's not the target of verbal abuse who normalizes but the bystander sibling; it's here that we can see the self-protection aspect most clearly. George and Tim, now in their sixties, were born just 15 months apart, but it was George, his father's namesake, who was in his father's crosshairs, not Tim. By their account, their father was a charming and affable man in public, well-liked by his neighbors and people at the country club, as well as his colleagues at work. where he achieved great success; at home, though, he could be cuttingly abusive to his older son, whom he deemed a continuous disappointment. He was also a binge drinker, disappearing at times, leaving behind a frantic wife who, in the days before cell phones, had no idea where he was or when he would come back. Fiercely protective of his mother, George increasingly took his father on as he got older, while Tim hung back, drawing as little attention to himself as possible. The stories these two men tell of their childhoods aren't just disparate but also basically irreconcilable; George's narrative is unflinchingly direct while Tim's is heavily curated and idealized, emphasizing his father's affability and charm. Tim learned young to deny his feelings and to push off from them—he knew the cost, after all—and, not surprisingly, has paid the price. Estranged from his adult children and twice divorced, he still maintains that his father "wasn't so bad" and that "anger is a wasted emotion."

Sometimes, both the circumstances and the length of exposure to verbal abuse stop normalization and denial in its tracks. That was the case for Billie, now 68: "I didn't normalize his abuse, but that's likely because I wasn't a target of my father's abuse until after my mother died, when I was 12. Before then, my relationship with my father wasn't particularly deep. He was a typical 1950s/early1960s father in that he left the better part of child-raising to my mother. It was only when my mother was no longer a buffer, and I had more direct dealings with my father, that he became abusive. So I had 12 years free of abuse in which I'd built a fairly firm self-image. That probably explains why my reaction to the abuse was more likely to be anger than anything else." And she fought with her father in response: "My father belittled me and criticized me, in a voice that was characteristically loud and angry. Many of his outbursts have been lost to memory, but a few favorites persist. Once, after I'd eaten all the ripe cherries from the bag in the fridge (mea culpa), he went on and on about how selfish I was (his favorite theme, when it came to me) and said, 'That's so typical of you. You eat all the ripe cherries of life.' He also once said to me, 'You're beyond help. I just want to make sure you don't pollute your sister.' Truly, I have no idea why he said that. I was a pretty good kid—always got A's, did my homework, and had a strong moral compass. But I always felt that my father had no control whatsoever over his anger, and that he never got irritated or miffed but instead went instantly to rage. And when he raged, he was mean. It infuriated me—my father and I had many a raging argument. And it made me feel very alone, very vulnerable."

But she went on to say: "If I normalized it—and my memory is cloudy here—it wasn't for very long. I have a very distinct memory of realizing, probably at the age of 14 or so, that children take everything their parents say as gospel. At the same time, I realized that what parents say and believe isn't necessarily the truth." But that realization, of course, offered scant protection: "Of course, my father's abuse couldn't have no effect on me. Early adolescence is a time when most of us are trying to figure out who we are, and it doesn't help to hear that one of the things we are is 'not good enough.' That, coupled with the devastating loss of my mother, no doubt contributed to a growing generalized anxiety that took me many years to get under control."

Verbal abuse always leaves a mark. There's no question.

Is Normalizing Dependent on Which Parent Is the Abuser?

This is a question that arises from the process of recognition, and it's one that I get asked all the time. As adult children stop normalizing and begin to plumb the patterns of abuse in their families of origin, they are often surprised by what they see. During the years that the young or older adult child stops normalizing, he or she may be shocked to realize that the constructed narratives about each parent's role are more fictional than factual. That was certainly true for Maria, now 45, who saw her father as the villain and her mother as yet another victim: "For years, I focused on my tyrannical father and how afraid of him I was. Mind you, my two brothers were scared of him, too, but they dealt with it by being the boys he wanted them to be. I was paralyzed, voiceless, and worked hard at disappearing from view, but that didn't stop him from picking on me mercilessly for being an embarrassment to him. It was only when I got into therapy that I started realizing my mother's role wasn't really passive. There's nothing passive about standing by and watching your husband abuse your children."

Other daughters and sons—remember how both Patch and Tim, the sons of abusive men, struggled to understand their mothers' roles in Chapter One?—find it very difficult to deal with the parent who stood by in the face of verbal abuse, retreating to a study or going to fold laundry or simply pretending that nothing much was going on. Even harder to deal with emotionally are those fathers and mothers who urged their daughters or sons to be accepting and understanding of the abusive parent, or who refuse to acknowledge, even years later, that any abuse took place.

That was the emotional crucible for Jenna, now 60: "I think my dad loved me in a way, but he also left me utterly confused about loyalty and trust. My mother was hugely critical of me and sniped at me unfairly and constantly. She never let an opportunity go by to put me down or, alternatively, ignore me. If I messed up, she'd go on and on how I was a failure. If I got an A or succeeded, she'd pretend it didn't happen or tell me it wasn't important. When I got older and started to push back, my father would step in. He'd appear to acknowledge that I was being hurt, but then he'd tell me to placate her or apologize. He'd say, 'It's just the way she is' or 'She's a good person deep down inside' or 'She's doing it for your own good' or something that made me feel as though he'd sold me down the river after I told him how much I was hurting. That was as damaging in the end as my mother's sniping and undercutting, even though it took me years to realize that his betrayal was, in some ways, worse than hers."

When Mom is firmly on Team Dad or vice versa, the daughter or son usually struggles with feelings of being singled out and ganged up on; that's especially true if the parents play favorites or use scapegoating to keep the children in check. That kind of dynamic creates a very specific kind of damage. But the parent as a bystander or one who acknowledges but palliates creates a deep mistrust of others and reinforces a sense that love is a quid pro quo, which can last long into adulthood. Becca, now 43, wrote: "My mother is my father's staunchest defender. My father is a control freak and a bully, but she considers him strong. She thinks his put-downs are a way of keeping us from getting too full of ourselves, his criticisms a way of motivating us, his authoritarian style the mark of a man who knows his mind. I don't think she is cruel by nature, but she also stopped thinking for herself. She is nothing more than his loyal follower, who victimized me as much as he did. I stayed blind to her active role for 20 years of my adult life, but that's over now. She may not be dishing out the abuse, but she's the one who hands him his megaphone."

Is It Culturally Easier to Recognize Paternal Verbal Abuse?

I think it may well be. "Am I focusing on my father, because I can't bear to blame my mother?" asked one reader, rather plaintively, and she's not wrong to ask. The cultural mother myths—that all women

are nurturers by design, that mothering is instinctual, and that maternal love is unconditional—provide a Teflon shield for mothers that
fathers lack, and as a result, maternal verbal abuse often gets normalized and rationalized more and for longer. In our culture, other than
the roles of the traditional breadwinner and the disciplinarian, father-
hood and fathering don't have a cohesive and protective mythology
as motherhood and mothering do. As a result, as a group, we're more
willing to accept the idea of a neglectful, deadbeat, or tyrannical dad
than we are of his maternal counterpart. While the Brothers Grimm
cleaned up the traditional fairytales and piously reassigned all the roles
mothers played to stepmothers, literature has a long tradition of genuinely awful fathers—whether it's the Greek myth of Cronos eating his
children (which ended up foiled), the raging King Lear, the tormented
James Tyrone *in Long Day's Journey into Night*, Bull Meechum in *The
Great Santini*, or the despicable Henry Wingo in *Prince of Tides*, to name
just a few —bullies at heart who loom large and scary over their small
children. So while all of the above is anecdotal and not research based,
it does seem that it's easier to stop normalizing your father's abuse
than your mother's.

Normalizing Verbal Abuse:
Revisiting the Role of Parental Narratives

You may remember the story of Patch, told in Chapter One,
whose birth supposedly was the negative tipping point for his family
and thus served as the rationalization for his maltreatment; there were
a number of stories submitted by readers that, while they had different details and arcs, followed the same lines. When there's a family
narrative of this kind—which is repeated endlessly by the entire family—recognition of how the verbal abuse is undeserved is delayed and
the treatment normalized. That was true for a daughter named Julia,
whom I interviewed extensively. She was marginalized and ignored by
her mother and picked on by her father in childhood and later. When
she went into therapy, the specifics of her story helped her understand
how her parents used her to duck responsibility for their own actions
and choices. Her mother had gotten pregnant in her freshman year

of college, which propelled her and the boy who became Julia's father into marriage. Her mother never finished school, and her father worked at a job that paid the bills rather than following his passion.

As Julia put it: "My birth was the cause of all hardship and strife. And I was never allowed to forget it. They chose to have two more children later, and it was always clear that unlike me, my sisters brought them happiness and pride. That was the family story, and they have never deviated from it, not in 50 years. I am still the source of all their disappointments, large and small, and that is part of their bond. In a weird way, their marriage has thrived, because they had someone to blame for their occasional unhappiness from the very start. My mother still dismisses me, and my father finds me lacking. It will never change, and I still find it painful and difficult to accept. I do what I can to minimize contact to minimize hurt. It's not ideal, but I'm not ready to let go of my whole family, which is what would happen. This is a story everyone in my family tells, and at the moment, I am staying a character in their story. Time will tell."

That is Julia's choice, but, it should be said, not everyone's. And it shouldn't be everyone's, I think.

If you are in any doubt about the choices you are making in response to either verbal abuse or its effects on you, please seek professional help. Going along to get along can have profound consequences.

Normalizing Verbal Abuse in Adult Life

As we've already seen, those who experienced verbal abuse in childhood and learned to cope with it are more likely to find themselves in adult relationships that echo the same patterns. It is a truism that, until you stop normalizing your past experiences, you will remain susceptible not just to repeating those old patterns in your relationships but also to continuing to be blind to them. When I asked one daughter, 52, who was belittled, marginalized, and gaslighted by her mother what she thought made her continue to rationalize verbal abuse by partners and others as an adult, she responded: "I think what made me vulnerable is my childhood. I was constantly being denied my reality. When I have experienced verbal abuse as an adult, all the well-formed childhood strategies kick in: I go small, and I freeze; I can't respond. I feel shame and lock down expressing anything externally, but the biggest reaction is an inability to respond. The thought of standing up for myself or calling out the behavior fills me with fear."

But we are not necessarily doomed to lock ourselves into our old childhood rooms. Therapy is an option, of course, as is self-help. I think the most important thing to realize is that there are so many reasons you look away from verbal abuse—and the culture does, too— that it becomes a question of how to outwit the tendency to duck.

Knowing what makes you duck is key, so let's start with one psychological process—yes, it is a biggie—that facilitates normalizing and denying. It actually has a name: intermittent reinforcement.

The Power of Intermittent Reinforcement: Yikes!

As demonstrated by B. F. Skinner in a famous experiment involving hungry rats, we humans actually become more persistent when what we want only happens some of the time. This is the reason gamblers stay at the slot machines when they win every now and again and why people stay in lousy relationships that, at odd moments, look vaguely like loving ones. Do remember that this experiment predates more evolved ideas of animal cruelty. Skinner put three hungry rats in cages, each of which had a lever. In one cage, pushing the lever delivered food all the time, and the rat understood that and went about his business. In another cage, the lever produced no food, and the rat understood that, too. He ran on the wheel provided and did whatever hungry rats do. But in the third cage, the lever produced food randomly, and that got the rat totally hooked. He stayed parked by the lever night and day, hoping for the food to drop. Intermittent reinforcement is incredibly powerful.

This applies to verbal abuse in a very specific way, as it does to all toxic connections. When your parent is suddenly nice to you and the ugly flood of words is dammed up, you feel incredibly positive and sure that you can garner his or her love; it also facilitates your rationalizing the abuse as a now-and-again thing or something the parent didn't mean or do on purpose. Since children don't have the power or ability to leave this particular relationship, they simply settle in and adapt to stay afloat. But intermittent reinforcement works in adult relationships, too, and will spur on optimism and rationalization of things balancing out and the false hope that the relationship has turned a corner.

Welcome to the world of rats and humans: Your inclination to stay the course is increased when you get what you want only some of the time.

That's counterintuitive but true, which is why when your lover/spouse/boss/friend says what you've been waiting to hear or acts the way you'd always wanted some of the time, you're much more likely to get so very hopeful and give him or her just "one more chance" or to "wait and see what happens." It's also true that if even if he or she didn't take Psych 101 and read about the rats, the verbally abusive person knows that the once-in-a-while strategy of handing out a bit of sweetness works. Because it does.

Empathy and Verbal Abuse: A Very Bad Combination

In the world of therapy and then filtered down through popular self-help, the ability to understand and share someone else's feelings is a key concept. Rightly, empathy is a highly regarded character trait, both in psychological research and in the real world. But as adults who are either making sense of childhood experiences or evaluating an ongoing relationship that includes verbal abuse, putting on our empathic hats is a terrible mistake. Yes, we may come to understand why the person acted as she or he did—that the mental models derived from his or her own childhood were deficient or that the steady stream of abuse is a way of protecting his or her vulnerable self, or that real circumstances make it impossible or difficult for this individual to genuinely understand the impact of his or her behavior—but playing amateur therapist will only strap you into the Ferris wheel even more tightly and buy you multiple tickets for a prolonged ride. Don't do it. Empathic understanding is best exercised with the benefit of 20/20 hindsight, once you are safely out of range.

The same thing goes for forgiveness, especially if the abuser continues to abuse. While it's true that our culture sees the ability to forgive as evidence of attaining a higher moral ground, studies on forgiveness make it clear that there are definite downsides. Psychological research provides a corrective to the cultural mishmash that equates forgiveness with forgetting.

For one thing, as pointed out by social psychologist Frank Fincham, forgiveness doesn't include pretending something didn't happen or that it was pain free; in fact, forgiveness confirms that the act was intentional because we don't have to forgive accidental acts. (If you lose consciousness and you fall on my treasured heirloom, I don't need to forgive you. But if you pick up a bat and deliberately smash my beloved heirloom on purpose, I might consider forgiving you—or not.) Fincham's article, which I cite in every book I write, also has a delicious title and sets up a brilliant paradigm; it is called "The Kiss of the Porcupines" because he imagines two porcupines trying to cuddle and, of course, the closer they get, the more likely it is that one will be pricked by the other's quills. It's a great metaphor for the benefits and risks involved in relationship or, simply put, the comfort of cuddles and the risk of emotional pain.

Forgiveness, Fincham argues, doesn't imply reconciliation or reunion; while it's true that reconciliation requires forgiveness, you can forgive someone and still have nothing to do with them in the future. Finally—and this seems especially important—forgiveness isn't a single act, but a process. It requires managing the negative emotions that are a consequence of the act and substituting goodwill for the impulse to strike back. It's a process that involves a considerable amount of emotional and cognitive work, and so, as Fincham notes, the statement "I am trying to forgive you" is particularly true and meaningful.

The problem, of course, is that the outcome is not in the forgiver's hands, but in those of the transgressor. That was the starting point for research conducted by Laura B. Luchies, Eli J. Finkel, and others, published under the title "The Doormat Effect," which investigated how forgiveness interacted with feelings of self-worth and respect. The team posited that forgiveness bolstered self-esteem if the transgressor made amends and changed his or her behavior. But, they hypothe-sized, if the transgressor continued to behave the same way after hav-ing been forgiven, the person who forgave would experience a drop in self-esteem, among other effects. This is what they called the doormat effect.

Over the course of four studies—one of them longitudinal and lasting five years—they found support for their hypothesis. Despite the body of research seeming to recommend forgiveness as a panacea, they wrote, "[T]he responses of both victims and perpetrators are influential following a betrayal. Victims' self-respect and self-concept clarity are determined not only by their own decision whether to for-give or not but also by their perpetrators' decision whether to act in a manner that signals that the victim will be safe or valued or not."

Clinicians and researchers agree that forgiveness of transgressions is a cornerstone of maintaining intimate relationships, especially mar-riage, but that certain caveats do apply: The relationship must be one of equals, without an imbalance of power, and with equal investment and recognition of the benefits of the connection. None of that is true of a verbally abusive relationship.

Both empathy and forgiveness without the abuser's absolute com-mitment to cease and desist simply keep you stuck.

The Sunk Cost Fallacy: Another Mind Trap for Normalizing

Our cultural tropes emphasize the gung-ho nature of humanity at its best, but psychological science knows that nothing could be further from the truth; as it happens, humans are a very conservative lot, and much more comfortable with the known, even if it doesn't make them happy, than the unknown future. Seen from that point of view, those who sailed the ocean blue and ventured into the darkness of space are the true outliers. Additionally, we are so risk averse—an obser-vation that won a Nobel prize in economics for psychologist Daniel Kahneman—that we will take risks to preserve what we have but not to increase what we have. That all ties into what's called "the sunk cost fallacy," which describes what we focus on when we are thinking about making a change. Rather than look to the possible greener pastures of the future, we end up thinking about what we have invested in whatever it is we are thinking about changing or replacing. It could be a car, a house, a job, or a relationship—it's all the same, but it's particularly pertinent when it comes to explaining why people stay in abusive relationships. What we've invested could be time, energy, emotion, or even money, and we're focused on losing that investment should we decamp. The thinking goes like this: "If I leave the relationship now, then all the years I have spent trying to make it work will be lost, and all my energy and efforts will have been for nothing." Please note that this kind of thinking is called a fallacy for a reason; the time, energy, and emotion are already gone and spent, whether you stay or leave.

Summing Up

It becomes clear that there are many reasons—cultural, psychological, emotional, and individual—that we normalize the face of verbal abuse.

If you are in an intimate relationship that includes some or all of these behaviors, please keep in mind that, one, verbal abuse is damaging to you and unacceptable and, two, normalizing enables escalation and perhaps even physical abuse. If you are hurting but telling yourself, "It's not so bad," or, "It could be worse," please talk to a professional immediately. If you think about verbal abuse as being on a continuum and *always* being about maintaining control, it's not hard to see that it's frighteningly easy to move on that continuum toward greater intensity for both the target and the abuser. Do recognize that the more subtle forms of verbal abuse—such as stealth control and others, especially if the effect is to alienate you from family, friends, and other support—have been called "coercive control" by experts. If you are reading this and feel you are in a bad place, call a professional immediately.

In the next chapter, we'll take an in-depth look at how verbal abuse changes us and the lives we lead.

Chapter Four

Effects and Affect:
How Verbal Abuse Changes Us

Famously, Leo Tolstoy began his brilliant novel *Anna Karenina* with these words: "All happy families are alike; each unhappy family is unhappy in its own way." Think about that for a moment, would you? My job as a writer is to discern the patterns that are common ground for those who have experienced or continue to experience verbal abuse, but at the same time, it's important to recognize the small differences that make each of our stories unique.

Verbal abuse shapes individuals in very different ways; some of that has to do with the kind of abuse (is it overt or the silent type?), the age of the person when the abuse starts, its frequency, the personality of the victim, and the specific dynamics of the abusive relationship. By homing in on the ways it shapes different people, we can gain insight into how it has affected each of us in particular and others who are close to us; it permits us to see important variations on the theme and gives us insight into how we can help ourselves and others. The point here is to get beyond the obvious—yes, verbal abuse damages—and see with more nuance and clarity. In truth, some of what we will discover will be counterintuitive.

Let's use the metaphor of a garden to explain the path we're on. You see a photo of what looks like a stunning and thriving garden posted by a neighbor, so you message her and ask to visit. She graciously allows you to come over and experience the garden in person, which, you discover, doesn't quite look as perfect as it did in the photograph. Yes, the beds of roses that frame the garden are just as stunning as they were in the photo, but you notice that there are spots beyond the roses on the left that look bare and scraggly, and you wonder why. It turns out that her neighbors graded their land so that every time it rains, the water sluices into that corner of the garden and it doesn't drain properly. The gardener has struggled to find plants that can survive the onslaught. In another area, you see that the perennials aren't thriving because they're surrounded by lemon balm and vinca, and the gardener ruefully admits that she planted those two without realizing how horribly invasive they were. She has tried for years to get rid of them, but so far, they're winning the battle, choking everything in their path. And toward the back, where once a tall oak stood, the plantings compete against old roots, and the struggle shows.

This metaphorical garden is the woman or man who's grown up with verbal abuse. She or he may look thriving and perhaps even terrifically successful at a quick glance, but introspection or closer inspection reveals something beyond the roses. Mind you, not everyone will have those symbols of success—those thriving beds of roses—to show off, but we're looking at the best-case scenario here, where, at least, external optics work if you don't look too closely.

The Damage Done: Looking at Direct Effects

The damage done by verbal abuse is complicated because it has two separate sources. First, there are the direct effects of the abuse itself—the damage inflicted by the words themselves or the neglect and willful ignoring in the case of silent abuse. We've already seen that the structure of the developing brain is altered by the experience, which may result in anxiety and depression, and that the messages conveyed by the abuse are internalized and accepted as truths by a child routinely exposed to it. Research by Natalie Sachs-Ericsson, Edelyn Verona, and others made clear that the experience of verbal abuse facilitates the development of a self-critical style that attributes failures and setbacks to indelible character flaws.

One of the first major inquiries into the effects of parental verbal aggression on children, an analysis of 3,346 American parents, was published in 1991 by Yvonne M. Vissing and Murray A. Straus, Richard J. Gelles, and John Harrop; it was the first to test, in an empirical way, the assumption that verbal abuse was deleterious. Perhaps not surprisingly, 63 percent of the respondents interviewed by phone admitted to being verbally aggressive at least once during the two waves of the inquiry, a year apart. The scenarios focused on what a parent might do if there were a problem with the child and here are the possibilities parents chose from: insulted or swore at the child; sulked and/ or refused to talk about the problem; stomped out of the room, house, or yard; did something to spite the child; threatened to hit or throw something at the child; threw or smashed or hit or kicked something. Just under 21 percent reported 20 or more incidents in the preceding year. Among the conclusions were that the more frequent the verbal aggression, "the greater the probability of the child being physical aggressive, delinquent, or having interpersonal problems." Note, too, that boys were subjected to only slightly more verbal aggression than girls. Finally, parents who used verbal aggression did so roughly 12.6 times a year or a bit more than once a month. There's some evidence that maternal verbal abuse specifically and significantly increases the risk of a child developing a personality disorder.

A longitudinal study on the effects of maternal verbal abuse published more than 20 years ago by Jeffrey G. Johnson, Patricia Cohen, and others specifically looked at maternal abuse separate from other kinds of maltreatment, including physical and sexual abuse. The study, which began in 1975 when the mean age of the subjects was five, continued to monitor them in waves until the mean age was 22. (The researchers specifically checked in with the participants during adolescence when the mean ages were 14 and then 16.) Mothers were asked specific questions on three separate occasions (when the participants were roughly 5, 14, and 16 years old), which they had to answer yes or no to: 1) Did you scream at your child during the last month? and 2) Did you say things like "I'll send you away" or "I don't love you" during the last month? In the later interviews (when the children were roughly 16 and 22), the mothers were asked to respond to the following statement: "I tell my child I will hit or smack him/her if he/ she does something I don't like." The possible responses were never, hardly ever, fairly often, and very often. Verbal abuse of the child was considered to have occurred if the mother responded yes to the first two questions or she habitually threatened physical violence in the third. Some 9.8 percent of the children were considered to be victims of childhood verbal abuse.

What the researchers found was that those who had experienced maternal verbal abuse were *three* times more likely to suffer from personality disorders, including borderline and narcissistic, than those who were not subject to it. In their discussion, the authors note that further investigation is needed to see if the timing of the abuse (meaning when it takes place in a child's life) and frequency of the abuse account for the three-fold increase in risk. They also write, "Alternatively, it's been hypothesized that childhood verbal abuse leaves deeper scars than other types of abuse because children tend to identify with their parents and therefore tend to internalize and self-inflict verbally abusive statements against themselves throughout their lives." Note the word "self-inflict" and remember the internalized echo of the mother's voice.

Covert verbal abuse appears to have a different range of effects on behavior than the overt variety, which was explored in a study by Shelley A. Riggs and Patricia Kaminski published in 2010. (The researchers use the term "emotional abuse," so I am sticking with their terminology.) This research is very pertinent to our inquiry since it specifically investigated the links among childhood emotional abuse, attachment style, and depression as predictors of difficulty and aggression in adult relationships. Using a battery of measures, this study of undergraduates, 71 percent of whom were women, yielded some fresh insights. While, not surprisingly, emotional abuse alone predicted high rates of adult attachment anxiety, emotional abuse combined with emotional neglect (overt and covert verbal abuse together) predicted high levels of attachment avoidance. We'll be exploring this finding in the pages that follow. The researchers' findings also confirmed what other research had found: namely that parental control was a strong predictor of adult attachment anxiety. Additionally, their study found that maternal control accounted for a five-fold increase compared with paternal control. Interestingly, paternal neglect contributed to attachment anxiety, not avoidance, which the researchers noted might be more harmful to adult romantic relationships. (Remember that those with a dismissive-avoidant attachment style need high levels of control and see needing a partner as a sign of weakness.)

While Riggs and Kaminski found no evidence of depression being a factor, they did note that childhood emotional abuse profoundly affects the adult attachment system, which, in turn, shapes the quality of romantic relationship. But all is not lost; as they write, "when people are able to establish secure romantic attachment styles, they have a better chance of circumventing the negative outcomes from childhood maltreatment and associated parent-child attachment styles." In the next chapter, we'll be looking at earned secure attachment which is one way of circumventing the effects of childhood experience.

When Abuse Is Disguised as Discipline

Confusion about what constitutes verbal abuse continues to be a problem culturally and personally.

Writing for a large platform like PsychologyToday.com, which used to permit public commentary, has given me insights that I wouldn't necessarily have sitting in the quiet of my apartment. I began one post about verbal abuse with this story, one I'd actually seen firsthand: "The boy is about eight, and a man stands over him, presumably his father, yelling on the corner of 72nd Street and First Avenue. The man towers over him, tall enough to cast a shadow on the boy on this summer day. The boy's knees are bloody, his cheeks tear stained, and a shattered iPhone lies on the sidewalk. The man's voice is loud enough to hear even as I cross the street: "How stupid are you? I told you not to run or fool around when you're holding my phone. It's not a toy. Dammit, you never listen. You always do what you want, not what you're told. You're a clumsy idiot." The boy doesn't answer, but his shoulders shake. A woman comes out of the bank behind them, sees the phone, and starts in: "Way to ruin a Saturday, Matt. Thanks a lot." She picks up the pieces of the phone and turns to the man: "The Verizon store is right down the block. Let's see what can be done." The man puts his arm around her, and they walk off, with the boy trailing behind them.

In the piece, I posed two questions, which I went on to answer myself: Necessary discipline? Understandable anger? Nope. Verbal abuse.

The comments flooded in with people saying that an iPhone is expensive and the father probably needed it for work. That the kid was lucky that all the dad did was yell at him. Others understood why the mother took her husband's side, saying "Kids have to learn responsibility." Many people disagreed with this statement: "What's not okay is what the father said. It's abusive to turn criticism into a litany of character flaws, as he did, especially with a young child. Yes, it's okay to hold children accountable but not to call them 'an idiot' or other names that shame them. And it's not okay to focus on your phone when your kid's knees are bleeding." A number of people thought I was dead wrong or that I clearly had never been a parent. But there were also comments from adults who had been verbally abused by a parent or both.

So, who's right? (I'd bet on me here, by the way.)

Even though the American Academy of Pediatrics came out categorically against any kind of physical discipline such as spanking or hitting (and against using language that "belittles, humiliates, denigrates, scapegoats, threatens, scares, or ridicules the child," aka verbal abuse) in 2018, the practice of spanking has not stopped, although the percentage of parents who do it has dropped significantly, according to a University of Michigan study published in *JAMA Pediatrics* in 2020. While 50 percent of parents in 1993 said that they spanked their child or children, the percentage dropped to 35 percent in 2017. The share of men who used spanking as a punishment fell from 52 percent to 36 percent, while the share of women dropped from 48 percent to 35 percent. That said, despite reams and reams of evidence that physical punishment does damage to children and to the parent-child relationship (and does little to dissuade the child from the behavior you are punishing him or her for), more than one-third of American parents still spank their kids. Once again, this statistic demonstrates the staying power of cultural tropes used to justify physical abuse such as "Spare the rod, spoil the child." This one is also commonly and wrongly attributed to the Bible. (If you're skeptical, look for it in the Bible. You will not find it.)

We don't have any current data on the prevalence of parental verbal abuse, but we do know that in 1995, when half of Americans still spanked their children, the percentage of parents who used what Murray A. Straus and Carolyn J. Field called "psychological aggression" was more than 90 percent! That is *not* a typo, and yes, you may imagine 90 percent of American parents cussing out kids under the age of two, if you can bear it, with some 98 percent of parents using one or more forms of psychological aggression in the child's first five years of life. These numbers, Straus and Field stated, suggested that "psychological aggression is a nearly universal disciplinary tactic of American parents." "Somewhat" reassuringly—yes, I have the word in quotation marks for a reason—the rate of *severe* psychological aggression was lower: 10 to 20 percent for toddlers and 50 percent for teenagers. Again, these percentages are more than 25 years old, and they may have gone down, but by how much? The decline in spanking is significant but not spectacular, and the cultural take on the damage inflicted by physical abuse is much more robust than that attributed to verbal abuse.

Straus and Field defined what they saw as the problem: For parental psychological aggression to be labeled abuse, it must be shown to be injurious to the child. (This is, as I pointed out in the opening pages of this book, the problem with the term "emotional abuse" as well.) They noted four reasons they felt that both researchers and the culture were hesitant to do so. I think these reasons still stand for the culture at large —even a quarter of a century later—so they are worth reviewing. Reason one: fear of prosecution or mandated intervention if psychological aggression is labeled as child abuse. The researchers point to countries where psychological aggression is illegal and enforced but without criminal penalties. Reason two: the assertions that kids are "resilient" and that an occasional incident of psychological aggression hurts no child. The researchers point out that there's no empirical evidence for that claim. Reason three: The argument here is that even loving and excellent parents occasionally lose it and shouldn't be labeled as abusers. The researchers point out that this is a possible explanation, not a justification. Finally, there's reason four: that for psychological aggression to be labeled as abuse, it must be chronic. But rightly, Straus and Field point out that finding an "acceptable" frequency that falls short of abuse is itself thorny. As they write, "Should it be not more than once a year, not more than once a month, or not more than once a week? We believe it should be never."

The cultural view hasn't shifted significantly in the two decades since their findings, and what changes have occurred have come slowly. Parents (as well as mentors, coaches, teachers, and other adults) use verbal abuse and label it as "discipline," "tough love," or even "punishment"; they see it an effective tool and feel utterly justified. (For more on "tough love" and its origins, see the discussion in Chapter Six, page 204.) A study by Ming-Te Wang and Sarah Kenny, published in 2014, used the term "harsh verbal discipline," which, in my opinion, is just a fancy euphemism for verbal abuse; the researchers specifically looked at the effects of this "discipline" on adolescents. They defined harsh verbal discipline in ways that make it clear that they were really looking at abuse: verbal intimidation (shouting, yelling, or screaming at the child), vulgarity (swearing or cursing at the child), and humiliation (calling the child dumb, lazy, or something similar). They note that, in addition to developing conduct problems and depressive symptoms, "Adolescents are likely to interpret harsh verbal discipline as indicative of parental hostility or rejection, behaviors that are defined by the absence of affection and emotional support." Gee, you think? Their study included 976 two-parent families with 51 percent sons and 49 percent daughters, 54 percent of European ancestry and 40 percent Black, and spanned two years. Forty-five percent of mothers and fathers used harsh verbal discipline with their 13-year-old children, and 46 percent of mothers and 43 percent of fathers used it with their14-year-olds. The researchers hypothesized that harsh verbal discipline predicted increased conduct issues and depressive symptoms, and they proved to be right. They wrote that verbal aggression can cause a cascade of effects, "leading to declines in self-confidence that in turn contribute to declines in self-directed social behavior and increase social avoidance." Since adolescence is a time of figuring out who you are, the damage done is considerable. Finally, echoing other research, they found that parental warmth did not buffer the adolescent against harsh verbal discipline.

The home isn't the only place where verbal abuse is justified as discipline. We'll explore that in depth in Chapter Six, "Who's to Judge: The Culture and Abuse."

But one thing is clear: Parental verbal abuse is a problem hiding in plain sight.

Indirect Effects of Verbal Abuse: Adaptation and Coping

But the second, and a wide-ranging, effect of verbal abuse is a result of the coping mechanisms—both unconscious and conscious—that the child adopts to stay afloat in his or her family of origin; most of these are, broadly speaking, maladaptive behaviors that have real consequences for the child and, later, the adult, including mental health issues such as anxiety and depression. Once again, I think the suggestion put forth by the anthropologists Kristen L. Syme and Edward H. Hagen is one that we should incorporate into our inquiry: seeing these behaviors as "aversive yet adaptive responses to adversity" rather than as "disorders."

When my daughter was in preschool many decades ago, mounted on the door was what looked like a regular mirror to the small children inside the room but was, in fact, a two-way mirror that allowed parents to observe their children and their interactions with the teachers and other kids without their knowledge. Psychological research, as well as people's stories, can be our two-way mirror, giving us a view of the verbal abuse that, in real life, transpires in the privacy—and secrecy—of the home.

From Defenseless to Unconscious Defenses

I've already mentioned the "Still Face" experiment conducted by Edward Tronick earlier (see page 65), but it's worth looking at again in depth, since it changed the view of the effects of maternal (and paternal) neglect and withdrawal on infants and toddlers. In that way, the experiment can be a primer for understanding the effects of silent verbal abuse. One of the reasons the experiment—since replicated many, many times—caught people's attention was that it was accompanied by a videotape, which was, in 1978, very cutting edge. (If you google "Still Face Experiment" or "Edward Tronick," you will find the video on YouTube. It's worth watching.)

The setup was simple, with the child sitting in an infant seat on a table and the mother on a stool so that they are face to face. The mother is animated—talking and smiling at the baby—and the baby is giving it right back in spades, doing all the cute things engaged babies do. Then, at the experimenter's signal, the mother turns away, and when she looks at the baby again, her face is still and emotionless. On the video, the first thing you notice is how quickly the infant reacts and starts doing all the things that worked with Mommy before—smiling, cooing, pointing. For a full two minutes, the mother's face stays still and we witness the baby's complete meltdown in stages—from protesting with her arms to agitated to wailing to slumping in the seat to turning her face away. Some babies bite their hands or scratch themselves as a way of distracting themselves from the flood of painful emotions. Of course, this is an experiment in a lab with controls, and so Mommy returns, smiling and cooing, and the work of reparation begins and the infant returns to emotional stability.

But when this happens in a bedroom or a living room—absent the controls of a laboratory—and is the most likely scenario for an infant's or child's experience, what are the consequences when there is no "reparation"? What about the infant or toddler whose mother turns to her or him with a perpetually still face and ignores the meltdown that ensues? Or, even worse, if the parent starts screaming at the baby to stop crying? Yes, that's the face of abuse. How long does the child keep trying, or put another way, how quickly does she or he give up, and what are the consequences?

What is nuanced here is that the effects of verbal abuse stem from both what *isn't* happening and what *is* happening. As we've already seen in the previous chapter, because we normalize what we know, it may be years—or never, in fact—before we recognize what should have been happening instead. Using the "Still Face" experiment as a model, though, we can clarify the two different threads that shape each and every one of us—what isn't taking place and what is. What's not happening is attunement—by which we mean the mother's paying attention to and reading of her baby's emotional cues so that she can respond to them—which lies at the heart of healthy emotional regulation. Infants learn how to manage stress on their own by seeing their mothers do it for them again and again; by being comforted by our mothers, we learn how to comfort ourselves. It is a dyadic dance. So what's not being learned or experienced affects the child in myriad ways, as we saw in the earlier discussion of attachment styles.

And then there's what *is* happening. Keep in mind that Tronick's experiment was conducted with both preverbal infants and older children who could use speech to try to get their mothers' attention, and the emotional effect was the same: a pattern of protest, then a flood of emotion, and finally, the infant or child turning away from the mother so as not to experience continued emotional hurt. This is an unconscious way of defending the self and, by doing so, the infant or child learns that he or she isn't safe around the parent and that the parent will not address his or her needs. The solution arrived at is to shut off from the feelings of pain of being ignored or rejected.

But there's a wrinkle worth discussing, which is the effect of being ignored on boys versus girls. This is an area that has yielded contradictory results from research but definitely merits a close look, especially since we have already seen that boys and girls aggress in different ways, much of which has to do with socialization. If, as infants, they react to covert abuse differently, is there a biological basis or is it a matter of socialization once again?

Girls, Boys, and Coping with Verbal Abuse

Even though it's culturally accepted that girls and boys are more different than not when it comes to emotion and emotional regulation—women are from Venus and men are from Mars, right?—the truth is actually more nuanced than the culture would have it. Additionally, what differences there are may be more a function of socialization than inborn traits. For example, a meta-analytic review by Tara M. Chaplin and Amelia Aldao on gender differences in the expression of emotion by children used data from 166 studies and found some surprising results. The researchers found that girls showed more positive emotion than boys but they were also more likely to cover up their feelings—putting a positive spin on things—when faced with a stressful or potentially hurtful situation. And while girls expressed internalized emotions such as anxiety, sadness, and sympathy more than boys, who showed externalized emotions like anger, that result actually reversed in adolescence, with girls showing more externalized emotions. That seems counterintuitive until you think about relational aggression. The research makes it clear that both age and context elude broad generalizations.

Numerous studies show that, in addition to being socialized differently, male and female infants are parented differently. Various studies, including those of Robyn Fivush, note that male infants tend to be fussier than their female counterparts and that, as a result, mothers tend to focus on containing and regulating their sons' emotions in ways that are different from how they treat their daughters. Additionally, male newborns are less responsive to auditory stimuli and less able to maintain eye contact than female newborns. But still, research on emotional expressivity yielded mixed results. That led M. Katherine Weinberg, Edward Tronick, and colleagues to explore gender differences in a 1999 study of 81 six-month-old boys and girls, which included the "Still Face" paradigm as part of three segments bracketed by a two-minute play session at the beginning and a two-minute reunion session at the end. Each segment was separated from the next by a 15-second interval, during which the mother would turn her back toward the infant.

The researchers hypothesized that boys would show greater difficulty regulating emotion and that they'd display more negative affect during the "Still Face" paradigm, and that is what they found. Compared with girls, boys got angrier, tried more often to escape from their seats or turn away, and cried more. (Keep in mind, as the researchers note, that this finding doesn't mean that some girls didn't show more negative affect than some boys.) Second, the team expected that, since boys need more help regulating emotion, mothers would use different and more frequent strategies to help their sons. This finding wasn't supported by the study. Finally, they anticipated that mother-son dyads would be more coordinated in their interactions than mother-daughter dyads. That only turned out to be true in the play period that preceded the "Still Face."

The work of Susan Nolen-Hoeksema established that girls and women are more likely to internalize and ruminate than boys and men and are more prone to depression as well. Since the main mental health effects of covert verbal abuse are depression and anxiety, does this mean that boys are less vulnerable to its effects? It would appear not, though it is surprising to discover how little psychological research there is on verbal abuse and mental disorders, as noted by Tamara L. Taillieu and others in an article published in 2016. These researchers note that one cause is what I've called the "gold standard" in this book—the emphasis on the effects of physical and sexual abuse, despite the clarity of current brain science—and they write that "the independent effects of emotional maltreatment on poor mental and physical health outcomes are rarely investigated and not well understood." Another problem is terminology, and what they are calling "emotional maltreatment" aligns closely with my definitions of verbal abuse (overt versus silent), since they include both acts of commission (emotional abuse) and acts of omission (emotional neglect). They note that most studies focus on one or the other but not both.

Their study included close to 35,000 people, large enough to be considered a sample representative of the U.S. population. They differentiated between abuse and neglect by the questions asked of respondents. For abuse, they asked if respondents had experienced an adult living in the home 1) swear at them or insult them; 2) threaten to hit or throw something at them without following through; 3) act in any way that made them feel afraid. For emotional neglect, there were five questions: 1) Was there someone in their family who wanted them to be a success?; 2) Was there someone in their family who made them feel special?; 3) Did they think their family was a source of support or strength?; 4) Did they feel part of a closeknit family?; 5) Did someone in their family believe in them? The answers were ranked by participants in a five-point ordinal scale comprising never, almost never, sometimes, fairly often, and often.

What the researchers discovered was that 14.1 percent of respondents reported having experienced emotional maltreatment; more women than men reported experiencing both (4 percent versus 2 percent); more women reported emotional neglect (6.3 percent versus 6 percent), while more men reported emotional abuse (4.9 percent versus 4.7 percent). Additionally, the researchers found that emotional neglect was associated with a lifetime of specific mental disorders (major depression, social phobias, and more), while emotional abuse had effects on what they called "a broad spectrum of disorders." They summarized by writing: "Emotional abuse may be particularly harmful to long-term mental health because negative cognitions are given directly to the child (e.g., you are worthless), whereas for other forms of maltreatment, including emotional neglect, the child has to find their own attributions regarding the cause." The researchers also cited studies showing that neglect is tied to externalizing problem behavior, as opposed to the internalized variety. Interestingly, the more educated the participant was and the higher his or her income, the less likely he or she was to confirm the experience of maltreatment. That may have more to do with confusion about what verbal abuse is or whether being fed, clothed, sheltered, and educated mitigates or negates maltreatment, which we've already explored in the chapter on normalizing.

I personally wonder whether the 14 percent prevalence rate they found—which seems low to me—was a function of the specificity of the questions they asked. Again, I'm neither a therapist nor a psychologist, but my experience of verbal abuse wasn't characterized by swearing or insults, nor was my primary emotional response fear. I probably would have ranked those low on the never-to-always scale given to participants. Then the neglect part doesn't delve into what the participants didn't get but what they did get from someone, and, again, in my case, I would have answered at least two of the questions positively. Additionally, we already know that most people, especially when faced with pared-down questions like these, are more likely to normalize. The most palpable takeaway, I think, is that overt and covert verbal abuse affect us differently and may impact women and men in different ways.

A Swedish study conducted by Johan Melander Hagborg and others and published in 2017 after the Taillieu study had different findings. It was a much smaller study (1,520 participants), based on self-reports, and focused on adolescents 12 to 18; the mean age for the first wave of data was 12.7 and 13.4 for the second. These researchers found that emotional neglect had a more powerful and long-lasting effect on girls than boys.

So what do we make of this as laypeople? First, we need to appreciate that there's still much to be discovered about the effects of each kind of verbal abuse. Second, the effects of each kind are different. Third, does it really matter which kind is *more* damaging? Many years ago, when I was in my twenties and estranged from my only surviving parent, I often spent holidays with a friend's family. The dynamics of her family were very different, but I was bemused by one of their activities, which I privately called "competitive suffering." The conversation would turn to setbacks—they could involve health or a tough situation at work or anything else that represented a hurdle—and all the family members would make the case for their suffering being "worse." Years later, I realized that this wasn't necessarily unique to this family, when I saw the movie *Notting Hill*, in which the characters compete for the last remaining brownie by telling their sob stories.

Instead of arguing about which is worse, let's look at the consequences of each. Keep in mind, too, that most people who are exposed to verbal abuse will experience both the overt and covert types; it's more a matter of what's the norm in the family of origin. For example, a parent may constantly name-call or gaslight—the aggressive variety of verbal abuse—but may use stonewalling or the silent treatment from time to time.

Self-esteem and Verbal Abuse

The problem with buzzwords—and yes, self-esteem has long been one—is basically that they're buzzwords, meaning that they are in vogue and subject to reinterpretation by people who don't know any better. Mind you, self-esteem is a psychological term that does have meaning, but when it made its way into the popular imagination, it pretty much lost its sheen. When I was raising my daughter in the 1990s, educators and parents were so invested in protecting that oh-so-fragile flower called self-esteem that kids got gold stars just for showing up, letter grades weren't given in more progressive schools, and praising your child for simply breathing was considered great for self-esteem. Piffle to all of that. Let's focus on what science knows instead.

Self-esteem is real, and as an English major person, I am going to ask you to mentally swap out the word "self-esteem" for "self-regard" for clarity because it loses the buzzword stuff and, just as shifting from "emotional abuse" to "verbal abuse" homes in, so does this. Once we've gone through this exercise, because all the research uses the word "self-esteem," I'll be using "self-regard." (Again, research studies will use the other word, of course. I am just switching for clarity). The following is drawn from a very smart article, drawn from longitudinal studies, written by Ulrich Orth and Richard W. Robins and published in 2014, which pretty much lays out what self-esteem (aka self-regard) is and isn't. As they point out, self-esteem refers to an individual's "*subjective* evaluation of his or her worth as a person." Those are their italics, by the way, and I'd like you to focus on the word "subjective," which means both "personal" and "reflecting personal views and feelings." It's the opposite of objective. Even more important to our discussion is their statement that "self-esteem doesn't necessarily reflect a person's objective talents or abilities, or even how a person is evaluated by others." Again, spend a minute thinking about that.

Finally, and perhaps most importantly, Orth and Robins underscore that "self-esteem is commonly conceptualized as the feeling that one is good enough" and "thus, self-esteem involves feelings of self-acceptance and self-respect, in contrast to the excessive self-regard and self-aggrandizement that characterizes narcissistic individuals."

Self-respect, self-acceptance, and self-regard are all whittled down to a nub by both kinds of verbal abuse, although with different behavioral results, as we'll see.

The *subjective* nature of self-esteem or self-regard needs to be underscored because our culture tends to conflate a person's worth with his or her achievements, successes, or talents and, of course, the opinions of others. This is especially salient in a world fixated on social media, influencers, celebrities, and fame. Even if we disdain those cultural attitudes, it happens on a micro-level in our individual lives when, worried about our self-worth, we compare ourselves to others, both those we know and those we don't. We've been taught to look over our shoulders when it comes to measuring our self-worth, but the reality is that we should simply be looking at our own shoulders reflected in the mirror. Even more important, the context in which both overt and covert verbal abuse takes place *always* equates the worth of the person with his or her achievements or toeing the line the parent or parents have drawn. Once you understand that, you will be quick to recognize that true self-esteem can't possibly survive the onslaught of either kind of verbal abuse, although its absence may be masked by achievements.

With overt verbal abuse, because we internalize the messages communicated by our parent or parents (and perhaps parroted by our siblings), our self-regard is always under siege in our family of origin; as we've discussed, this underlying doubt about the self can result in feelings of fraudulence or Imposter Syndrome, which absolutely coexist with real-world achievement and success. Equally, fear of failure may make it well-nigh impossible for the verbally abused son or daughter to achieve anything at all; what is worse, after all, than actually proving your parent or parents right about you? But these are the relatively easy-to-see effects of overt verbal abuse; Magnum's story illuminates the very complicated ways in which sustained abuse can affect a person.

Now 55, Magnum was the youngest son of three boys with a sister two years younger; the brother he shared a room with was autistic, which, in addition to the verbal abuse his mother rained on him personally, made him a witness to her treatment of his brother, which was venomous and cruel. His father was more or less a silent partner to his mother's abuse and preferred not to engage, but when challenged, he, too, was verbally aggressive. As Magnum tells it: "I rarely witnessed love-based feelings from my parents. I often experienced feelings of anger. Hugs were rare. Criticism and sarcasm ruled. I couldn't express my feelings because 'children are to be seen and not heard.' I can't tell you how many times I heard that growing up. If my emotions were heard they were met with anger and/or physical violence. My parents couldn't handle their own emotions, and certainly didn't want to handle their kids' emotions."

His mother was hypercritical and demanding, even of a son who did well in school because it was his means of escape: "Mom: 'You always do things the hard way.' 'You never get anything right.' 'Other kids are getting better grades.' 'You shouldn't . . . (fill in the blank).' 'You're never going to get it right if you keep doing it that way,' 'Why can't you do it right the first time?' 'Starving kids in Africa will eat anything on their plate. Why aren't you?' 'If you don't (fill in the blank) then you are going to go to hell.' 'Satan likes kids like you.' 'Santa doesn't give gifts to rotten kids.' Grades, too, had to be perfect; no C's or B's allowed."

School was his lifeline until he turned nine and got a record player and music became another; as he hit puberty, he discovered pornography, and that became another outlet. But the damage done by the verbal abuse couldn't be tamped down. As we've already seen, though, one of the biggest obstacles to his healing was his own denial and his normalization of the behavior of his family of origin: "I was working with a counselor while in my late twenties. The counselor explained in great detail how the actions and behaviors of my parents were not normal and contributed to my anxiety, depression, OCD, and relationship issues. I was indifferent to what was being explained to me. I thought I loved my parents, and that they loved me, and I found it hard to grasp that they were consciously cruel to me. At one point I sat down with both parents to discuss what I learned and to ask questions about why they raised me like they did. Looking back on that sit-down meeting now I realize they refused to acknowledge that they did anything wrong, and I was minimizing to them the effects their actions and behaviors had on me."

Hindsight, as they say, is 20/20, and the trauma specialist whom Magnum started seeing not only gave him understanding of what had happened to him but also the tools to begin to heal himself: "The verbal abuse manifested as low self-esteem, a dislike for myself, and a strong desire to be liked by others that opened me up to being bullied and abused by others. I was a good student, and consistently verbally and emotionally abused myself as I entered adulthood. I unconsciously chose women partners that exhibited similar behavior patterns as my mother, thereby continuing the abuse. If I dated someone that did not exhibit those behavior patterns, they typically left me. Up until I started working with a trauma counselor, I continued to allow others to walk all over me and use me. I didn't enforce any boundaries because I wanted anyone I came in contact with to like me. Now, after intense therapy, I enforce boundaries and have a love for myself I had never felt in my 55 years." He has not been in contact with his family of origin for more than 13 years; it is, as he puts it, a necessary boundary.

When overt verbal abuse—including shaming and name-calling— coexists with the outward trappings of what appears to be a healthy and functional family, a child (and later adult) experiences terrific emotional and psychological confusion. That was the case for Erica, 58, who recounts that the family looked great from the outside—going to public school and to church and living in a nice house in an average suburb—with parents who were bright and socially engaged. "On the one hand, we were involved in the arts, learning about history, family camping trips, etc. But on the other, my mother was abusive, much more to me than to my brother, both physically and verbally, interspersed with 'nice' moments when she would do the commendable, loving-looking things like birthday parties, bringing goodies to my school class, etc. So I would always be looking to her to get what I desperately needed, enticed by what seemed promising in her behavior, and then would get a bait-and-switch, which was devastating for me, and meant that I took in the message not to trust my perceptions, that I was the problem, etc. And my father was a bystander. He took advantage of having me as an adoring, bright, pretty daughter when we were alone, and when my mother was present, he became a spectator and hunkered down into 'hear-nothing see-nothing' mode. I now see that their marriage was some kind of nefarious emotional contract. So despite outward appearances, my family was a sick secret hiding in plain sight."

Her mother's verbal assaults were relentless, and it's only with the benefit of therapy, hindsight, and over 14 years of estrangement that Erica is able to see their effects in fullness: "I learned—probably out of self-preservation—not to have a self that was too evident. I was pleasing enough not to be embarrassing, but never as strong, intelligent, or insightful as I truly am, which would have been threatening. I didn't express anger; I became accustomed to her belittlement of me and so grew to anticipate it. I also created small spaces for myself—not enough to stop the damage—but spaces like a trail of breadcrumbs: my desk, writing, journaling, exploring the woods near our house, playing with friends. But I think it was too hard to feel too much. By the time I was a teen, I was over-programming myself, making sure every hour was full and planned, which was probably both my own nature but also a bulwark against too much room to feel."

When asked what the greatest effect of verbal abuse was, Erica answered directly: "A decimated sense of self and an inability to know the inherent validity of my personhood and experiences, especially in disagreement, conflict, or poor treatment by someone else. I will always struggle to know that, whether I'm 'right' or 'wrong,' I'm valid and needed in the working-out of whatever situation I'm in. I think I'm more 'there' now, but it will always have to be a conscious process, like someone who must always use a leg brace to walk."

Felicia's story illuminates a counterintuitive truth, which is that overt verbal abuse is sometimes easier to deal with than the covert variety. Now 43, she hasn't officially gone low-contact with her parents, but since they live on the other side of the country and they make no effort to see her or her children, there hasn't been, in her words, "any need to make a formal announcement. My mother has made her feelings clear in the same manipulative way she always has—by saying and doing nothing." On the surface, her parents seemed like polar opposites—he was hot tempered and quick to anger, and she was cool, calm, and collected—but they both had one thing in common: "They both thought that showing emotion was a sign of weakness and even frailty, and if you cried or whined or showed any sign of pain, they'd attack as a pack but in their own imitable ways. He'd be blustering and shouting, calling you a crybaby, but she'd turn to stone and look right through you. My brother and I both knew that tears would earn you a week of the silent treatment, maybe longer."

For all of her father's screaming, though, it was her mother's covert abuse that affected her more: "My dad didn't scare me because you knew why he was angry, and that just wasn't true of my mother. She'd shut me out and then refuse to tell me why when I asked, and throw it back on me by saying, 'You know why. Don't play dumb,' or something similar. The truth is that, starting when I was small, most of the time I had no idea why I disappointed her or made her angry, and that was very scary. I tiptoed around her, trying to figure out how to avoid displeasing her. By the time I was ten or so, I had learned not to stick my neck out by expressing thoughts or likes or dislikes; it was just easier to take my cues from her. To belong to the family, I had to erase myself, and I pretty much did."

While her brother fought back against their mother's treatment—challenging her, calling her the Ice Queen—Felicia just floated through life at home. If her mother didn't like a friend, she ended the friendship; if her mother looked disapproving about her joining the theater club, she didn't join. Of course, she didn't realize the effect it was having on her: "I was only vaguely aware of how she was controlling me; I thought I was just keeping the peace and avoiding the pain of those horrible silent treatments. You have no idea how awful it was to be ignored in that way for days on end and sometimes even weeks. And of course, there was no one I could tell. Our family looked normal from the outside, and my mother was an admired member of the community. If I had told, I would have been called a liar or a drama queen."

Everything came to a screeching halt when Felicia went off to a large state university and couldn't begin to function even on a superficial level: "I was absolutely paralyzed by having to make choices for myself, even small ones. My mother's face—her icy glance—would float into my head and the voice in my head would say, 'You're gonna screw this up because you're not good enough to do it right,' and I'd freeze. I actually stopped leaving my room so I didn't have to make choices. Luckily, my resident advisor noticed and literally took me by the hand and walked me into the counseling office; she knew I wouldn't be able to get there on my own." That was the beginning of what has been a long road for Felicia: "It took me a long time to recognize that my mother actively hurt me by using withdrawal and silence as her weapons of choice. When I began therapy, I talked about my dad's anger issues, but my mother was much harder to pinpoint because she'd never yelled. My therapist had to convince me that she had treated me this way deliberately, and even then, I didn't entirely believe her." What progress she made during the school year eroded over the summers at home, and whenever she tried to discuss the issues with her parents, she was met with denial and, yes, the silent treatment.

Felicia deliberately went to graduate school on the East Coast where she met her husband and settled, far away from her West Coast family of origin. The story of her journey will be familiar in its broad outlines to many who have experienced silent abuse: "I'd say it took about ten years for me to see the myriad effects my mother's behavior had on me, along with the effect of the tag team of both parents. I basically had to learn to trust my feelings and my thoughts because the loudest voice was the one that said I wasn't capable of making sound choices. I had to learn to feel safe enough to challenge people's opinions. I had to learn how to respond without reverting to pleasing or silencing myself. And finally, hardest of all, I had to learn to stop erasing myself when there was a disagreement or stress. I know I've made a lot of progress, but I'm still working on it. To be clear, had I not moved away, I don't think I would ever have made it this far."

Self-Regard and the Two Kinds of Verbal Abuse

While it's true enough that healthy self-regard can't grow in the scorched earth of either kind of verbal abuse, the effects of each are different. Let's paint a picture in broad strokes, keeping in mind that these are generalizations and that, yes, there will be notable exceptions in individual cases. Also remember that most verbally abusive people avail themselves of both so it's really a question of which style—overt or covert—was used most often.

With overt verbal abuse, the internalized messages often usurp the space that healthy self-regard is supposed to occupy and fill it with the words and labels that have been pinned on you—that you are stupid, ugly, unlikeable, inadequate, or any other variation on the theme. The messages function as foundational "truths" about the self, which facilitate the habit of self-criticism and profound self-doubt, and enable you to "self-inflict" verbal abuse. While the messages often lead to low achievement—fear of failure inspired by the so-called "truths" tends to trump every effort to set goals—they may also coexist with real-world achievement. (That's the imposter syndrome we discussed on page 84.) While it may look from the outside that this woman or man has healthy self-regard—the trappings of outside success and it are conflated in the culture as we've seen—whatever sense of self-worth she or he has is always tenuous and under siege. Seen through the lens of attachment theory, this is the fate of the anxious-preoccupied style, always in need of validation and super-sensitive to criticism and slights.

But this isn't the only possible behavioral response to overt verbal abuse. An individual may respond to the emotional battering of a parent or parents by developing a deep mistrust of others and an even deeper need for being the controller him- or herself. The shame and self-loathing associated with the internalized messages are buried deep inside; much energy is devoted to building an armored persona to face the world where true self-regard ought to be. And, as Joseph Burgo has pointed out, it gives him or her a way of wielding power that hides the deep shame he or she feels. While this persona has no true foundation and is more like a house of cards than not, it works because it permits him or her to bury the pain of the abuse experienced in the past and to exert control over the future. In terms of attachment theory, this is the dismissive-avoidant style—with a high opinion of the self and low opinion of others—and, if you're wondering, a description of an individual high in narcissistic traits. We'll be talking about the spectrum of self-regard in the pages to come and where the narcissist is on that spectrum, but in the meantime, it should be noted that one of the hallmarks of someone high in narcissistic traits is his or her curation of the past, including childhood. This is different from what psychologist Jennifer J. Freyd called betrayal trauma; this is conscious curation that accompanies the creation of that face to meet the world.

Covert abuse affects people in more insidious ways because it's even harder to recognize and pinpoint as abusive in nature; it takes a great deal of self-confidence and sophistication to label a person abusive when nothing is being said, especially since the working definitions of verbal abuse focus on words and tone. If the space where self-regard is supposed to reside has been under fire by covert abuse, as it was in Felicia's case, the space is filled with lack of trust in one's perceptions, doubts about one's thoughts and conclusions, and one's supplying the "reasons" for the parent's treatment. It is emotionally and psychologically confusing. These generalized feelings of worthlessness—not being important enough to be seen or heard, being so inadequate or unlikeable that one can be ignored or attention isn't warranted—instills terrific fearfulness and self-doubt and solidifies both fear of rejection and a sense of complete isolation. Unable to trust his or her feelings or perceptions, the child, and later the adult, keeps hiding in plain sight. Covert verbal abuse contributes to the fearful-avoidant style of attachment and, using other terms pertaining to self-regard, which we will explore next, echoism.

Again, many people are exposed to both kinds of verbal abuse, but covert abuse appears to affect individuals in ways that make them even more insecure at some fundamental level than those who were most often blistered by words. Covert abuse is like being shadow-boxed, and the child, and later the adult, may not even be able to realize it is real. That's what Laura, now 59, wrote: "It was the coldness of it all as I painfully and slowly realized in therapy that made it so hard to label her behavior as cruel and, even more, for me to be able to see the effect on me. It was as though the sound had been turned off in the house—

no yelling, no screaming, and no explanation ever—as though I was watching pantomime. I didn't trust myself enough to be able to label her behavior as abusive for years and years. Being yelled at or even hit clarified things for me."

The Strange Case of the Scapegoat and Self-Regard

How detrimental the scapegoat role is to a daughter's or son's development depends, in part, on personality and awareness of the dynamic, either at a young age or later in life. One daughter confided that she understood what was going on by the age of seven or eight: "My mother made no effort at being at all even-handed; she favored my older sister who could do no wrong, and she blamed me constantly for not being good enough. The unfairness of it all rankled me, and I actively looked for outside positive feedback to offset what was going on at home. My father also didn't join in on the bullying, so that helped." But another daughter, now 46, describes how she went down for the count: "I honestly believed every word my mother and siblings said about me until I went into therapy at a friend's suggestion when I was 30. I blamed myself for everything and couldn't take credit or feel pride in anything. When something good happened, I thought it was a fluke. When someone liked me, I doubted it. When something went wrong, I knew I'd made it happen because I was flawed and deficient."

Almost all scapegoated children develop a thick hide emotionally and are prone to self-armoring, even when they're conscious of how they're being bullied and mistreated and how unfair it is. Being robbed of a sense of belonging in their family of origin leaves a real mark and may dog them into adulthood. They can become high achievers, on the one hand, actively working to disprove their parent's vision of them, or, on the other, they may have so internalized the negative messages about themselves that they set their sights low, avoid failure at all costs, and have problems both setting and accomplishing their own goals. They may become "echoists" who hide in plain sight so as to duck under the radar. (For more on echoism, see page 148-150.) There's no question that significant emotional and psychological wounds are sustained.

Yet in all of this, there may be a silver lining. Of all the children growing up with a verbally abusive parent or parents, it is the scapegoated child who's more likely to come to terms with and recognize the toxic patterns of the family dynamic. He or she is more likely to seek help healing from these patterns and their effects than her or his siblings who have bought into the family story, lock, stock, and barrel. Paradoxically, the scapegoat is often the only child in the family who has a shot at being able to have healthy and sustaining relationships once she or he has sought help.

That's because, even without being scapegoated, the other children in the family are learning at the verbal abuser's feet. They learn that being safe from abuse and being supported are transactional and not a given; they are reminded of that by seeing how the scapegoat is treated. They develop deficits in empathy by normalizing verbal abuse, being bystanders, or sometimes joining in on the blame game. They learn to tamp down their emotions and hold their tongues to go along to get along. If there is a favored son or daughter, or one of each, these trophy children know that love is earned by fulfilling parental expectations. They live in a world governed by external achievement and how they look to others; who they actually are is of no import so that their own self-regard rests on the most fragile of foundations. Trophy children know nothing about introspection and even less about their true selves. They carry those mental models into their adult relationships since they're disinclined to look beyond what the family mythologies tell them.

Not to mix up our barnyard metaphors, but once they've achieved adulthood and left home, scapegoats grow up to be the black sheep of the family. What efforts they make to try to dislodge the family mythologies will be met with vehement denial and reprisal; they move from justifying the family dynamic as scapegoated children to unifying the other family members by challenging their truth as black sheep. What happens usually is a hardening and solidification of the party line ("She was always crazy, even as a child"; "No one could ever deal with him. He was always a liar given to fantasy"; "The most ungrateful human being you've ever met"; "She never wanted to be part of the family to begin with"). Additionally, the family isn't likely to go quietly and ignore the threat; they will often mount a smear campaign and use other tactics to discredit the adult black sheep. Often, the scapegoat is left with no choice but to go no-contact with all of them.

But as many of them have reported, the scapegoated child often is able to forge a very different kind of adult life, free of verbal abuse and a sense of self that is born out of coming to terms with the abuse he or she experienced. In that sense, the scapegoat is more like the phoenix rising from the flames than not.

Healthy Self-Regard Lies on a Spectrum

Perhaps the most useful and clear discussion of what I'm calling healthy self-regard (popularly known as self-esteem) was formulated by psychologist Craig Malkin in his book *Rethinking Narcissism: The Secret to Recognizing and Coping with Narcissists.* Given that his book is about narcissists, he uses what he calls the spectrum of narcissism in a very different way, but with his permission, I'm using it in another context. And if you haven't read *Rethinking Narcissism*, you should, since it's pertinent to our discussion of verbal abuse and control. Spoiler: Those at the very far right end of the spectrum are high in narcissistic traits controlling and, yes, indulge in verbal abuse. It's true, too, that many of them experienced it in childhood.

Imagine, if you will, a line—that's the spectrum—that goes from zero on the left to ten on the right. As you think about the line, please keep in mind the definition of self-esteem/self-regard that we are using: a person's *subjective* evaluation of him- or herself as a person, separate from his or her talents or abilities and the opinions of others—or put another way, your own assessment of your worth as a person. In the middle of the spectrum—at around point five—is the person with healthy self-regard, as well as secure attachment. This person can look at him- or herself with a certain amount of equanimity and see someone who's not perfect in every way but certainly "good enough." He or she knows that mistakes happen and that the occasional setback or failure is a part of life, and this individual's ready to roll with the punches and deal when they happen. He or she doesn't devolve into self-criticism or self-loathing but takes responsibility for the actions he or she owned and separates out the factors he or she couldn't control. When setting a goal, the person with healthy self-regard thinks, "Why *not* me?" instead of having a long list of reasons as to why it would never be me pop into his or her head. Another way of looking at self-regard, as we'll see, is to focus on motivation and whether the person is oriented to approach a goal (and the possibility of failure) or to avoid it (and the possibility of failure). We'll be talking about that in the coming pages, too.

But that is the middle of the spectrum. While the word "narcissism" has certainly gone mainstream—google it, and you'll be offered up no fewer than 57 million entries—the term "echoism," popularized by Malkin in *Rethinking Narcissism*, is now beginning to get the recognition it deserves. Mind you, echoism isn't a diagnosis, but a trait.

The term derives from the same Greek myth as narcissism. The story is a morality tale about the gods, overstepping bonds, unrequited love, and the dangers of self-absorption. A wood nymph named Echo is punished by the goddess Hera for distracting her from spying on one of her husband, Zeus's, paramours; Echo is deprived of her voice and only able to repeat the words said by another. The other thread in the myth is the beautiful Narcissus, who is granted eternal life as long as he doesn't catch a glimpse of himself; again, there is a glitch because the gods notice that he's rather a cad, and he leaves a trail of spurned, dead lovers in his wake. Mind you, all of this was via Ovid and other sources long before chick flicks and Lifetime movies. Yes, as scripted, destiny is cruel: Echo falls in love with Narcissus, who sees his reflection, becomes besotted with his own pretty face, and dies (but he does get to turn into a flower, which is more than Echo gets), and the spurned Echo becomes, yes, an echo.

In Malkin's view, if narcissism is seen as a spectrum—with healthy self-regard in the middle—the grandiose, self-absorbed, and empathy-deficient Narcissus is on one end, and the disempowered and voiceless Echo is on the other. While none of us needs convincing that it's bad to be a narcissist and even worse to be involved with one, it's really no better to be at the self-effacing end, where the person is incapable of seeing her or his own needs, much less addressing them. And yes, being in a relationship with an echoist has its own set of perils.

Both overt and covert forms of verbal abuse, alone or in combination, can produce an echoist. Parental control and intrusion—along with the battery of hurtful words or the stinging silence of being ignored—make ducking under the radar a safe place to be. Verbal abuse delivers the message that speaking your piece will only result in more abuse and alienation. Echoism also sheds more light on why so many verbally abused women and men become chronic underachievers and underscores a motive that amplifies the usual suspects science rounds up, namely low self-regard, fear of failure, and self-doubt. According to Malkin, the extreme echoist doesn't want to be noticed; he or she is much more comfortable hiding in the shadows where it's safe, and what better way to do that than to underachieve? Interestingly, while the echoist doesn't want to draw attention to her- or himself, the echoist is caring and does for others. He or she is the friend you have who's always willing to go the extra mile for others, but who cringes at a compliment.

In my view, echoism sheds even more light on the verbally abused people who are high achievers. While on the surface, at least, they seem to have fully recovered from their childhoods and appear to have overcome being ignored or marginalized, put down or criticized, they continue to be plagued by self-criticism and doubt. Their feelings of being "less than" absolutely coexist with accolades and honors and high-paying and prestigious positions, not to mention advanced degrees. Their achievements don't bring them the kind of satisfaction and sense of wellbeing they would to someone who has a secure attachment style and who's in the healthy middle of the narcissism spectrum. They often feel like imposters or frauds, attributing their successes to flukes or luck instead of talent and effort. Echoism explains all that; despite their standing in the outside world, they're still echoists at heart, especially if they fear being mistaken for or labeled as a narcissist like their mothers or fathers. Alternatively, since the echoist knows better than to ask anyone for anything— childhood has taught her or him that needing something is a weakness or dangerous—outside achievements may serve as protection, a declaration to the world that she or he is fine as is and needs nothing from anyone. Of course, deep down, that's not true,

Please keep in mind, especially if you think you are an echoist, that as Malkin explains it, echoism is a trait, not a diagnosis. It's not the same as being introverted either; you can be introverted, still have healthy self-regard, and also dislike or feel uncomfortable hugging the spotlight or being center stage. An echoist ducks under the radar and silences her or his needs and desires for protection. Malkin underscores that echoists on the far left end of the spectrum and narcissists on the far right end are made, not born.

Verbal Abuse and the Making of a Narcissist

Yes, like "self-esteem," "narcissism" and "narcissist" have become buzzwords—the little black dresses of pop psychology—but rather than focus on the effect of the bad gal or guy who will ultimately do you wrong, let's look at self-regard and the spectrum Malkin describes. We've already looked at echoism—the left end of the spectrum where there's not enough healthy self-regard—so now we turn our attention to the right end of the spectrum, above the healthy middle, where, to use Malkin's phrase, individuals who crave feeling special all the time are found. At the very end are those who are diagnosable as having narcissistic personality disorder (NPD); buzzwords notwithstanding, keep in mind that NPD is relatively rare, thought to affect roughly 6 percent of the population. That said, the number of people who are high in narcissistic traits is much higher.

The kind of parental control and/or neglect that makes the echoist duck for cover can also yield someone who decides, suffering the hailstorm of verbal abuse if perfectionist standards aren't met or who's taught that looking weak or less than perfect will bring on conflict, that the best answer is to join them if she or he can't beat them. The damage done by overt or covert verbal abuse is tucked deep down, away from prying eyes, and this individual makes it her or his business to be the most powerful person in the room—loud enough to be listened to and admired—and the one who's always in control. It's as though he or she has learned that you can either dominate or be dominated, and the choice is clear. Again, Joseph Burgo identifies the hidden aspect as profound feelings of shame.

I think it's important to remember the suggestion made by anthropologists Kristen L. Syme and Edward H. Hagen, adduced earlier, that it might be more fruitful to understand certain disorders not as they are described in the DSM but as "aversive yet adaptive responses to adversity." What do we gain in understanding by seeing depression, anxiety, PTSD, and even being high in narcissistic traits as responses to the specific adversity we are calling verbal abuse? Using this understanding as a lens permits us to comprehend why children, growing up in the same household with verbal abuse, may have such differing responses—such as the one who becomes an echoist and the other who learns that there is safety in being on center stage, flexing his or her muscles as a narcissist. What they have in common, deep below the surface, is a lack of healthy self-regard.

Given that individuals in any particular family will, as we've seen, adopt different but equally maladaptive behaviors to deal with verbal abuse, one of the most under-discussed effects is what verbal abuse does to the structure and functioning of the family. Our myths about family might have you think that adversity would actually end up creating stronger bonds among and between siblings—just like Hansel and Gretel—but the reality is that rarely happens. We've already explored, in Chapter One, how siblings can ape parental verbal abuse, taking on the role of the bully down the hall, but this is a bit more subtle, since it involves adaptation, normalization, and motivation. Ted, 41, wrote that: "The party line is that Dad is a great guy and that his way of talking—laced with contempt and put-downs—is just the way he is and that it's my problem that I'm too sensitive and that I need to man up. Mind you, I am the oldest of three sons and my father's namesake to boot, and his criticism of me is never-ending and withering, despite the fact that I am the most successful male in the family by far. He's not nearly as tough on my brothers, but I wouldn't call his treatment of them much better. It's created a terrific rift between us because I'm not taking the old man's garbage any longer."

We'll be discussing this more in the next chapter as well.

How Verbal Abuse Hobbles Motivation

Different psychological constructs provide specific lenses through which we can see the effects of verbal abuse. Attachment theory permits us to grasp the damage done to the processing of emotion, the formation of mental models about how relationships work, and the ability to forge dyadic and intimate bonds. Looking at healthy self-regard and where it sits on the narcissistic spectrum illuminates the damage done to the very foundations of the self. Yet another perspective emerges from looking at how individual motivation and the ability to set and achieve goals are affected.

We've already talked about the effects of internalized messages on healthy self-regard and how even high-achieving adults who were verbally abused in childhood may suffer from the imposter syndrome and be dogged by self-doubt despite their apparent success. Another view is provided by the work of Andrew J. Elliot and Todd M. Thrash, who suggested that, rather than simply defining personality by traits (traditionally extraversion, agreeableness, openness, conscientiousness, and neuroticism), it would be more illuminating to see temperaments as essentially motivated by either *approach* or *avoidance*. Once again, these two temperaments are shaped by childhood experience and align closely with secure and insecure styles of attachment.

The easiest way to think about this construct is to imagine yourself at the base of a mountain you have to climb to get to your destination. Do you look up at the mountain and find yourself thinking through possible strategies, jazzed by the challenge ahead, if a bit nervous? Do you begin planning for the climb, anticipating both possible glitches and setbacks as well as ultimate success? Do you feel relatively confident that if your plan A doesn't work, you'll come up with a plan B because getting where you're going requires you to scale the mountain? This is pretty much what the approach temperament looks like.

Or do you look at the mountain and feel utterly done in, sure that this mountain foray is going to be an utter disaster and nothing more than a foolproof opportunity to prove to the world, once again, what an abject failure you are? Do you immediately start thinking of ways *not* to climb the mountain—is there a way around the damn thing or something else you could do? —so that you can save yourself from your inadequacies and utter humiliation? And is your next thought about whether the destination—the one that requires you to climb the mountain in the first place—is really important to you after all? Note the descending cascade of thoughts, all focused on finding ways to duck out, as the task ahead looms large. This is the avoidant temperament in action.

There are a few things to keep in mind about approach and avoidance so that we understand the difference between hardwired animal impulses and this theory of personality. Remember that we humans and the rest of the animal kingdom, including one-celled creatures, avoid the dangerous and unpleasant and approach the yummy, inviting, safe, and sexy. And all of us will, for perfectly good reasons, decide to avoid situations that involve danger or a high degree of failure. That's not what avoidance temperament is about. Instead, it describes deficits in motivation, resilience, and drive that can be caused by overt verbal abuse, neglect, or both. Securely attached children who aren't subject to verbal abuse or other kinds of neglect become adolescents and adults with an approach temperament. No one has laughed at them for failing, mocked them for belly-flopping in a pool, or doing anything that has been declared untoward; instead, they have been listened to, validated, taught boundaries, criticized and praised, and loved well enough.

I think this approach-avoidance perspective is valuable because it gives us another way of looking at how the kinds of verbal abuse affect the individual and the area of achievement in the broadest sense; avoidance temperament would appear to exert more power on motives and actions than either the internalization of the messages conveyed by verbal abuse or the habit of self-criticism. Another study by Elliot, this time with Harry T. Reis, specifically looked at the connection between attachment styles and their connection to adult exploration and goal-setting in adulthood. You'll remember that one of the hallmarks of a securely attached infant is feeling protected enough by his or her primary caregiver to explore his or her surroundings by crawling or walking, even in an unfamiliar setting. The researchers hypothesized that, while securely attached adults would see achievement goals as potentially validating, insecure adults would respond to achievement goals as potentially threatening and would "self-protectively seek to avoid incompetence." (In that experiment, 50 percent of participants identified as securely attached, 30 percent as avoidantly attached, and 20 percent as anxiously attached.) They found that anxious-preoccupied individuals had a low need for achievement and a high fear of failure and thus used avoidance as a strategy. Yes, this aligns with figuring out how to circumvent the mountain in my earlier example and ultimately deciding to ditch the destination, too.

But as we've already seen, the faces of insecurity aren't all the same, since the researchers also found that those with an avoidant style of attachment set mastery-approach goals just like their securely attached counterparts. Parenthetically, this explains why those high in narcissistic traits are capable and high achievers as well as being very goal oriented, despite their emotional deficits and exposure to verbal abuse.

Ignoring and Dismissal as Withdrawal of Love

Another study, this one conducted by Andrew J. Elliot and Todd M. Thrash, explored how parents, especially mothers, transmitted the fear of failure to their children. Specifically, the researchers hypothesized that fear of failure is transmitted from parent to child via "love withdrawal." Let's begin by looking at what they considered "love withdrawal" to be: "For example, the parent may look coldly at the child, turn away from the child, refuse to speak to or look at the child, express dislike of the child verbally, move away from the child, send the child to another room, or threaten to remove the child from the home." You will note that all of these examples are, in fact, verbally abusive in nature, so keep that in mind as we explore Elliot and Thrash's findings. Their definition of fear of failure is worth paying attention to as well: "fear of failure is defined as the dispositional tendency to orient toward and to seek to avoid failure in achievement settings because one feels shame at failure. It is not failure per se that is feared and avoided but the shame that accompanies failure." Furthermore, they write: *"For the high fear of failure individual, failure indicates global incompetence and carries the message that the self is unworthy of love and in danger of being abandoned."* I have added the italics for emphasis.

Using undergraduate participants and reports from the participants' parents themselves, Elliot and Thrash found that, indeed, parents' own fear of failure was replicated in their offspring, especially with mothers who specifically used "love withdrawal" during childhood. Interestingly, love withdrawal was not associated with fathers in the survey, even though they, too, influenced fear of failure. The researchers did not think that inducing fear of failure was actually a conscious parenting strategy, writing that "most who use it are simply responding to their children in a reactive manner out of their own deeply engrained self-evaluative processes."

Many of the respondents to my questionnaires did directly connect their own fear of failure to their parents' shaming and mocking of mistakes during childhood and, more important, wrote about how they were able to manage their avoidance *after* they had stopped making excuses or normalizing a parent's treatment. In some cases, such as Kathy's, they'd gone on to repeat the same patterns in a partnership or marriage, and their ability to take on challenges began only after they'd extricated themselves. This is Kathy's story: "I lasted six weeks in college, thus fulfilling the prophesy my mother had always promoted—that I was too lazy and stupid to succeed, and it was a waste of money to even try—and got married at 19 instead and immediately had two kids by the time I was 25. My husband put me down in the same ways as my mother did, and I just accepted the words as familiar truths. But when he started putting my then ten-year-old daughter down, I knew he was wrong about her because she was bright and ambitious. He had no business calling her names while he praised our son to the heavens. And while I could sit still while I was being abused, I couldn't stand watching her get ripped apart. I sprang into action and got a job as a receptionist in a lawyer's office, and he got me my divorce. I went to community college at night and then to state college and got my Bachelor's degree at the age of 42. I earned my MSW at age 46, and I have been a counselor ever since. I'm 55 now, and I help men and women deal with abuse."

Amen to that.

In Process: From Normalizing to Understanding to Dealing

As difficult and painful recognizing verbal abuse is, the hardest part is deciding how to deal with it. There is, alas, no one-size-fits-all or even one-size-fits-most for this process. It is territory that most definitely includes gains but, equally, real losses.

Chapter Five

Breaking Free:
Dynamics and Strategies

If life were like a made-for-television movie, the moment at which
you recognize the verbal abuse in your life and how it has affected
you would be one of those aha! moments of clarity, accompanied by
chords of music—Beethoven, perhaps, or maybe Lady Gaga?—and
a closeup of your face registering both relief and resolve. But guess
what? That isn't what happens in real life to most people; many of you
will experience a cascade of emotions, many of them conflicting, without a clear takeaway on what exactly you need to do next. Denial and
normalization are self-protective, and recognizing how you have been
victimized by someone you deeply care about—and who you thought
cared about you—can be emotionally devastating.

In fact, your first (and automatic) response to recognition may be
more denial, as we've seen in some of the stories in these pages illus-
trating how women and men alike pushed back against their therapists'
analysis of the dynamics in their lives. In the previous chapter, recall
how, in his younger years, Magnum just didn't want to hear what his
therapist had to say; at that moment in time, he opted for the façade of
normalcy and pretense, and decided what the therapist called abusive
was just well-meaning "tough love." The truth is that when we love
our abusers and think that we need them, the cold, hard truth may be
highly unwelcome in the moment. That what was Kelly, 52, wrote in
her questionnaire: "When my therapist started enumerating how my
husband systematically used put-downs and mockery to make me toe
the line, I sprang to his defense. I literally started shouting at her that
she didn't know him, that she'd never met him, that she'd misunderstood what I'd said about him, that he was a good man, and that she

was pushing me to a place I didn't want to go. My carrying on didn't faze her one bit. She kept talking, in her calm voice, reading from her notes, reminding me of all that happened in the past two years, and I kept yelling that she was wrong until I ran out of steam. And then the strangest thing happened. I heard this terrible wailing—it sounded like a wounded animal—and I swear to you that it took me a minute or two to realize that the sound was coming from deep inside me. Like a dam had finally given way."

You might be among those who feel mainly relieved when you recognize abuse for what it is, but if you're not, it may be of help to you to think about the possible range of emotional responses you may have at this cusp moment.

Facing the Reality of Relationships Fortified with Verbal Abuse

The common thread in these relationships is always the imbalance of power, and the sad truth is that the abuser has to be willing to give up that power—and whatever rush it gives him or her—to make things different. Is that person—whether it's your parent, your partner or spouse, a sibling, a friend, a coworker or boss—really going to make that leap and decide, miraculously, that a connection forged in mutual respect and equal power is really what she or he wants? Think about it for a moment.

You may remember that I mentioned the work of researcher and psychologist John Gottman and the remarkable accuracy with which he's able to pinpoint whether a marriage or relationship can last or crash and burn. That's largely based on whether what he calls the Four Horseman of the Apocalypse are present; they are contempt, criticism, defensiveness, and stonewalling, all of them stars in my verbal abuse pantheon. Again, the fragility or strength of a relationship isn't measured by the absence of conflict but, rather, how conflicts are tolerated and resolved. Gottman calls a relationship or marriage an ecosystem, and of course, both people have to sign up to be caretakers of that ecosystem. It's at the moment of recognition that each of us confronts whether our abuser is willing to be a coworker in a mutual enterprise.

Those who use verbal abuse as a way of managing a relationship would need to have a major epiphany about redirecting and reimagining their idea of relationship; that is the sobering realization that comes with the recognition of the abuse. Of course, you can no more force that epiphany on someone else than you can find a way to give pigs wings; the only behaviors you can control in any relationship are your own.

We'll be looking carefully at whether the verbally abusive relationship can, in fact, be changed in the ways that actually matter as we delve further into what happens when the music stops and look at whether verbal abuse follows some of the same cyclical patterns experts have discerned in domestic violence.

Understanding the Mix of Emotions

Many of us defend ourselves from verbal abuse by pushing off from our feelings, especially if we were raised in a household where it was the norm. In addition to having problems regulating emotions, it's entirely possible that you have trouble distinguishing what you're feeling with precision. (The ability to name and distinguish specific emotions is a function of what's called emotional intelligence.) It's not uncommon to feel hugely rattled, panicked, or even trapped when the full import of recognizing both the abuser and the effect of the abuse dawns on you. Because this experience can be so intense and emotionally daunting, the safest place to explore these feelings is in the company of a gifted therapist. If you can possibly do that, you will be better off for it. This is not to say that self-help doesn't work—it does—but a gifted professional can help in untold ways.

That said, let's look at some of the possible and even contradictory emotional responses to recognition, what sets them in motion, and how they affect you as you work toward beginning to deal with both how verbal abuse has affected you and what to do next.

Anger and Its Variations

Anger definitely plays a role in jumpstarting recognition, but paradoxically, it can equally become unproductive and keep you stuck when you need to get moving. Anger is usually the first strong emotion experienced, especially when the verbal abuse was experienced during childhood. The recognition that you were victimized and targeted by the very adult who was supposed to care for and protect you can stir up enormous amounts of feeling, as the question posed to me by Angie, age 42, made clear: "How do I stop being so angry? Now that I understand what went on in my childhood, I am just so angry. I'm angry at my mother for treating me so cruelly. I'm angry at my father for standing by. I'm angry at my siblings for falling into line and torturing me. I'm angry at my relatives who never spoke up."

Let's spend a moment looking at the positive energy of anger, especially when it comes to recognizing and calling out verbal abuse. Anger at the unfairness of how you've been treated or continue to be treated clarifies how denial was an act of self-protection; anger also helps you focus the blame and responsibility where it belongs rather than landing on the old default positions of normalizing, self-blame, and self-criticism. This is especially important given the lopsided nature of power in the parent-child relationship, since the child is literally powerless in every sense. Adult-on-adult verbally abusive relationships differ in some significant ways, so let's begin with the adult child-parent recognition first.

We've already discussed how verbal abuse can affect whether we're more motivated by approach or avoidance, and there's an argument that's been set forth by Charles S. Carver and Eddie Harmon-Jones that anger—especially when contrasted to fear or anxiety—is strongly associated with approach goals. They adduce much research from different fields of inquiry, including brain science, to posit that anger—especially when sparked by the idea that you were kept from achieving or getting something you deserved or "ought" to have had or that was intentionally thwarted by someone else—strengthened approach motivation. Another possibility is that in the face of a crisis—such as recognizing the presence of an abuser—anger helps facilitate action and gets us out of the avoidant mode many of us have long occupied.

But the positive energy anger can bestow isn't all that's going on. There isn't one of us who doesn't know what anger feels like in the body—"seeing red" isn't just a metaphor in this case—and all of us have experienced the hot flush, the heart-pumping moment that accompanies anger. Our bodily sensations are the external manifestations of a process that's going on in our brains and disrupts our ability to think, as the work of Sarah N. Garfinkel, Emma Zorab, and others made clear. The researchers wanted to test what priming for anger would do to a specific thought process—in this case, identifying real words from nonwords. During the course of the experiments, after priming the participants subliminally either with the word "anger" or "relax," both blood pressure readings and MRIs were performed to see the prime's effect on lexical ability. As it happens, the anger prime didn't just raise blood pressure, but it also changed activity within the brain itself; additionally, anger increased the reaction time to lexical cues and interfered with semantic decision-making, a relatively high-level cognitive process. So, if you're trying to sort things out and figure out what you are going to do about the verbally abusive relationship, continuing to be angry isn't just unhelpful but it will also hold you back.

While some anger is necessary to the process of recognition—we *should* be angry at maltreatment—it quickly becomes a detriment on the emotional level. The problem with anger is it ties us to the people we're angry with; it's not unusual for verbally abused daughters and sons to think about wanting to hurt back, to give their mothers or fathers a dose of their own "medicine," and even wanting revenge of some sort. This is what Lydia, 52, shared: "I did want her to hurt the way I hurt, and for a while, that feeling was consuming. I thought about her constantly, in fact—much more than I had over the course of 20 years of my adult life. It was as if someone had uncorked a bottle with all this toxic, explosive stuff, and I was the bottle. Finally, my husband confronted me and convinced me to see a therapist. Thank goodness he did. The anger was eating me alive. It was just as destructive as my mother, if in another soul-sucking way." Similarly, Tim's anger at his father (whose story we told in Chapter One) spilled over into the rest of life, which propelled him into therapy. Generally, sustained anger just puts us on another merry-go-round with different horses and music.

Even worse in some ways is the anger daughters or sons often feel at having played along to get along for years and sometimes even many decades; they may berate themselves for being stupid or chumps, ironically reinforcing the internalized self-critical voice that is both a legacy and an echo of a verbally abusive childhood. That was Amanda's struggle "What kills me is that I can't get the years back, years I could have been working on myself, being happier. My mother died 10 years ago, and it's only now, at 64, that I am finally seeing the truth of it all. How could I have been so blind? How could I have been coopted by denial?"

In answer to Amanda, it's remarkably easy to be coopted by both denial and hopefulness, as many adult children can attest. That said, time can't be recaptured, of course; what you have is the present. If this is happening to you, and you are beating yourself up, you must address that immediately. It's holding you back. And no, it's not weird or strange; in the context of recovery, being angry with yourself isn't unexpected. Unexpected doesn't make it good, however, and working with a gifted therapist is the best solution.

Needless to say, the tendency to self-blame can even be more intense when the abuse emanates from an adult-on-adult relationship, where, in theory at least, you could have headed for the door at any time. We'll be looking at whether that "theory" about the exit holds true in real life.

Anger in Men and Women:
Are There Important Differences?

A number of female respondents to my questionnaire expressed great discomfort with the anger they felt as a result of recognition, worrying whether it testified to their own ability to become verbal abusers themselves or whether it was yet another maladaptive response to abuse. It was Kaitlyn's comment that really caught my attention: "Because both of my parents were incredibly angry people, I spent my childhood trying never to get angry with anyone; I pushed my feelings away because anger frightened me. I still have trouble accepting those feelings as legitimate; my anger makes me feel bad about myself, and I end up backing down and reverting to pleasing and papering things over instead. My therapist says I've taken on the role my parents had—marginalizing my feelings of anger and telling myself they're not valid."

Again, while anger can play a positive role, especially in the stage of recognizing and dealing with verbal abuse, there are twists and turns that need to be paid attention to, especially when it comes to gender. While there's no science that shows that one gender is angrier than the other—despite the culture's pinning the tail on the male donkey—there's enough nuance and research on socialization and cultural influence to warrant entertaining the question, particularly when it comes to dealing with our own anger or someone else's.

Let's begin with the socialization of boys that, unintentionally, makes men comfortable with anger. This is brilliantly explained in William Pollack's book *Real Boys*, which we've already discussed in other contexts. Anger is one of the few emotions considered "masculine" and permissible within the narrow confines of what Pollack calls the "boy code." He notes that most boys express their vulnerability and powerlessness through anger "in order to mute and rein in the full range of emotional responsiveness they would otherwise exhibit. The more tender feelings seem too shameful to feel and thus boys turn to anger."

As we've seen in the discussion of bullying and aggression, girls tend to use abusive tactics that are more subterranean than not (gossip, stonewalling, and the like), even if they are fueled by anger. But the idea that women are somehow not capable of the same volume of anger as men is contradicted by numerous studies, including one conducted in the Netherlands by Agneta H. Fisher and Catharine Evers. Additionally, that study suggested that an imbalance of power within a relationship affects a woman's expression of anger more than any fac-

tor having to do with gender; needless to say, this observation is pertinent to our inquiry and may explain the discomfort with this emotion
some women experience.

The researchers wondered how the experience of anger was mod-
erated by relational context, and they divided participants (the parents
of psychology students) by the kind of relationship they had: egalitarian (a partnership model) or traditional (male wage-earner, etc.). The
study was based on self-reports and focused on two kinds of conflict,
one financial and the other a relational issue. They found that while all
women, regardless of the kind of relationship, reported more intense
anger than men, women in traditional relationships suppressed their
anger more. All men reported that women initiated conflict more,
which all women disagreed with, regardless of the kind of relationship.
Women in both kinds of relationships reported more indirect expression of anger—sharing one's anger with others, gossiping about it, or
crying in conflict. Perhaps not surprisingly, women in more traditional
relationships expected more negative consequences from the expression of anger than those in more egalitarian ones. As the authors note,
"In other words, the social costs of direct and critical confrontation
are considered higher for women than men in traditional relationship
contexts, as indicated from the women's stronger negative social appraisals." Of course, a traditional relationship is one which, by definition, incorporates an imbalance of power, since financial dependency
is inseparable on many levels from other kinds of dependence. This
is especially true—and yes, I am extrapolating here—in relationships
that include verbal abuse.

Finally, since we are all influenced by the culture we live in—whether we are male or female— we need to look at the broader cultural attitude toward women and anger. Daughters are more likely than sons
to become pleasers and apologists, in part because our culture is much
more tolerant when boys (and later men) express anger than when
girls (and women) do, and there's a tendency to mistrust or think less
of women who get angry. That is the point made by Harriet Lerner in
her book *The Dance of Anger*, first published in 1985 and revised three
times since and still very much in print. While aspects of her book do

seem dated—yes, some cultural attitudes have shifted over the past 35 years—her explanation of why women still have trouble not just expressing anger but also using it directly and productively still has merit. She divides women into "The Nice Lady Syndrome" and "The Bitchy Woman"; I know they sound lame all these years later, but it's the self-help categories that are dated, not her descriptions of them.

The so-called "Nice Ladies" are the ones who avoid open conflict and, even worse, avoid being clear about what they think or feel in order to keep the peace. This is what we've already seen in those who are avoidant-oriented or have learned to be echoists, to use slightly different terms. As Lerner writes, "in situations that might realistically evoke anger or protest, we stay silent—or become tearful, self-critical, or 'hurt.'" The other stereotype, "The Bitchy Woman," is one she underscores is considered "unfeminine" in cultural terms, a female who's not shy about getting angry or stating her difference of opinion. The problem, she writes, is that these women vent their anger ineffectively, a situation she attributes to being "caught up in unsuccessful efforts to change a person who does not want to change. When our attempts to change the other person's beliefs, feelings, reactions, or behaviors do not work, we may then continue to do more of the same, reacting in predictable patterned ways that only escalate the very problems we complain about." She concludes by noting, "Thus, our fighting protects the old familiar patterns in our relationships as surely as does the silence of the 'nice ladies.'"

Lest we think Lerner's assertions are so last century, we need only look at a study published by Jessica Salerno and Liana Peter-Hagene in 2015 and their findings. Participants in the study thought they were part of a real jury, but the scenario was scripted, with four jurors supporting the verdict and one supposed holdout. The holdouts were given a male or female name and expressed their opinions with no emotion, anger, or fear. It turns out that the holdout didn't change the jurors' original opinion, except that when a supposed male holdout expressed anger, the participants' confidence in the verdict dropped. But when a "female" holdout expressed anger, participants became significantly more confident in their original verdict. Note that both the "male" and "female" holdouts expressed the same opinion in the same way. It's worth remembering that the English language has a raft of gender-specific words for women who express anger such as "shrew," "fishwife," "battle ax," and "bitch."

Whether you are a woman or a man, anger is not the only emotion you are likely to feel at this moment of recognition.

Feeling Powerless

This is particularly bewildering because, after years of inner conflict, denial, and normalization, we thoroughly expect that we will feel empowered by recognizing verbal abuse and realizing that we have to take action. Again, remember that this is also the moment that the lack of sustainability of the relationship becomes clearer than it has been. The fact that you now have to do something may, paradoxically, make you feel powerless.

That was the case for one reader, whose recognition was sparked by her therapeutic sessions: "When my mother's verbal abuse was brought home to me, I felt hopeless as well as powerless. I still remember the moment the counselor asked me if I really accepted that my mother was toxic for me, and although I knew it was true, the feelings of bewilderment, sadness, and helplessness hit me. I'm one of those only children, and she was my only living blood relative getting quite elderly so my distress was compounded by that fact. If there was ever a decision to be made about her health, finances, anything really, I was the one named on documents or called on." But that wasn't the thing that made her feel powerless, as it happened. She continued: "It was made more difficult because of the way she presented to other people: as a sweet, little old lady with curls, a lively sense of humour and delicate. In fact, she was as tough as old boots when it came to getting what she wanted. However, I didn't feel I could contradict the people who would compliment me on having such an interesting and charming mother. This was part of the powerlessness: the inability to express myself to most people about the situation."

But feeling powerless may also be the result of not getting what you wanted—which is for your abuser to stop abusing you. That was true for one of my readers who answered a callout for interviews, and I think you will find it as moving and revelatory as I did: "I never felt powerless until now. Now I have to let go. I have to walk away. . . . There is nothing left I can do to protect my sisters from my mother's abusive, narcissistic ways. I am powerless. I am the successful oldest daughter that can no longer protect my mother from herself and her bad decisions in her old age (she still drinks and has mild dementia), but I need to walk away if I want to save myself and my wonderful family. I didn't feel powerless when she beat me as a child. I didn't feel powerless when I left home at 18, I didn't feel powerless when she divided my sisters and me over the years. The powerless feeling is the result of realizing there is nothing left to do but walk away." I think this testimony speaks for itself.

Joseph, 54, was shocked both by the emotionality of his reaction and his sense of having the wind knocked out of him; his story illuminates how relatively benign verbal abuse—nitpicking and criticality—can escalate in a time of crisis: "I honestly believed for a long time that my wife's anger and put-downs were just a function of the setback we'd experienced and that, on some level, she didn't mean what she said. We had a marriage that seemed good enough until I lost my job four years ago; I was the primary wage earner, and to be honest, we lived higher on the hog than we should have, with mortgage and debt, in a nice neighborhood. She didn't work until the kids were in school and her job as a receptionist in a local law firm didn't pay much, but she ran the house, and the kids were cared for well, and she wanted it that way."

But then life served up a twist: "Out of the blue, my company got bought and I got pushed out, and while I did get another job, it didn't pay as much. A close friend and colleague of mine held on to his job, and my wife was enraged about that; she insisted we no longer see him or his family which was painful because he'd been a friend for the eight years I worked there. She was adamant that we weren't downsizing, and holding on to the house meant cutting back on everything else, and she blamed me and me alone. It was nonstop carping, every day and every night, and while I applied for other, higher-paying jobs, I didn't land one. In her eyes, I failed miserably, and she held me accountable. She berated me in front of the kids, my parents, and anyone who would listen to her story of the loser she'd married."

As they say, hindsight is sometimes 20/20, as Joseph continues his story: "Looking back, I can see that she was always a harsh taskmaster, but somehow, I thought that berating me and raking me over the coals for little things I forgot, for how I loaded the dishwasher, got too focused on work, or didn't do enough for the kids wasn't really abusive, even if it was unpleasant. She called me names and swore at me, and mocked me when I tried to make up with gestures. I wrote it off to her being a perfectionist and me being laid-back and a bit of a slob. But I didn't get how much contempt she had for me until we went into counseling to try to rebuild the marriage and her utter disdain for me filled the room. And she took the position that she had every right to call me whatever she wanted because I was nothing but a flop. There was no talking it through, no nothing. Since then, my parents and siblings have all said she always held me in contempt. So, yes, recognizing the abuse and being the only one who didn't notice it knocked me to my feet. She divorced me, by the way, and that is as powerless as it gets."

Desolation and Loss

In addition to making you feeling powerless, recognition may also bring with it feelings of terrific loss. This may seem counterintuitive—you are opening the door to a life without the pain of verbal abuse, after all—but the recognition is one fraught with the loss of the hope that things can ever be made right. This observation has come up constantly in my work on unloved daughters, by the way.

And then there are hard choices about the relationship with the abuser, which can induce deep sadness and even panic. All the upsetting questions you've held at bay for years or the things you looked away from as Joseph did may float to the top with alarming force and fill you with distress. It may seem strange to mourn a connection that ultimately hurt you but it's likely that the good moments you had will also come to mind at times.

Again, if you need help, please seek professional counsel.

Self-doubt and Second-guessing

Faced with the scary need to act, some will find themselves back-tracking from their recognition and just sliding back into the familiar core conflict if the verbal abuser is a parent or plain denial fueled by hopefulness if he or she is an adult intimate. This backsliding is a function of the need to keep the relationship going and the hope that there's a magic wand out there somewhere that will somehow change it in all the ways that matter. If you are someone who experienced verbal abuse in childhood and have reencountered it in your most in-timate adult relationships, you're even more likely to fall back into the habit of doubting yourself and using old coping mechanisms to stay afloat. While it's not surprising that you're rolling back down the hill under stress, be kind to yourself and get support, either from someone who loves and cares for you or a professional. This is a big emotional moment in your life, and there's no shame in admitting you're having trouble dealing.

Feelings of Shame

While one of the tactics of the verbal abuser is to induce shame in his or her target, you may also experience deep shame at having permitted yourself to be abused in this way once recognition takes place. This is especially true if you have been involved in an adult-on-adult relationship that has included verbal abuse and you've confided in no one and have worked hard at maintaining a public façade that hides the truth of your situation. While there is a sense of relief in being able to confide the truth, it may equally be matched by feelings of shame. Tamara, 46, discussed what she called "deep humiliation: "Telling my parents and sister why I was seeking a divorce and, more specifically, why I was so concerned about Ron being alone with the kids was the most painful thing I ever had to do in my life. My father looked absolutely dumfounded when I told him how Ron treated me, but he became enraged when I told them about how he tore our oldest son apart on the daily. I could see how disappointed he was in me—

that I allowed Ron to put me down and make me cower, all the while never saying a word. My mother kept saying 'Why did you stay? You had enough money to leave,' which made me feel even worse because she's right. There wasn't a financial reason; I make good money and that made me all the more ashamed for tolerating his treatment for so long. Even worse, if he hadn't really escalated his abuse of our son, I might have just gone along for even longer. I wanted this marriage to work. I didn't want to be part of some divorce statistic. But I think those are all excuses. Somehow, he managed to plug into some deep insecurity or need I have hidden inside. I am going to find a way to dig out of this, but I have to say, admitting it fills me with shame."

Closely allied with feelings of shame may be regret and guilt, especially if children are involved.

Regret and Guilt

While it's true that most of us worry about regret most when we're contemplating taking action or making a significant change—our conservative spirit kicks in and we wonder if it's something we're going to regret in the long or short term—research by Thomas Gilovich and Victoria Husted Medvec showed that, in fact, the deepest regrets are rooted in moments of inaction and what we didn't do. And anecdotally at least, that's what I heard from those who deeply regretted not dealing with verbal abuse; this observation echoes what I have heard from daughters who spent decades trying to please or placate unloving mothers or fathers, rather than taking action. Ironically, since these defensive actions, such as setting strict boundaries, going low-contact, or even initiating estrangement have the very real potential of destroying whatever shards of maternal or paternal relationship existed altogether because of parental pushback, it was those defensive actions they worried most about regretting.

But that's not what happened to most; instead, it was their inaction that they regretted deeply, as well as the time, often years, they spent placating or trying to repair a relationship that wasn't reparable. Additionally, adults with verbally abusive parents felt deep guilt about exposing their children to abuse because of their inaction. Many daughters and sons specifically said they'd initiated estrangement out of the need to protect their children from either witnessing verbal abuse or being verbally abused themselves.

Those feelings of regret and guilt are, of course, intensified when the verbal abuser is a spouse and the children are coming of age in a place of emotional and psychological unhealth. That was what Krista called her "burden": "I guess it's just a cliché at some level but I kept minimizing Jordan's angry outbursts, telling myself that no family is perfect and that our family was better off than most. And it was true. Pretty house, nothing to want for materially except, of course, peace of mind. I don't think I understood how often I walked on eggshells— careful not to set him off—because I got so used to tiptoeing. I shut down mainly. But the cracks showed in the two kids, both of whom had trouble concentrating in school. My daughter started acting out with other kids and my son lost interest in pretty much everything he used to like. It was their pediatrician, who'd taken care of them since birth, who finally confronted me and started asking tough questions about what was going on at home. She recommended I go into therapy, which caused Jordan to hit the roof, and things got even worse for a while. But I couldn't unsee what was going on with my kids and that gave me purpose to push forward and to stand up to Jordan. Are things better? Only slightly but we are finally getting help."

What Comes Next?

Here's the place where real life diverges from the movie script any target of verbal abuse is looking for —the one in which the confrontation is calm, the abuser has his or her epiphany, and order is restored to the family and the verbal abuse just stops on a dime. While there's no one-size-fits-all scenario, it's smarter—and safer—not to imagine a best-case scenario. This isn't just a doom-and-gloom point of view but one that is in sync with the ties between verbal abuse and physical abuse, and the possibility of escalation. Not every verbally abusive relationship will necessarily escalate into physical violence, *but* it is important for you to keep that possiblity in mind as you consider the paths open to you after recognition. Even if the verbal abuse you've been subjected to doesn't devolve into physical harassment, it *can* escalate.

It's the cyclical nature of abuse—both verbal and physical—that effectively traps victims into a pattern of denial and hopefulness; if the abuse was 24/7 and literally constant, it would be increasingly hard to find the energy to hope. But that isn't what happens. Beginning with Lenore Walker's work on battered women in the 1970s and then significantly expanded to include male victims and a more nuanced vison of how abuse includes coercion and verbal tactics in addition to the use of force, the cycle is usually divided into three or four distinct phases. My description is deliberately broad because I am adducing it for reasons that are slightly different from the ones usually intended.

The first phase is that of *tension-building* in the relationship, with the abuser's complaints, dissatisfaction, blaming, and control amplifying. The target responds by trying to avoid confrontation, walking on eggshells, and often coming up with reasons outside of the household that are responsible for the increased tension. It's been pointed out that the victim's avoidance only serves to ramp up the abuser's need to control, especially if he or she fears the target will leave and perhaps expose him or her.

The second phase is the *violent incident* itself. Once it is over, both the victim and the abuser may minimize the damage done, though for entirely different reasons.

The third phase is called the *honeymoon,* and in some models, a fourth phase called *calm* is added. It's at this moment, in an effort to blame-shift and maintain control over his or her partner that the abuser appears to make amends, becoming charming and caring, and promising that the "anomalous" behavior will come to an end and that he or she will change. It goes without saying that this honeymoon period reminds the victim of why she or he first fell in love with the abuser, feeds hopefulness as well as denial, and reinforces the decision to stay. (We have discussed the power of intermittent reinforcement, and this honeymoon phase is proof positive of how it works.) Some experts add a phase of calm, which, again, helps to keep the cycle intact until the wheel turns again and tension begins to build.

In case you don't know, the Centers for Disease Control (CDC) states that one in four women will experience physical violence by an intimate partner in their lifetimes, as will one in seven men. It's thought that 10 percent of children experience domestic violence annually and that 25 percent of children will experience it at least once in their childhood.

Perhaps the most cogent—and counterintuitively obvious—observation comes from Rachel Louise Snyder in her book *No Visible Bruises*, in which she who points out that when we envision a victim of physical abuse, we never imagine ourselves in that position. That is true of victims as well. She writes: "What we might conjure, if anything at all, is a punch. Someone we're dating, one punch, and we'd be gone. That's not how it happens. It evolves over time. A partner who might not like your makeup. Or a suggestive outfit. Maybe he'll say it's for your own protection. Then, a few months later, maybe he yells a little louder than you've heard before . . . But neither the control nor the abuse tend to come at once, lit up like a punch. They leak out slowly over time, like radon."

All of this is meant to be cautionary but, still, it's important to realize that verbal abuse also works by the slow process of accretion or leaking. It works like a tipped-over can of invisible stain, that colors your world, your sense of yourself, and even what you believe to be real, without your ever being fully aware of its impact.

Expectations: What Comes Next in the One-on-One Adult Relationship

Years ago, I went to talk to a very experienced marital counselor named Susan when my last marriage was very clearly in tatters. One of the first questions I asked her was whether she believed couples counseling really worked, which, when you think about it, was a pretty out-there question to ask someone who'd been in practice for 35 years. Doubtless a testament to her being seasoned and good at what she did, she answered me calmly and directly. "Not usually," she said, smiling. When I asked her to explain, she did so in detail, saying that by the time a couple got to her, the behaviors in the relationship were entrenched and it was really likely that one or both of them was simply worn out. She paused. "Battle fatigue is very real," she said, explaining that, often, one spouse has really decided, deep down, to bail on the relationship but isn't quite ready to say so or feels the need to show that they've "tried everything." She went on to say—or so my notes tell me—that "Being in my office is the ultimate proof for showing that you've tried what the culture calls 'everything,' even though you're really unwilling to do any of the work that would actually change the relationship. People do it so they can justify divorce or just feel better about their choices."

I wondered aloud whether that was the real reason couples counseling didn't work—because the commitment to the work was absent or not totally sincere. She shook her head and said that, while that was partly true, it was also a huge oversimplification. She went on to explain that it wasn't just that each person's behaviors were entrenched but also that each was highly invested in having the reason for the marriage's failure be crystal clear. Once again, my notes tell all: "Even though the meeting in my office is private, the people in my office often use it to serve a public function, which is to either assign a role to the spouse or to place blame. If the couple shows up at the first sign of trouble, there's a good shot at restoring good will and improving communication. But late in the game, it's not about repair or restoration. That's why, too often, it's just a question of moving their cars from my parking lot to the ones outside their lawyers' offices."

Take a moment to absorb that, and keep in mind that when you are dealing with a verbal abuser, it's not just his or her behaviors you want to change but his or her underlying need for power and control, which drives the abuse. When you think about it, that's a pretty tall order and would not just take a tremendous amount of inner work and introspection but also a true sea change of great magnitude. That isn't to say that this can *never* happen—both the Egyptian pyramids and Stonehenge attest to the dint of human effort—but frankly, it's not very likely. *Do* talk to a therapist about your thoughts, feelings, and expectations. *Do* be aware that the cycle associated with physical abuse can also happen in the context of verbal abuse; most particularly, be conscious and aware of any pattern of escalation.

You may also want to ask yourself the following questions to keep your expectations as realistic as possible. Base your answers on your understanding of your abuser.

Is he/she willing to acknowledge the verbal abuse without resorting to blame-shifting or defensiveness?

Is he/she willing to listen you thoughtfully without pushing back, objecting, or arguing?

Will he/she accept your pointing out abusive behaviors and instituting boundaries that are respected?

Is he/she willing to work on learning new ways of communicating and resolving conflicts?

Is he/she willing to go into counseling and commit to working on change?

Is he/she willing to commit to a set of steps you mutually decide to take if he/she backslides into old behaviors?

If there are children involved, is he/she willing to apologize for his/her past behaviors and work on acquiring new parenting skills?

The truth is that if the answer to any of these questions is "no," recovering and repairing the relationship will be next to impossible.

It's worth pointing out that in her book *The Verbally Abusive Relationship*, which was originally published in 1992 and remains in print, Patricia Evans specifically singles out couples counseling as being largely ineffective, writing, "Unfortunately, many couples counselors have been trained to see any problem in a relationship as belonging equally to two persons." Alas, there is simple wisdom in that statement when you are dealing with a relationship that has its foundations in an imbalance of control and power. In her book *Gaslighting*, Stephanie Sarkis has an even more blunt message: "Gaslighters are all talk, and will always be all talk. It is time to give up the idea that the two of you can work this relationship out. It ended with the first signs of control and abuse." I asked Dr. Joseph Burgo, a therapist and author of *The Narcissist You Know* and *Building Self-Esteem*, to weigh in on whether a verbally abusive partner can transform his or her behaviors and re-sponses: "The abuser's ability to change depends upon his tolerance for bearing shame and vulnerability. Serial abuse points to a massive defense against those emotions; as with the extreme narcissist, will-ingness to change is rare and usually depends upon feeling at risk of losing all that matters in one's life—relationships, career, family. An abusive character reflects a kind of entrenched defensive structure akin to a personality disorder; such individuals rarely change, mostly because they are too heavily defended against their own vulnerability and incapable of tolerating it."

That assessment is direct, clear-headed, and realistic, and you should keep it top of mind, even though it does deny you any chance of breaking out the bubbly.

Expectations and Strategies

I turned to Craig Malkin, the expert on narcissism I have cited numerous times and a working therapist, for some insight and advice on what you might expect if you confront a verbally abusive part-ner. Let's begin with his most salient and powerful statement about strategies: "What the most effective strategies have in common is this: They're meant to help the person being abused, first and foremost. They may or may not reduce episodes of verbal abuse. But they cer-tainly will reinforce your sense of which of your partner's behaviors are unacceptable. And that's the key to protecting yourself. You have to be *clear in yourself* emotionally that you're being abused. In that sense, effectively dealing with verbal abuse is always about what helps you in the moment *regardless* of whether or not your abuser can change his or her stripes." This is yet another way of beating that same drum more loudly, reminding yourself that the only person you can change is *you.*

Malkin makes the point that, since "verbal abusers are seeking con-trol, empowering themselves by making others feel vulnerable," any action you take to take back control will end up with their "stepping up their efforts at regaining control and disempowering you, which means more abuse." That said, he advises that, "if you feel strong enough to bear the possibility of more name-calling, blame-shifting, or gaslighting—a likely retaliation—you can and should name the abusive comments as they are happening. Try holding a mirror up to your partner with statements such as, 'You're calling me stupid right now and that's abusive and unacceptable.'"

We'll take a look at Malkin's other suggested strategies, but it is vital for you to keep in mind that they all boil down to the same thing, as he writes me in an email: either setting limits (by naming or calling out unacceptable behaviors) or protecting yourself emotionally. These are *not* strategies to make your verbal abuser change because that's not in your power; only he or she can choose to change him- or herself and, as we've seen, experts agree that there's a really limited possibility of that happening. Apparently, rock bottom needs to come first.

I have left out quotation marks, but all of the following are Malkin's suggestions. My comments are in parentheses.

Set limits and boundaries.

Try a connection contract in which you spell out ahead of time—in specific detail—all the comments that will end the conversation: "I'm willing to discuss this, but if I hear you call me stupid or crazy, or if you accuse me of causing the problems or tell me I'm misremembering, that will show me you can't talk productively with me and we need to end the conversation and try again later."

Holding up a mirror to the abuser, as mentioned, embraces the power of reflection: "You're calling me dumb and crazy"; "You're yelling at me"; or "You're blaming me." If your partner has any healthy shame at all about his or her verbal abuse, this will at least slow the abuse down. If not, at least you're reinforcing your crucial awareness that the problem lies in your partner's actions and words, not whatever real or imagined mistake he or she claims you made.

Assert your boundaries in a clear and articulated way, such as, "I won't stay in a conservation where someone is speaking to me like a child"; "I can't remain in the room while being yelled at. It hurts my ears"; or "You're finding fault and I don't see how that gets us anywhere so I'm stepping away." *And* keep in mind that you are free to leave the room if the boundaries or limits you have set are being ignored. No, this is not abusive behavior or stonewalling, for that matter; if you're feeling uncomfortable and you don't feel like explaining why, bear in mind that you don't have to stay where you are. Just say, "I need to step aside and come back to this later." In healthy relationships, this should always be an option; there are good times to talk and not-so-great ones. So in exercising your right to leave the moment, you're once again just practicing behaviors that should be in your repertoire for your own self-care and safety. *Do* keep in mind that it's not a requirement that the verbal abusive person agrees.

(Again, if any of these efforts simply escalates his or her abuse, stop on a dime. It is a sign of health to admit defeat or failure instead of rationalizing. If your partner or spouse physically threatens you or your children or escalates in ways that frighten you, withdraw and get help immediately. Do not doubt your own perceptions.)

Develop self-protection.

It is especially important that you access healthy anger. You don't have to show your anger to your partner—and again, it's not advisable if he or she habitually resorts to verbal abuse, but you do have to feel the anger and tolerate it internally. This is all about holding your center. As long as you can safely feel anger in the face of abuse, you can keep your wits about you even if you decide, for emotional safety—e.g., not wanting to be yelled at—not to say anything in the moment. Anger puts you in touch with your strengths and your clarity—about right and wrong—and your needs for safety and dignity. Without it, you're likely to question yourself— "am I being overly sensitive?"—which makes you vulnerable to further abuse. The anger will help you whether you express it directly to the abuser or not. (This is harnessing the power of righteous anger, which we've already discussed in terms of recognition on pages 160-162.)

Use a shift in perspective: If you're having trouble maintaining clarity about whether or not the way you're being spoken to is acceptable, ask yourself if you'd tolerate someone treating your child or someone else you love this way. This can often snap you out of self-doubt. Vividly picture the same conservation happening to someone you care about and you'll likely see the problem with how you're being spoken to much more quickly.

Make up your mind: to stay or to leave.

Finally, Malkin ends with these words: "In every case, insight is the first step. If the abusive person in your life can't acknowledge how hurtful he or she can become, you can't possibly be safe interacting with him or her. If your abuser can't see how or where he or she learned to be abusive, he or she lacks the self-awareness to change. You can try limit-setting and boundaries as an active form of assessment. If such steps slow the person down, there's some hope, but only if they're willing to seek help. Without proper treatment, verbal abusers can't change their abusive behaviors."

(I cannot emphasize more strongly that these strategies are for you, not the abuser. Be aware of escalation and threats at all times and take them seriously. Stay safe and get help.)

What to Anticipate When You Leave

Verbal abuse may not end when the relationship ends; it's counter-intuitive but true. It depends on the intensity of the relationship and what the abuser gets from it in terms of his or her feelings of control and power. While some verbally abusive partners will simply move on, others will not—initiating smear campaigns and other forms of getting back at you for leaving. If you are seeking a divorce, do tell your attorney about your spouse's patterns of behavior, especially his or her need to win. Be prepared for the fact that he or she may make the divorce process hard, drawn-out, or painful. If one partner has more earning power, the divorce process can become an economic cudgel as well. We will be looking at the courts and legal system's take on verbal abuse in the next chapter.

If you will be co-parenting with a verbal abuser, please discuss the issue and his or her behavior with your attorney as well as a psychologist; needless to say, if minor children are involved and your spouse has been abusive to them and is likely to continue to be, this is an issue that needs to be front and center.

Verbal Abuse After Divorce:
Dealing with Parental Alienation

While parental alienation is most usually discussed as a cause of adult child/parent estrangement, I think it's more valuable to see it as a form of verbal abuse that is part of a continuing power play, even after the formal dissolution of a relationship, most usually through divorce. That said, it's not just spouses who may strive to alienate a child from his or her parent; equally, it may be a grandparent or other relative. And it may happen in degrees, too, outside the formal confines of court proceedings. As a divorced mother, I have witnessed firsthand how children can be made to be critical or disdainful of one parent by an angry or embittered or combative ex-spouse, creating emotional distance without full-fledged estrangement. I am moving outside the formal definition of parental alienation here, but I think it's important to recognize any form of verbal abuse in all of its variations.

Recognition of this form of verbal abuse is relatively rare (and relatively new, for reasons I will explain), but it doesn't make it any less real or damaging; again, unlike the irritated or bitter remark any divorced person might say within earshot of a child whose other parent he or she is describing—"Larry flies off the handle in the blink of an eye" or "Lucy has never been able to budget because 'Spend, spend, spend' is her mantra, so I'm not surprised she's hurting financially"—parental alienation is highly motivated and more like a dedicated smear campaign than not. It usually happens in the context of highly contentious divorces—which are estimated to be about 5 percent of all divorces, the ones that end up in litigation and, often, continuing court battles even after the divorce decree—and the goal is to maintain control and punish the other parent by effectively turning the child or children against him or her.

Of course, while the ex-spouse is the intended target of the abuse and does, indeed, suffer, the other victim is the child, who is used as a piece on an abusive parent's chessboard. Young children are relatively easy to coopt in this way because of the power a parent has, and having been asked to choose one parent over the other, will do so either out of fear of losing the alienating parent or because he or she genuinely loves and obeys him or her; with young children, the parent the child thinks is the center of his or her universe wins. Older children—and that includes adolescents—can be seduced and coopted by blandishments, such as the promise of more freedom (compared to the "bad" and "controlling" parent who is "caging you") or, of course, material goods by the parent who can fork over luxuries. Yes, children can be bought in this way without realizing they are being bought and may internalize lies and criticisms about the offending parent as absolute truths. Do keep in mind that the brain matures between the ages of 25 and 30, so while a young teen or an eighteen-year-old may look "adult," that's not true in terms of emotional regulation and decision-making.

For those of you who haven't been divorced, know that every divorce decree has some wording in it akin to "Thou shalt not speak ill of the other parent," so that part is pretty clear. *But* since the culture still is figuring out what verbal abuse sounds and looks like, it's not surprising that the system *can* be gamed, especially since, in the United States, most judges will use the rule of thumb "in the best interests of the child," which, state to state, may be defined highly specifically or in completely vague terms. Most important—unlike the divorces of the 1950s, 1960s, and 1970s, when children always ended up living with their mothers, who had custody of them, and saw their fathers occasionally or not at all—a child's best interests are generally defined as having equal access to both parents. That most usually comes down to 50/50 custody. What this means, of course, is that a verbally abusive parent (and in some states, a physically abusive one) may still have access to his or her children.

The best interests of the child, as defined by the courts, may not be in his or her best interests at all.

The Problem with Defining and Dealing with Parental Alienation

It should be said that formulated as a syndrome, parental alienation syndrome, or PAS, hasn't fared so well and has encountered more than its fair share of naysayers; it was rejected for inclusion in the DSM—the bible of the American Psychiatric Association—and has been countered in legal circles as "not real" enough to be included in testimony. But as a form of verbal abuse and a tactic used to maintain power, it is much easier to identify and grasp, and I think it's valuable to see and understand it in this context. First, as a behavior—and not a syndrome—it seeks either to extend the imbalance of power that existed in the original relationship or to eke out revenge and continue the power play, despite the fact that the marriage has been dissolved. The motivation is to keep the game going even though the parties have left the field, and the goal is to manipulate, control, or punish the ex-spouse, who is the real target, not the child or children. Second, the weaponry is words, which effectively continues both control and abuse despite the end of the relationship. The child or children are collateral damage, as the military would put it, although the alienating parent is very unlikely to see it that way. Like all other forms of verbal abuse, parental alienation is rationalized and justified.

But once again, terminology has given us a cultural muddle.

The Origins of the Mess

A bit of history illuminates why, once again, terminology leads to confusion, which, alas, has real-life consequences. Richard Gardner, a very prolific writer and psychiatrist who wrote and self-published more than 40 books, invented and popularized the term "parental alienation syndrome" (abbreviated as PAS and later also called parental alienation disorder, or PAD) in 1985. Never subjected to peer review, his description of this disorder, which he posited affected children in custody battles, was drawn anecdotally from his own practice and, as it turns out, was founded in a series of assumptions that were not borne out by scientific research. Despite this lack of scientific standing, PAS became a talking point, one that was hotly debated until it was finally debunked and firmly rejected for inclusion in the DSM. But that did not prevent PAS from finding its way into the offices of therapists who testified at custody trials and, of course, the offices of attorneys who wielded it like a cudgel.

The story of how this all came about is both weird and fascinating, as outlined in a research paper by Joan S. Meier, a professor of clinical law, published in the *Journal of Child Custody* in 2009. Among the things Gardner asserted was that the allegations of parent-child sexual abuse were prevalent in 90 percent of divorce cases and that the majority of these were false claims, invented by mothers to vilify fathers. (Meier points out that sexual abuse allegations at the time were relatively rare, appearing in about 2 percent of cases, and that roughly 50 percent of those were proved to be true.) The misogyny of his assertion was obvious. But it was also off-kilter and weird in other ways, though it would appear that many who jumped on the PAS/PAD bandwagon didn't know the full extent of Dr. Gardner's thinking—or maybe they did.

Gardner's views on human sexuality were both abhorrent and aberrant; he wrote that it was only society's "overreaction" to pedophilia that made children suffer (!!!) and that "children are naturally sexual and many initiate sexual encounters by 'seducing' the adult" (!!!). He also wrote that "sex abuse is not necessarily traumatic; the determinant as to whether sexual molestation will be traumatic to the child, [sic] is the social attitude toward these encounters." What can I say other than to note that these statements are part of his self-published work.

None of this impeded his career as an expert witness in some 400 custody cases and, in a 2012 commentary by Timothy M. Houchin and others titled "The Parental Alienation Debate Belongs in the Courtroom, Not in SDM-5," the authors note how lucrative the PAS was to the industry that is divorce litigation.

Sorting out the Muddle

But how to prove that one parent has deliberately made efforts to alienate a child from the other parent without the argument devolving into a "he said/she said" game of accusations? One expert, psychologist Amy J. L. Baker, has done much to elucidate and clarify what parental alienation is and isn't by outlining four necessary factors to establish that it has taken place, rather than an estrangement between parent and child that has other roots:

1. There has to have been a positive relationship between the child and the now-rejected parent in the past. As she writes, "This factor precludes parents who were habitually absent, uninvolved, and uncaring from claiming that they are victims of parental alienation. There has to be proof that such an emotional bond between the child and the parent existed."

2. There must be an absence of parental abuse or neglect.

3. There has to be proof of one parent actively behaving in such a way as to alienate the child from the other parent. Baker and her coauthors have, in a series of articles, established 17 primary behaviors, which I will discuss separately.

4. The child must exhibit eight behaviors that differentiate children who have been alienated from parents from those who have not.

Baker went on to test these criteria in an experiment with mental health professionals to see whether these factors permitted participants to identify true cases of parental alienation.

Additionally, she identified 17 parental behaviors that needed to be present (part of factor three), which were:

1) denigrating the other parent to make it seem he/she was unsafe, unloving, or unavailable

2) limiting the child's contact with that parent

3) limiting communications with that parent when separated

4) making it difficult for the child to talk about that parent

5) withholding love and affection when the child expresses love or affection for the other parent

6) presenting time spent with the other parent as optional or undesirable

7) pressuring the child to reject the other parent

8) telling the child the other parent doesn't love him or her

9) creating the impression that the other parent is dangerous

10) sharing adult details (personal, financial, legal) so the child feels taking sides is required

11) asking the child to spy on the other parent

12) asking the child to keep secrets from the other parent

13) referring to the other parent by given name, not "Mom" or "Dad"

14) making the child call a new significant other "Mom" or "Dad"

15) changing the child's name to remove connection to the parent

16) withholding information from the parent

17) undermining the parent's authority

In addition, Baker outlined eight behaviors a child would demonstrate from efforts to alienate him or her, including echoing the words of the alienating parent about why rejection is right; painting one parent as "good" and the other "bad"; lacking remorse about being cruel to the other parent; trashing the rejected parent and always supporting the favored one; claiming that he or she has reached his or her own conclusions, absent of any influence; echoing words and phrases the alienating parent has used; and extending the animosity and rejection to the alienated parent's friends and family.

To test these assumptions, Baker surveyed 71 randomly selected members of the Parental Alienation Study Group to assess 16 vignettes (written by Baker) as constituting parental alienation or not; 54 percent of the participants had doctorates in law, psychology, medicine, family therapy, and counseling, while 46 percent held Master's degrees. There was broad agreement (88 percent) that parental alienation had not occurred when one or none of the four factors was present. That said, one-third of respondents identified parental alienation as having occurred if only factors three and four were present; as she notes, the presence of substantive efforts to alienate one parent was given more weight than the factors of whether the rejected parent had had a close relationship to the child before and whether he or she had been abusive or neglectful.

So even in a controlled research setting—with specifically tailored examples—getting a consensus on whether parental alienation had occurred wasn't easy or without bias.

This doesn't mean, of course, that it doesn't happen. It does mean that it's hard to prove, especially in a court of law, as we'll see in detail in the next chapter.

The Stories Alienated Adult Children Tell

Of course, the cultural muddle doesn't mean that children aren't alienated from one parent by another. I asked readers who believed they'd been alienated to fill out a questionnaire, and while this is un-scientific and anecdotal, these stories illuminate much in the way of the overall dynamics of family life when there is verbal abuse. The first thread is how the children didn't see what transpired as manipulative; what they felt was pressure to do what they were told. The second thread is that, by and large, they accepted what the alienating parent told them about the other as truth, even when their own perceptions varied.

It's a reminder that verbal abuse always depends on an imbalance of power. And a parent wields great power over a child for good or ill.

Elizabeth lives in the United Kingdom and is now 42 and the mother of two, ages seven and five. Her father became the alienat-ed parent when she was 11, and she didn't see him for close to two decades. Her memories of her father from childhood are scant—he wasn't home much since he ran a successful business and enjoyed his hobbies—but what memories she has are good ones, filled with genu-ine attention and fun. She remembers wishing, as a child, that he were around more, though in hindsight, she suspects he wasn't because of the disastrous state of her parents' marriage. Her parents separated when she was eight or nine, which was surprising to her since nothing was ever said or discussed; that said, she knew that her parents weren't happy in each other's company as her friends' parents were.

As she describes it, once her father moved out, her mother began telling her and her older brother stories about things her father had done, things Elizabeth actually didn't remember: how he would turn off the lights in the dining room and force them to eat in the dark if they didn't finish their meal and how he verbally abused them, especially mocking her brother when he had trouble with his homework. And then there were the stories of how her father had physically abused her mother, so often that the family doctor had noted her injuries. But Elizabeth didn't remember those bruises or the fights. At all.

Elizabeth wrote: "My mother would repeat these incidents to us again and again, in such detail, that I'd imagine them, and the more I imagined them, the more they became etched in my mind. But looking back, they weren't real memories; they were simply scenes that had been created. Even now, I couldn't possibly say, with any certainty, that they actually happened." Additionally, contact with her father became limited: "While this was going on, we barely saw our father and I didn't feel able to ask to see him, not after everything my mother told us about him. It would have felt like I was betraying her, and anyway, she was my main caregiver and I didn't want to upset her or make her angry. I didn't really have anyone else."

All of her mother's prep work was actually about custody, and when the Family Welfare officers came to interview Elizabeth, she was carefully coached in what to say. She remembers sitting on the couch, with her mother standing in the doorway, listening while "I repeated what we'd practiced saying." Her mother won custody, the house, and a large sum of money, and promptly moved hundreds of miles away. Elizabeth's father was given no information about how to contact his children. At this juncture, Elizabeth noted that her mother's narrative shifted: "She used a lot of words such as 'escaped' or 'we're safe now' and 'it's just us now' as if we had gotten free. I remember being confused. I liked my old life. I never felt unsafe." Her mother's sister had gotten remarried to a man with kids whom they saw regularly, and these relatives brought up the fact that her mother had effectively disappeared the father of her children as a sharp criticism, which sent her mother into hours of raging. That, too, affected Elizabeth: "Seeing her reaction cemented the idea that we shouldn't bring up our father as it simply wasn't worth the fallout."

Elizabeth's getting back in touch with her father happened accidentally; she joined an Internet website from where she used to live, and her father contacted her and suggested they meet. She hadn't mentioned her father to her mother in years, but when she told her about this communication, her mother ranted and raved. Elizabeth was cowed and decided not to meet her father but did continue to email him. Ultimately, it was the man she married—someone who enjoyed the benefits of close ties in his own family of origin—who encouraged her to meet up with her father. As she wrote: "My father was kind, gentle, and soft-spoken with a certain vulnerability now that he was in his late seventies but still fun with a brilliant sense of humour, We sat and talked for hours. I asked him about the divorce as well." What he told her was devastating. He said that her mother would stop at nothing to get what she wanted, even threatening to accuse him of sexually abusing Elizabeth. He felt that the threat—even if untrue—would ruin his life and he simply gave up, hoping that his two children would have a good life.

Elizabeth stayed in touch with him, even vacationing with him, but she did not tell her mother. It was only when she had children herself that she emailed her mother, saying that she wanted her father in her life and those of her children. Her mother has never responded to that email, and it has been over two years since she's heard from her mother, who continues to send her grandchildren gifts and cards. Her relationship to her father, her stepmother, and her stepsiblings continues.

Elizabeth's assessment of how she was affected by the alienation of her father is vivid and echoes that of other adults with similar experiences. She wonders whether her father might have protected her from the bullying she experienced at school. She wonders whether the early years of her career—when her mother belittled her efforts and she was plagued by low self-esteem and anxiety—would have been easier if she'd had her father by her side. Finally, she mourns the difficulty she still has with feeling as though she belongs; she continues to struggle with fully understanding healthy family ties despite her love for her husband and children. As she wrote, "I still find family relationships very complex and stressful."

Lisa S. is 51 and mother to an 11-year-old, and her story of alienation is a web of tangled lies that is worthy of a Lifetime movie. She was two or three when her parents divorced, and her mother remarried soon after. She was adopted by her stepfather at the age of four, and it was at this time that she started calling her stepfather "Daddy" and the man who was her biological father by his first name, something that she was told about but has no memory of. She was raised believing that her stepfather was her biological father and that her biological father, his new wife, and his parents were "friends" of the family. It was as "friends" that Lisa S. visited them, even spending a few weeks each summer with the "friends," who were actually her grandparents.

Of course, the truth will out, as Shakespeare noted, and by the time she was eight or nine, she started asking questions about the arrangement and was swatted down by her mother. Then, when she was ten, her biological father told her the truth. Her mother and "father" (actually her stepfather) were furious at his so-called "breaking of a promise," and she was no longer allowed to see him. They smeared him in every way they could—calling him lazy and unaccomplished—and told Lisa S. that she should be grateful she wasn't being raised by him. Oddly enough, she was allowed to visit her paternal grandparents, but on the condition that she never tell anyone about this family "secret," especially her three half-siblings. And she obeyed the rules.

When she was in her twenties, a friend convinced her to get in touch with her father; it hadn't even occurred to Lisa S. that he would want a relationship with her. But he did, and what evolved is what she calls a "wonderful" relationship that extends beyond the two of them, includes a friendship between her husband and father, and what she calls "storybook" grandparents for her only child. Of course, a painful past that is unaddressed has a way of rising to the surface, and when her daughter turned 11—the age at which Lisa was forbidden to see her own father—Lisa began experiencing flashbacks of those years and the enormity of what her mother had done hit her. She is now only in distant contact with her mother, through texts and emails. She reports having had trust issues all of her adult life as a result of her mother's actions. When I asked her what might have motivated her mother not just to alienate Lisa from her father but also to concoct such an elaborate tissue of lies, she wrote: "I talked to my husband about it (he knows my mother well), and we could only conclude that it was to protect her image. My mother has a very specific image of how she wants the world to view her, and she will do or say just about anything to protect that image. My mother once told me that she did it to protect me from my schoolmates thinking I was strange or weird, but I don't believe that for one second. To this day, my mother doesn't understand why I feel the need to tell people 'such personal stuff.'"

While these stories are personal, they do echo the findings of a 2005 study by Amy J. L. Baker, which, by the way, relies heavily on Gardner's work. Her sample was small, with 38 recruited participants between the ages of 19 and 67; 14 were male and 24 female. Three-quarters of the participants experienced divorce during childhood; notably, in 31 out of the 38 stories, the mother was the alienating parent. Baker found high rates of low self-esteem and even self-hatred; she attributed the latter to both being the offspring of a "hated" parent and believing that they were unloved and unwanted by the targeted parent. (This rings true from all the interviews I've conducted for *Daughter Detox*; if your parent doesn't love you, who will?) Finally, self-hatred was compounded by their adult understanding of how they had betrayed and abused the targeted parent. Some 70 percent of the sample reported significant episodes of depression in their adult lives, and roughly one-third struggled with substance abuse at some point. Just under half of the participants discussed not trusting either themselves or other people.

Stunningly, half of the participants were alienated from their own children. And two-thirds had been divorced at least once, a statistic well above the national average.

An even smaller study, conducted by Caitlin Bentley and Mandy Matthewson in Tasmania, sought to see whether Baker's research from the United States held true in other populations. This was an admittedly tiny study—composed of eight women and two men between the ages of 26 and 54—but what the researchers found echoed other research. The participants described being abused by the alienating parent and being frightened or feeling guilty if they showed any empathy for the targeted parent, as well as having to take sides (and being parentified) in custody disputes. In addition to feeling emotionally neglected, the adult children reported feeling compelled to suppress feelings, thoughts, and even memories of the targeted parent. The researchers' findings on the effects of being alienated from a parent are both stark and unsurprising, with myriad effects. All the participants reported mental health issues, including, among others, anxiety, depression, and panic attacks. They suffered from low self-esteem, and many reported substance abuse as a coping mechanism. The effects on their ability to form and sustain relationships were myriad, including difficulty with peer relationships, fear of loss and rejection, and both difficulty exiting abusive relationships and staying in healthy ones.

Not surprisingly, the majority of alienated adult children in the study struggled with guilt, both that induced by the alienating parent and self-imposed guilt that they went along and treated the targeted parent so badly. And yes, they grieved the loss of the relationship to the targeted parent.

Finally, in a 2018 article published in *Psychological Bulletin*, Jennifer J. Harman, Edward Kruk, and Denise A. Hines argued that parental alienating behaviors should be acknowledged as a form of family violence.

Prevalence of Parental Alienation and Cultural Attitudes

Jennifer J. Harman, Sadie Leder-Elder, and Zeynep Biringen conducted two studies, several years apart, to determine the prevalence of parental alienation and reached some startling conclusions. Because not all children who are exposed to alienating tactics actually become estranged from the targeted parent, they took the tack of polling respondents in the United States and Canada to determine the prevalence of adults who felt that they were being alienated from their children; additionally, they focused on the mental health issues, including depression, faced by these targeted parents. Using different measurements, they found that over 30 percent of parents felt that they were targets of "abusive strategies to harm parent-child relationships," and that very high percentage held true for those polled both in the United States and Canada. Half of the respondents also said that being targeted in this way led to negative mental health outcomes such as depression and traumatic stress symptoms.

Interestingly, Harmon and her colleagues looked to their findings to draw distinctions between situations in which *both* parents engage in alienating behaviors and estrangement; their distinctions bear directly on my argument to see alienating behaviors as a form of verbal abuse. They write that when both parents use alienating strategies, it should be considered "a loyalty conflict," since it involves two parents with similar levels of power who are each inserting their child or children into a conflict that is between them. In contrast, alienating behaviors directly aimed at an ex-spouse involve unequal power and are not easily countered or reciprocated. Similarly, they emphasize that it's important to distinguish between parental alienation and parental estrangement. Estrangement, they state, arises from issues that are built into the parent-child relationship, such as a parent's abusive behavior or poor parenting skills.

For parental alienation to take place, you need both an imbalance of power and someone willing to abuse, no matter what the cost to anyone, especially the child or children.

In the next chapter, we'll explore how the culture deals with this form of verbal abuse.

Expectations: Parental Verbal Abuse and the Adult Child

Dealing with parental verbal abuse is different from adult peer verbal abuse, though it has its own pitfalls and peculiarities. The imbalance of power in the adult child/parent relationship can be remarkably impervious to change even though both parties are now adults;

counterintuitively, the parent-child relationship often retains the same imbalance of power it had during the adult's childhood. Many parents and adult children never become full equals, even in healthy relationships, for reasons we'll discuss. While it's true that the parties involved aren't likely to live in the same household, so the 24/7 aspect of intimate peer abuse is missing, and their contact may be limited by geographical distance, the issue of confronting abuse may not seem as urgent. *But*—and this is a big but—the relationship has a psychological centrality that gives it a special firepower of its own.

Confronting a parent may be hindered or rendered futile by cultural beliefs about filial duty and the special status of the parent, magnified by that commandment that tells us to honor our fathers and mothers. Those beliefs appear to support a parent's contention that a child, even an adult one, has no right to challenge his or her authority or behavior. Additionally, remember that all the various forms of verbal abuse are rationalized and justified by the parent over the course of many years—the mantras of calling it "discipline," "necessary to the child's not being too full of him- or herself," among others—and those rationalizations are unlikely to be abandoned now.

Parents who thrive on control and who consider it their due are equally unlikely to be willing to pay attention to an adult child's setting of boundaries, much less criticism. Telling a parent that she or he has acted abusively isn't exactly going to be considered with an open mind, much less welcomed with open arms.

It is a sad reality that trying to set boundaries and limits with a verbally abusive parent is often an exercise in futility; efforts to get the parent to acknowledge his or her behavior and articulating complaints and criticism often spawn a cycle of threats and one-upmanship. As a result, the preponderance of adult child-parent estrangements are initiated by adult children, and yes, verbal abuse is often cited. Going no-contact is often the last-ditch effort to protect the adult child and his or her family from ongoing abuse after repeated attempts at setting boundaries and low contact have failed.

From that point of view, it's interesting that Joshua Coleman—an expert in estrangement and a therapist whose practice is devoted to helping parents whose adult children are estranged—begins his new book, *Rules of Estrangement*, with the story of Ralph and his estranged son, Frank. While Rachel, Ralph's wife and Frank's mother, is at the meeting with Coleman, she is very much a bystander, for reasons that become clear (and are pretty much par for the course, as we've already seen). Frank has tried to set boundaries and failed; his father is controlling and demanding, and his constant criticism of his son and his choices makes Frank feel terrible about himself. Ralph, on the other hand, believes Frank owes him an apology for challenging him; he also is adamant that he will not, under any circumstances, apologize to his son for his behavior. Coleman deftly tries to steer Ralph in another direction, saying, "It's not exactly that you have to apologize. It's more like this: you're saying that you didn't know when you were raising him that you hurt him. And now you do. Now you wish you'd communicated differently."

Given what we've already seen about verbal abusers and their love of control, it's not altogether surprising that Coleman's redirect has precisely the opposite effect on Ralph, who doubles down and says it was all purposeful because Frank was too much of a momma's boy and needed to be toughened up and hurt. Ralph actually says, with some pride, that he hurt his son with purpose. Coleman bobs and weaves like a skilled prize fighter in the ring, trying his best, and enlists Rachel, who misses her son and grandchildren. Of course, Ralph tells her she's free to see them but—duh—she knows better because she's just as cowed and beaten down by Ralph as Frank was as a boy. No go.

Keep in mind that Coleman is in the reconciliation business— that's literally true, since his practice and workshops are devoted to the issue—and he has the honesty and integrity to begin with a story that explains how it may sometimes be out of reach. (Yes, he does include others that are more hopeful, if you are wondering.) Anecdotally at least, the story of Ralph and his son, Frank, dovetails with my own findings over more than a decade; this isn't to say that reconciliations don't ever happen, but the reality is that when verbal abuse is involved, they are few and far between.

The bottom line: Verbal abusers are loath to give up the power and control. Remember that verbal abuse is goal oriented and, deep down, sincerely meant and highly motivated, even when wielded by a parent on a consistent basis. Please remember the distinction I drew in the opening pages of this book between the one-off verbally abusive comment uttered in anger or distress and a consistent pattern; it's the latter no one should normalize.

Estrangement Initiated by the Abusive Parent: Pushback and other Fallout

Long a taboo subject and wrongly considered rare, adult child-parent estrangement is finally getting the attention it deserves, thanks to new research. And it's much more common than you'd guess; in fact, one researcher, Richard P. Conti, has opined that it may actually be as common as divorce, a finding that is echoed by other research conducted in the United Kingdom. Blood, it turns out, isn't always thicker than water. Each estrangement is, of course, unique, but research has unearthed broad generalizations about the process, the reasons behind it, and who initiates it.

The reality is that, while most parental estrangements are initiated by the adult child, some 12 percent of estrangements are estimated to be set in motion by parents, usually mothers. It's worth saying that cultural attitudes—and the amount of support the decision is likely to get—very much depend on who engineers the rupture; a mother who cuts an adult child out is always given the benefit of the doubt because of the myths pertaining to motherhood and its sacrosanct bond. A father is usually given the same pass, especially if there's been a significant investment in schooling and education and other visible kinds of support. People cluck and murmur, sympathize and listen, figuring there must be a very good reason indeed for a parent to cut ties. A study by Megan Gilligan, Jill Suitor, and Karl Pillemer found that dissimilar values held by mothers and adult children were the strongest predictor of estrangement.

In contrast, the adult child who goes no-contact is immediately labeled an ingrate—after all, who fed, clothed, and sheltered him or her?—and is thought to be impetuous, immature, or selfish. (This isn't a surmise, by the way; it's what researchers Christine Rittenour, Stephen Kromke, and others found in their survey of American adults and the stereotypes pertaining to estrangement.) Based on my own research and that of others, the reality, though, is that adult children spend years, even decades, thinking about the decision, usually choosing to set boundaries and limit contact before moving to estrangement. They are, moreover, likely to "cycle" in and out of estrangement, as research by Kristina M. Scharp and others shows; I did it myself for close to 20 years.

Even though they are anecdotal and not scientific, stories shared by those who answered questionnaires and who comment on my Facebook page illuminate possible currents that underlie a mother's or father's taking action and sending a family member into permanent exile; it's uncommon, no matter who initiates the estrangement, that any extended family ties are maintained. Not surprisingly, family members take sides, especially since they are often urged to. It's relatively rare that someone in an extended family can maintain a position of neutrality.

Payback for Pushback

Among the stories collected for this book were those about payback: When adult children set boundaries about verbal abuse, some mothers and fathers simply cut all ties. Sometimes, estrangement is just an extension of the scapegoat role the daughter or son has played during childhood and after. As we've noted, the presence of a scapegoat, as the work of Gary Gemmill made clear, facilitates a family narrative, allowing a parent or parents to believe the family would be the picture of perfection if it weren't for the presence of the scapegoat. Casting that person out serves to solidify the family mythology and unites its remaining members with a shared narrative. While some parents estrange from an adult child with nary a word, maintain a stony silence, and may not even acknowledge that the son or daughter ever existed, other parents use the allied tactic of the smear campaign in an effort to set the record straight.

The smear campaign is born out of a combination of factors, including the need to be right and have his or her "truth" become the prevailing script, retaining status and standing (making sure that his or her inner hidden shame doesn't become public), and maintaining control of his or her image and the narrative of the parent-child relationship. The verbally abusive parent curates her or his public persona very carefully, and feeling attacked by an adult child will make the need to control that image even more urgent; the smear campaign may be retribution for the adult child's criticisms, even though smear campaigns can be mounted in response to the adult child's initiating a cutoff as well. All smear campaigns recast the parent or parents as victims and rely on a litany of all that was done for the ingrate son or daughter.

It's hard to exaggerate the viciousness of some of these campaigns. I have to say that, in the course of writing *Daughter Detox* and this book, as well as corresponding with readers over Facebook, nothing has been as surprising as the lengths mothers who consider themselves spurned by their adult daughters will go to in order to eke out revenge, get the upper hand, maintain power or control, or hold on to their social standing by maligning their children. I heard about mothers who tried to break up their daughters' marriages by inventing illicit affairs, mothers who notified social services of trumped-up charges of child abuse, and mothers who insinuated themselves into divorce proceedings, taking the about-to-be ex-husband's side, and more. Some mothers also contacted bosses and coworkers. It was unreal, and, frankly, some of the stories were so mindboggling that I felt that if they were included in a novel, an editor would demand they be taken out because they are unrealistic—except, of course, that they happened. Anecdotally at least, fathers tend not to be as aggressive, but of course, that doesn't mean it *never* happens.

Dealing with Parental Payback

This is likely to be an emotionally painful moment, even if you'd already come to the conclusion that you would have to initiate estrangement yourself. That sounds counterintuitive intellectually—if you thought you'd made peace with the possibility, why would it matter who initiates the cutoff?—but the wallop here is that, once again, you are being made to feel insignificant, rendered powerless, and being controlled. Of course, that's the point; that's what motivates the parent who continues to abuse even as she or he is waving goodbye. Following are some strategies to consider if your parent has taken the initiative and additionally launched a smear campaign.

Work on managing your emotions, especially anger.

As we've already noted, anger can be a positive emotion at one stage and serve to keep you stuck in another; it can keep you tied to your parent in much the same way you once sought to gain his or her favor so that the verbal abuse would stop.

Also keep in mind that our cultural take on venting is largely wrong. It's a cultural trope that letting off steam—aka venting—and engaging in some physical activity (running it off, punching a pillow, etc.) is a good way of letting go of anger, but did you know that's actually not true? That's exactly what a study by Brad Bushman found 17 years ago—yes, cultural myths die hard—when he challenged the idea of anger and catharsis in a series of experiments. In his handy introduction to the subject, he traces the idea of catharsis back to its Freudian roots—Freud believed deeply that repression was the source of many of our psychological maladies—and lists research studies, one after the other, that failed to validate the claim that venting decreases anger. To put the icing on the proverbial cake, Bushman conducted a series of experiments, with more than 600 participants, to either prove the truth of the assumption or expose its falsity. Anger was primed by a supposedly critical review of a paper by a peer; angered participants were told to think about the person who angered them while hitting a punching bag (rumination group) or told to think about getting physically fit by punching (distraction group). There was also a control group who were just left to chill out. After completing the punching part, those in the first two groups were offered the chance to administer loud bursts of noise to the people who'd angered them. Well, guess what? The people in the rumination group not only stayed angry but also were the most aggressive, followed by those who just punched the bag. The least angry? The ones who chilled. So is venting necessarily a good thing? No; the chances are good it'll just make you angrier, unless you vent and let go. Easier said than done, especially when it comes to your being verbally abused. This is especially true for those among us who tend to ruminate.

Part of the work ahead is that of letting go and focusing on the positive changes you can make to your life.

Reread the Serenity Prayer and don't engage.

This sounds corny, but it cuts to the chase. Yes, dig out the old reminder to "accept the things I cannot change/[have the] courage to change the things I can." You cannot change the course of a smear campaign, nor will you be able to change the thinking of those who have already made up their minds. Trying to retaliate will only amp up the volume. Obviously, if lies have been spread about you in your place of work or anywhere they may have a direct impact on your life or on your children, *do* act and hire an attorney if you need to.

Focus on what you *can* change and plan for your future. Pay close attention to those relationships outside of your family of origin that will be a source of sustenance and support, both now and in the future.

If You Initiate Estrangement in the Wake of Parental Verbal Abuse

You will expect to feel better—empowered and resolved—but don't be surprised if, instead, you feel terrific conflict, a sense of loss, and other more complex feelings; estranging yourself from a parent, even a verbally abusive one, is a decisive and painful act, one closer to self-orphaning than not. The loss of other family relationships is usually inevitable, including those of siblings who take a decidedly different point of view. While the idea of being out from under is intellectually liberating, it's neither weird nor unusual to still feel uncomfortable about your decision. Humans do what they can to avoid loss, as we've seen, and this moment—while positive in myriad ways—involves great losses. It's neither unusual nor strange to feel both pangs of regret and feelings of relief at once.

George, age 60, has been estranged from his parents for close to 15 years and was taken aback by how the Covid-19 pandemic reawakened doubts he thought he'd long put to rest: "I found myself wondering whether I had been too reactive, too sensitive, not man enough to roll with the punches—which was the old tape that echoed everything my father ever said about me. I started wondering whether it was appropriate to stick to my guns when the whole world had been turned upside down. I even replayed old events and started rationalizing my father's behavior. Luckily, my wife and my two adult kids have excellent recall, and they didn't let me wander down that dead-end street. Their recitations of chapter-and-verse made me realize that my loss of nerve had nothing to do with my father or me, but it was a reflection of the last year. I stuck with the status quo."

But it need not take a pandemic or other major crisis for you to ruminate, second-guess, and yes, even reinstate relations with a verbally abusive parent despite there being no real substantive change or ownership of his or her behavior. Research shows that adult children often cycle in and out of estrangement, as I've already noted; it took me just short of 20 years to stop and maintain estrangement. In his book *Rules of Estrangement*, which is largely aimed at and addressed to estranged parents, whom he counsels, Joshua Coleman describes how he writes to the adult children who have initiated the cutoff, offering to initiate a discussion, and reports that roughly 60 percent of those adult children agree to speak with him. His conclusion: "Most adult children don't choose estrangement lightly and probably hold, somewhere in their hearts and minds, a wish that it could be otherwise, even those who refuse to speak to me." While there is certainly much Coleman and I disagree about, his observation is absolutely true.

To those of you who double back and return to the well even though you know intellectually the well is dry: There are no right and wrong answers because the dynamic of every relationship is unique, except that whatever you decide, you must keep the high cost of being exposed to verbal abuse in mind. Do not kid yourself into thinking that "it wasn't really so bad" or that you've finally grown a skin thick enough to tolerate it; if necessary, reread the pertinent sections of this book.

Recognizing What You Need to Do for Yourself

Although I'm neither a psychologist nor a therapist, I do know—as a writer of self-help—that self-help has its limitations and that working with a gifted therapist who understands the deep and lasting effects of a verbally abusive relationship is, without question, the very best road out. It is crucial, I think, if you have been in a marriage or partnership with a verbal abuser, and even more so if there are children involved, that you and your ex or former partner will end up coparenting. In the next chapter, in the overview of how society and the culture deal with verbal abuse, we'll have an opportunity to discuss the court system as well.

But recognizing that self-help can't do what good therapy can doesn't mean it's utterly without value. Following are some strategies you may want to avail yourself of as you move forward:

Understand why you normalized verbal abuse.

In Chapter Three, we looked closely at why and how people rationalize abuse, and it's important that you locate yourself in that group. Knowing what motivated you either to choose the nonabusive partner (in a peer relationship) and/or to make excuses for the abuser, whether a peer or a parent, is key to moving forward to an abuse-free future. Ask yourself the following questions; in the best of all possible worlds, you will write your answers down so that you can review them and emend them over time:

Did you mistake his or her need for control as a sign of strength?

If you were controlled by a partner, were you initially relieved not to have to make decisions?

Did what your abuser said about you find a sympathetic listener in your mind? Did your own habits of self-criticism or blame make his or her words and assessment sound true?

Were you more afraid of being left or abandoned than of being abused?

What motivated you to tolerate the pain of being verbally abused?

Articulate what you have learned about identifying verbal abuse.

It's important that you become fully conscious and aware of abusive behavior, that you're able to recognize red flags in someone's behavior that may presage abuse, and that you become comfortable asserting yourself and necessary boundaries. Again, ask yourself the following questions and write down answers; discussing these with someone you trust, if you're not in therapy, will help, too, since speaking out loud helps us become more aware:

What, if any, behaviors would you now no longer tolerate that you did before?

Which behaviors would start alarm bells in your head?

Are you confident that you can identify what is abusive and what is simply angry talk?

What boundaries do you wish to set going forward when dealing with others?

Begin dealing with your own behaviors
that facilitated your tolerating verbal abuse.

Whether it's the habit of self-criticism, a lack of self-regard, or even an unwillingness to stand up for yourself or break the peace, now is the time for some honest self-reflection and goal-setting. Be kind to yourself in the process, but remember that advocating for your own happiness and peace of mind is key to making sure that you build kinder connections in the future.

Verbal abuse has no place in anyone's life. Period. End of story.

Looking at the Broader Culture

In the next chapter, we'll shift away from the personal and see how cultural attitudes aid and abet verbal abuse in some ways and deter it in others.

Chapter Six

Who's to Judge:
The Culture and Verbal Abuse

In these pages, we'll turn away from personal experiences and, since we are all influenced by the cultural environment, take a close look at how the culture deals with verbal abuse, defines it, and, yes, tolerates it. We are all influenced by the environment of ideas that surrounds us, as a number of psychologists and sociologists have noted in published papers, but we may also be directly affected by how those ideas inform attitudes, policies, and laws. On a most mundane and intimate level, we may find that friends to whom we turn for support minimize our experiences, either by diminishing the damage done by words or telling us that we need to toughen up and not be so sensitive. We may find ourselves in the office of an attorney who keeps asking if we were hit or feared for our lives or those of our children when we describe the verbal abuse of a partner or spouse. Those of us dealing with verbally abusive parents will face culturally-freighted consequences from intimates, bystanders, and even therapists as they remind us that no parent is perfect, that we have "only one mother" or "only one father," or that we were fed, clothed, and sheltered. Those of us coparenting with a verbally abusive ex need to be educated about the culture of the courtroom and to recognize that it can be friend or foe, with laws and statutes that vary from state to state. Those of us wrestling with verbal abuse in the workplace may be surprised to find that it is more tolerated than not for reasons that are both simple and complicated at once.

In truth, the cultural thread is tangled and messy.

Now starring "Tough Love!"

Other than the "sticks and stones" rhyme and the human propensity to justify and rationalize bad behaviors, no single cultural idea has contributed more to the flourishing of verbal abuse than the concept of "tough love." We've already seen that both abusive parents and adult children have referred to tough love as a way of looking past the true nature of control and cruelty, but both the genesis of the idea and its influence—still present despite what science knows—are worth looking at. Today, Merriam-Webster defines the term like this:" Love or affectionate concern expressed in a stern or unsentimental manner (as through discipline) especially to promote responsible behavior." Of course, the word "tough" combined with the word "love" is enough to set a rational mind spinning. And that is precisely what we need to look at it because the concept of improvement or correction linked with an improbable combination of shaming and revelation supposedly inspired by love filtered down through the culture in myriad ways, providing nutrients for subcultures of verbal abuse and abusers in positions of power, who often hide in plain sight. We will see that positive narratives of tough love not only coursed through communities but also became a staple for television shows for decades, despite the fact that there is no evidence—and never has been—that what is called tough love works in any context, including addiction.

The idea of tough love legitimized verbal abuse as a tool for changing people and their behaviors; it was hailed as a motivational tool.

The book that started it all—published in 1967 when I was 18—was *Tough Love,* written by Bill Milliken with Char Meredith, and for a book that had outsize influence, it is remarkably dull in many ways except for Milliken's belief that he was not just destined to find Christ but also that his own work with the "ghetto people" (his words) of New York City's Lower East Side was ordained by Christ himself. Skim-reading this book 50 years later, it is impossible not to recognize that it is more like the books and letters written by the 19th-century imperialist European colonizers of the Indian and African continents than not; the smug superiority of the two white guys, Milliken and his colleague, bringing the "light" to the less fortunate brethren in the slums is patriarchal in spirit and frankly paints the two of them as mini-saviors in the service of the Savior himself. As Milliken puts it on the very first page: "It took me a long time to discover that love could be tough. . . . I found out that loving is tough—it costs; [sic] and the love itself has to be tough, too, tough enough to hurt if the hurt can heal." But his message resonated somehow, reinforcing the idea of hurting someone, stripping him or her down, so that he or she hits rock bottom and can be redeemed by new choices and, yes, love. And it was all served up with a heaping side of Christianity and Jesus as the Redeemer.

The cultural ripple effects were enormous, despite the fact that "tough love" wasn't and isn't founded in any psychological principles that actually work. The idea picked up even more steam as the concept of the addiction intervention, popularized by Dr. Vernon Johnson, a recovering alcoholic and Episcopal priest, entered the mainstream. Claire D. Clark, a historian of medicine, wrote a scholarly article called "Tough Love: A Brief Cultural History of the Addiction Intervention," which sheds even more light on the phenomenon and its effects, with a fascinating discussion of how the intervention (and tough love), revised and revived in a dramatic format, became a staple of both the media and the cultural imagination. In Clark's analysis, it was former first lady Betty Ford's story of intervention in April of 1973 that launched it; she was confronted by her husband, her two adult children, and a Navy doctor about her use of alcohol and her dependence on prescription drugs. Mind you, there was nothing mean or sensational about this confrontation, as was revealed in Ford's 1978 autobiography, but intervention became a buzzword not just because of her stature as the wife of a president and vice president but also because she was a respected figure for having already gone public about her battle with breast cancer and her mastectomy; her honesty was rare for the times.

The story of her intervention gained even more traction when it became the subject of a made-for-television movie. In time, her name became synonymous both with addiction and successful treatment, and the idea of tough love got a big boost.

As Clark notes, the intervention (and tough love) became staples of television shows in the 1980s, replacing the sitcoms that had dominated the 1970s, and continued to thrive into the 1990s and the new century as the bread and butter of reality television. Mind you, this wasn't the compassionate intervention as imagined by Vernon Johnson or experienced by Betty Ford but as a mano-a-mano confrontation on shows like *Ricki Lake, Jerry Springer, Geraldo,* and *Sally Jessy Raphael.* As Clark notes, the formula used by these shows "encouraged participants to cross-examine, question, even ridicule each other about their personal behavior patterns." There were shouting and tears, humiliation and anger. Clark points out that the show itself became a kind of fake "therapy session," with the television viewer as an active participant and with chyrons exhorting people to get help for themselves or others if needed.

In the 2000s, shows such as Dr. Drew Pinsky's *Celebrity Rehab* and A&E's *Intervention,* which has been running pretty much for the last 16 years as I write this, cemented the appeal of watching either the formerly famous or ordinary folk with outsize problems struggle on camera. What began as tough love and intervention with a side of Christianity ended up as a sideshow with a helping of schadenfreude.

In the real world, for a time, the tough love/intervention model spawned an entire industry that preyed on anxious parents who couldn't deal with kids who smoked pot, had addictions, acted out, or who were just not willing to go along to get along and who could, with the wave of a check or a credit card, send their kids to a boot-camp retreat modeled on "tough love" environments that promised results. (I actually knew one or two teenagers who were awakened in the middle of the night and whisked off by strangers to one of these places. No, they weren't "cured," but they were angry and terrified even when they got home.) Just because these kinds of interventions are known by psychologists to be damaging doesn't mean they no longer happen, either.

You don't need to be a scientist to see how familiar patterns of verbal abuse—ridiculing and shaming, ignoring boundaries, violating privacy, and more—gained credibility in the eyes of the public, since they were supposedly being used for a higher good. Again, this isn't altogether different from the rationalizations verbal abusers, especially parents, tell themselves, but it happened on a cultural level when all eyes shifted to the ultimate prize, rather than the pathway through which that prize might be acquired. Alas, in terms of recovery, this path was a dead end, but the culture didn't pay that any mind.

Tough love found cultural acceptance, and not surprisingly, it hid in plain sight for decades in gyms, schools, ballet studios, theater clubs, playing fields, swimming pools, and anywhere else young people trained to attain new heights and relied on mentorship. Remember that verbal abuse is always about an imbalance of power.

Cautionary and Revelatory Tales

Not surprisingly, the public reckoning began with physical and sexual abuse, beginning with priests and trickling down to teachers, mentors, trainers, doctors, directors—in short, anyone who wielded power over others. The moment of reckoning picked up steam, fueled by the #MeToo movement, which toppled the once high and mighty. For a culture used to keeping its eye on the prize—whether that was artistic or athletic achievement or simply fame and fortune—looking at what someone did once they achieved those heights, especially how and whether they took advantage of their positions of power, was a new take. After all, Harvey Weinstein worked in an industry which was said to have "a casting couch" when film was still on reels and in black and white.

Since physical abuse is the gold standard, it still took real time for the culture to look at verbal abuse in the same context. As discussed in the first pages of this book, some of the delay and hesitation has to do with the blurriness of the term "emotional abuse" and the need to prove its presence by its effects. And as the examples show, in order to substantiate verbal abuse, there usually had to be some physical abuse to move things along. In this sense, the implosion at USA Gymnastics is instructive, since it began with sexual abuse but, in the end, revealed a training culture that was based on verbal abuse. It should be said that this is not an American phenomenon, although the scandal started here, and while we've focused on gymnastics, verbal abuse has been part of the training ground in other sports around the world.

Between the Balance Beam and the Floor: Gymnastics and Abuse

The cultural acceptance of tough love as a technique that worked and delivered results was, in retrospect, an important thread in the twisted story of USA Gymnastics, the sexual predator Dr. Larry Nassar, and the culture of verbal abuse that enabled and empowered that abuse. In the end, Nassar was sentenced to 40 to 175 years in prison, a term that the presiding judge rightly admitted was her signing his death warrant, after 150 women—some of them former Olympians—came forward to substantiate the claims of sexual abuse. Perhaps the most salient part of this story is that we only know about it because a team of newspaper reporters at the *Indianapolis Star* pulled it out from under the cover of darkness where USA Gymnastics and Michigan State University had systematically and methodically kept it. The sexual abuse perpetrated by Nassar, a doctor in the employ of both, had been the subject of complaints to USA Gymnastics by minors and parents since the 1990s, but until the story was published in 2016, no action was taken. While the chances are good that you read or heard about Nassar's conviction even if you weren't an aficionado of the sport, the story in its complicated entirety testifies to the many themes we've already touched upon in these pages, among them how verbal abuse facilitates physical and sexual abuse.

After combing through many articles and watching the superlative Netflix documentary *Athlete A,* which recounts the *Indy Star*'s reporting and its effects, I've come to realize that the story really begins in 1976—more than 40 years before the abuse was finally reviewed and judged—when a 14-year-old Romanian gymnast named Nadia Comăneci took the world by storm at the 1976 Montreal Olympics with her perfect 10s; her coaches were Béla Károlyi and his wife, Márta, who were immediately thrust into the limelight along with their tiny star. Károlyi would defect to the United States in 1981, along with his wife, and would build his adopted country into a gymnastic powerhouse. Do keep in mind that Károlyi and his wife were never charged with aiding or abetting Nassar or, for that matter, anything else; it's how Károlyi coached that is pertinent to our discussion, and how long it took for action to be taken against abusive coaching. Note, too, that by the time Károyli and company established themselves in the United States, tough love had already had a decade to put down roots in the popular imagination.

Put-downs, manipulations, coercive control, insults, body-shaming, minimizing physical injury as well as pain, and, yes, ignoring what his minor charges were feeling or mocking them were all on the menu at the Károlyi ranch where the gymnasts trained, along with other deprivation such as not having enough to eat, being watched 24/7, and—since we are talking about minors—being isolated from parents and family. Parents were not permitted at the ranch, and its remote location made cell phone service spotty or impossible. Nassar treated—and molested—the gymnasts at the ranch, often playing good cop (sneaking in food and candy, making a fuss over a girl, being affectionate) to the coaches' bad cops. Nassar played the same game with another coach, John Geddert, who committed suicide in February of 2021, right after he was charged with 24 crimes, most of them centering on abuse and coercion. The key point is that the steady diet of verbal abuse fed into the confusion these preadolescent and adolescent girls experienced, so it's little wonder that they either rationalized what Nassar was doing (because he was, in comparison, a nice guy and a renowned doctor) or were afraid to tell anyone. In contrast, Károlyi's method of coaching was deliberate and calculating, and he offered no apologies then or at any time because it produced results. Keep in mind that the whole appeal of tough love is hurting someone in the name of a higher good.

In an interview he gave to the *Harvard Business Review* in 2012—after gymnast Dominique Moceanu accused him and his wife of abuse—the coach was decidedly unapologetic and forthright when the interviewer noted that he could be both enthusiastic and tough and asked how he decided which motivational tactic to use: "Criticism and encouragement have to be alternated and used at the right time and in the right situation. If there is ignorance or lack of interest, then make the critical remarks. If criticism isn't working, you have a more concrete discussion about the reason we're competing. If that fails, we say good-bye to each other." Remember that these are kids who are spending seven to eight hours a day practicing highly specific skills. Even more revelatory was Károlyi's vision of what really worked: "So I was always fighting for a centralized training program. I came up with this in Romania, and it's the most efficient way of creating high-quality athletes. Bring me a six-year-old, and I'll send them home when they're 21. In this country there is no way to do that." I personally find this remark chilling when it becomes clear that he is speaking about a human being; in honesty, I think a sculptor has more respect for clay or marble than the coach did for the feelings of his young charges.

In her book *The Girls: An All-American Town, a Predatory Doctor, and the Untold Story of the Gymnasts Who Brought Him Down*, Abigail Pesta details in mind-numbing—and soul-wrenching—detail how these young gymnasts were sexually abused by Larry Nassar and verbally abused by their coaches. She interviewed many of these gymnasts, years after the fact, and their continuing pain is palpable. Of course, what validated the verbal abuse was the incredible success of these coaches—national champions and Olympians made and delivered—in a variation on the tough love theme. With just a few exceptions, parents looked away because of their daughters' passion and because they wanted them to succeed as there were full college scholarships in the offing and perhaps Olympic fame and fortune; it should be said that Nassar ingratiated himself to many of the parents as well. As to the coaches' treatment, alas, most parents—and their children—normalized it.

Reading through these accounts, I felt keenly that even though the words "tough love" are never mentioned on the pages of *The Girls*, the idea clearly animated many of the stories survivors told Pesta, leavened only by the power of 20/20 hindsight. One haunting comment came from Sara Teristi, who might have been the first girl Nassar victimized: "People don't understand how many broken girls it takes to produce an elite athlete. . . . A coach can easily go through three hundred girls or more." Absorb the chilling truth of that statement and try to square it with a child and her dreams. Sarah Klein was eight when she started training and was "treated" by Nassar at Geddert's gym, and her adult self understands what happened completely: "We were all in perpetual terror in John's gym. He is personally responsible for why none of us developed a sense of self. We developed no boundaries. He robbed us of our voices even before we got our voice. . . . Then you have Larry saying, 'Come here, little girl. I'll help you.'"

More in line with what we've seen in the pages of this book—though counterintuitive nonetheless—the girls and women Pesta interviewed all said that the verbal abuse they endured was more damaging than the sexual abuse and made them doubt their perceptions that there actually had been sexual abuse instead of the "treatments" Nassar claimed to be performing. Pesta writes of Sara Teristi: "She wrestles more with the psychological abuse from her coach than the sexual abuse from her doctor. She continues to blame herself for getting injured." This is not surprising to me, and if you've been reading along, it may not be to you either.

Another Look at the Culture of Abuse (and the Confusion it Sows)

You would have thought that USA Gymnastics had learned its lesson, but the organization proved to be a slow learner, especially when there's "only" verbal abuse involved, and continues to be very slow to act. This case is interesting because it doesn't include sexual abuse and the physical abuse is, as the standards go, relatively minor; it's also important because the coach is a woman, and as mentioned in the opening pages of this book, when we imagine the face of abuse, it tends not to be female. In April of 2020, Maggie Haney was formally suspended from coaching gymnastics for eight years after USA Gymnastics conducted hearings on her behavior. This case is especially important because it highlights the confusion children (as well as their parents) experience in the wake of verbal abuse and reveals the cultural confusion about defining the damage verbal abuse inflicts.

The whistleblower was Wanda Hernandez, the mother of an Olympian named Laurie Hernandez, who basically hounded USA

Gymnastics for four years after her then fifteen-year-old daughter con-
fessed to physical abuse she'd witnessed and verbal abuse she'd experienced. In an interview with *The New York Times* which was published
in May 2020, Hernandez's recollections echo those of the men and
women who answered my questions for this book and who weren't
Olympic medalists and who experienced verbal abuse in domestic
settings. When Hernandez complained to her coach of her maltreatment, she was told she was taking things too personally, and predict-
ably, she would back down and eventually apologize. Haney had been
her coach since she was five—a position of power very akin to that
of a parent—and the coaching was, by definition, unsupervised; parents were not allowed in the gym. Hernandez went on to say that "I
thought I deserved it all. . . . The toughest part about it was there were
no bruises or marks to show that it was real. It was all just so twisted
that I thought it couldn't be real." This is an echo of a familiar theme
we have heard again and again on these pages.

Not surprisingly, it was Laurie's witnessing Haney's pulling another gymnast by the hair, talking about it to another girl over FaceTime,
and having her mother overhear the conversation that finally toppled
the house of cards in 2016. Wanda Hernandez not only fired Haney
immediately but also registered a complaint with USA Gymnastics. It
took them *four years* to take action against Haney! On December 10,
2020, an arbitrator reduced her suspension to five years and ruled
that four of the gymnasts' testimonies had been improperly included.
Haney's attorney stated that they were exploring their legal options.
Two other gymnasts have filed legal complaints against Haney and
others; since the complaints demand a jury trial, it won't surprise you
that physical abuse is front and center in both, even though emotion-
al/verbal abuse is included. I suspect the attorney is well aware of the
cultural bias.

In November of 2020, Maggie Haney, who'd maintained her silence since her suspension, agreed to an interview with *The New York
Times*; she intends to appeal her suspension. What she had to say
echoes the familiar patterns we've already seen and which we can file

under the "lie of tough love" folder we've already assembled. Among them were these:

The yelling and demeaning came out of "caring."

This is a direct quotation from Haney in *The New York Times:* "I think my mistakes were that I cared too much, and I wanted them to be too perfect every day, when maybe that's not possible." As someone trained in English literature, not psychology, I'd draw your attention to that "maybe." You screamed, yelled, demeaned, and shamed children so that they'd attain perfection in their sport, and "maybe that's not possible"? She hardly sounds convinced.

She attributes the charges to a cultural shift, not to her behaviors.

Another direct quotation: "Maybe what used to be OK is not OK anymore, and maybe it shouldn't be. I think maybe the culture has shifted." Two "maybe"s in this one, and actually, shaming, body-shaming, ridiculing, and other forms of verbal aggression have never been okay unless your goal was to terrorize children. Ditto hair-pulling and forcing gymnasts to practice when injured.

She points to her defenders and says she's being scapegoated.

Ah, the old blame-shift—another form of verbal abuse—being used as a defense. She points to the fact that the mothers of two of the gymnasts suing her never complained about her behavior, even though they were sometimes in the gym. What she doesn't mention is how, when years ago Laurie Hernandez did complain to her mother and Mom called, Haney shamed Laurie for "telling" and "punished" all the gymnasts with extra exercises. A parent is quoted as defending Haney—one who is identified as managing his five children by "screaming, not coddling"—saying, "I don't think it's fair to say that Maggie is an abuser. It depends on how much any child or any person can tolerate." Please think about that. Should abuse be defined by what a person can tolerate or withstand, rather than the wreckage caused?

Once again, that's the myth of tough love; discipline and verbal abuse are not synonyms. Maggie Haney sued USAG in federal court in March of 2021 to have her suspension overturned entirely.

These were not isolated incidents but evidence of a culture so permeated with verbal abuse and tough love that it could swallow a young person's self whole. That's ultimately what got Katelyn Ohashi off the merry-go-round, as she revealed in an interview with ESPN. com in 2019. Katelyn began gymnastics at the age of three, and when she became an elite gymnast at 12, she says, "everything became less about me and what I wanted and more for everyone around me. The Olympics was the ultimate goal but it was never my goal. It was put in front of me because of my talent, and my coaches kept pushing me toward it." She felt she couldn't quit because her family had made so many sacrifices, but she was desperately unhappy: "My voice was so suppressed. I still loved the sport, but the joy was diminished. I believed the medals were worth so much more than I was."

She was fat-shamed, and she began starving herself and engaging in disordered eating, and that, in turn, led to absolute exhaustion, given the intensity of her training. She describes how her world and sense of self was ultimately narrowed down to the sport and winning: "Every gold medal, every international competition I won—that gave me my worth." A series of injuries forced a hiatus, which she describes as a relief because she was so miserable, and she began to see being hurt as a way out of the elite training without the onus of quitting. But the break allowed her to miss the sport, and by going to UCLA—a step down from the Olympian heights—she was able to rediscover the joy gymnastics had once given her. She's since become an outspoken critic not of the sport but of the culture that she deems abusive.

An investigative article titled "The Medals Keep Piling Up. But at What Cost?" by Lauren Green, published in *Sports Illustrated* on July 30, 2021, revealed that little had changed, despite all the efforts of gymnasts and their parents to push the sport out of the Dark Ages. It was published after Simone Biles, a victim of Larry Nassar, in case you'd forgotten, pulled out of various events during the 2021 Tokyo Olympics, citing "mental health issues" which, alas, showed how conflicted the culture really is about whether "mental health" is just a wuss's way out or something real. Green interviewed 16 gymnasts and parents from the 1990s to 2020 and found that little had changed and that, indeed, coaches—for all the uproar—were still not being held accountable or had changed their tactics. As Green writes: "This wasn't a public relations nightmare. It was a system that may have created champions but also left a trail of gymnasts who were beaten down and broken in its wake. Gymnastics did not have a Larry Nassar problem, the SI [*Sports Illustrated*] sources say. Instead, the sport has an abuse problem that existed long before Larry Nassar became international news." Additionally, she writes: "Gymnasts are trained to be silent. They are taught to just keep training through injuries and that they aren't really *that* hurt. They realize that fear isn't tolerated. Athletes are manipulated into believing that this is normal. *This is just how gymnastics is. This is just tough coaching.*" As we already know, it's the perfect cocktail for verbal abuse, mixing up gaslighting, manipulation, need to please, insecurity, and tough love served up to young girls separated from parents. It is truly appalling.

Tough Love, Abuse, and the Fertile Soil of Elite Endeavors

It wasn't just gymnastics, of course, nor did it just happen in the United States. Thanks to gymnasts speaking out, as of 2020, national gymnastics federations in Britain, Australia, the Netherlands, and Belgium have begun investigations or requested inquiries into alleged abuse. Perhaps most revealingly, as part of her requirement for earning a Master's degree at UCLA, an elite synchronized swimmer named Alison Williams did a study of rates of depression and emotional abuse; she turned to research to amplify and explore her own experiences in her sport, since renamed "artistic swimming." Tellingly, she begins by writing that the public perception is that athletes are immune to mental health issues because of all the exercise they do, but she points out that research studies show that elite athletes are highly vulnerable to anxiety, depression, eating disorders, and substance abuse. Echoing the observation of gymnast Sara Terisi, which I quoted earlier—that it took 300 broken girls to produce one elite gymnast—Williams writes that, "But for every athlete that succeeds, there are dozens or hundreds more who invest the same amount into their training and never make it on to a Wheaties Box or into a Nike commercial." Verbal abuse—calling a swimmer a "fat cow," shaming her, and the like—was on the menu the coaches served up. Keep in mind that her findings echo the experience of Katelyn Ohashi as well—the confining bubble of elite training, which includes a suspension of other activities and isolation from other people and "normal" social activities—and a coach's outsize position in and influence over an athlete's sense of self.

The findings of her survey—which, while accepted for her degree, were not peer reviewed as they would be in a journal and are a small sample, but a focused one—are eye-opening, especially when you keep in mind the idea of tough love and the normalization of verbal abuse as a means to an end. She had 56 respondents, all between the ages of 15 and 42, all of whom had participated in elite levels of artistic swimming. She begins by laying out the statistics on depression, the rate of which, in the general adult population, according to the National Institutes of Health, is 7.1 percent. In the college athlete population, depression jumps to 18.3 percent. Among the U.S. national synchronized swimmers, 37 percent were diagnosed with depression by a doctor, but when self-diagnosis was added in, the percentage leapt to 64.3 percent. Painstakingly, she unpacks the emotional toll of elite sports in relationship to depression—from isolation from family, friends, and age-appropriate social activities to the dependence on coaches and the narrowing of self-definition. Just as in gymnastics, injury was categorized as weakness and 67.9 percent of the respondents reported feeling an obligation to perform in order to please a coach against the recommendation of a doctor; among the depressed, the percentage grew to 95.2 percent. Among depressed swimmers, more than 71 percent reported that they couldn't speak to their coaches about issues, either personal or professional, and 61.9 percent of them felt that they had lost sight of everything but their identity as an athlete.

Her survey explores the experience of what she calls emotional abuse defined in eight ways (belittling, humiliating, shouting, scapegoating, rejecting, isolating, threatening, and ignoring), which are all within the purview of what I have called verbal abuse in this book; she had participants rate the prevalence of abuse by checking "rarely/never" or "sometimes/always." Among those who had been diagnosed with depression by a doctor, just under 74 percent checked off "sometimes/always." In those who had not been diagnosed, the percentage fell to 42.5 percent for "sometimes/always," while 57.5 percent said they experienced abuse rarely or never. That said, she writes: "Negative behaviors experienced by athletes were normalized, inefficient, and often felt like personal attacks." Finally, she quotes one athlete as saying: "It's like a cult. You get sucked in and are isolated from everything and you take the word of your coach as the end all and be all. It's not healthy." Amen to that.

Once again, when tough love meets up with verbal abuse and eyes are stuck on the end goal, and not how you get there, people get damaged. As this book goes to press—too late to write about it—an investigative report about the National Women's Soccer League (N.W.S.L.) released by Sally Q. Yates, a former deputy U.S. attorney general, noted that "Abuse in the N.W.S.L. is rooted in a deeper culture in women's soccer, beginning in youth leagues, that normalizes verbally abusive coaching and blurs boundaries between coaches and players."

Stay tuned and aware. It is clear that there is much left to be done when it comes to verbal abuse in sports.

Next, we'll turn to other kinds of verbal abuse and the culture's take on them.

Verbal Abuse and the Courts

In our earlier discussion of parental alienation in Chapter Five (see pages 180-192), we've already noted how much confusion there is about what it is and isn't, despite the efforts of experts to come up with working definitions that would permit relatively easy identification without devolving into a he said/she said situation. We've also seen that there's a direct and potential conflict in the determination of most judges, who interpret the dictum of "the best interests of the child" as meaning equal contact with both parents except for cases of clear physical violence. To understand why cultural acceptance of parental alienation as yet another form of verbal abuse has been slow in coming, we'll turn to the research. It is a complicated question, but at the same time, it should be, since it involves children and their connections to their parents.

Some Common Fallacies About Parental Alienation

In a compelling study published in 2015, Richard Warshak examined the prevalent assumptions about parental alienation that, in his words, "lead therapists and lawyers to give bad advice to their clients, evaluators to give inadequate recommendations to courts, judges to reach injudicious decisions." Warshak, as you might guess from this opening sentence, doesn't pull any punches about the cultural mess. As both a psychologist and an expert on parental alienation who has testified in many court cases, he notes that when a fallacy is mentioned in a professional presentation or publication, "it becomes a commonly accepted idea that lacks grounding in persuasive evidence yet gains traction to the point where people assume that it's true." (By the way, this phenomenon of an often-repeated untruth standing as truth has a name; it's called a "wozzle," taken from an incident in A. A. Milne's *Winnie the Pooh*.) There are, of course, other biases professionals bring to the table—the confirmation bias, among them—but there are ten most common fallacies Warshak lays out in detail. Here they are, in all their ignominious glory, with a summary of his arguments.

1) *Children never unreasonably reject the parent with whom they spend the most time.*

That parent is often the mother, but Warshak cites studies that show that, in 16 percent of cases, the alienated parent had either primary or joint physical custody. He points out cases in which the father was able to manipulate the child, nonetheless.

2) *Children never unreasonably reject mothers.*

Nope. One-third of alienated parents are mothers, as numerous studies show. (This particular bias is part of the bundle of cultural myths pertaining to motherhood, which includes the idea that mothering is instinctual, that all women are nurturing, and that a mother's love is always unconditional.)

3) Each parent contributes equally to a child's alienation.

No again. In at least one-third of the cases, one parent was solely responsible for initiating and sustaining conflict. From a legal point of view, Stanley Clawar and Brynne Rivlin looked at 1,000 cases and identified a parent's "programming" of a child as the primary dynamic of a child's alienation. (Their book was published by the American Bar Association and was called *Children Held Hostage.)*

4) Alienation is the child's transient, short-lived response to the parents' separation.

This is misguided and ignores the active and committed nature of a parent's alienating behaviors.

5) Rejecting a parent is a short-term healthy coping mechanism.

Actually not. Even though estimates of alienated children are high, the truth is that the vast majority of children who have experienced divorce want contact with both parents.

6) Young children living with an alienating parent need no intervention,

Again, not true. This is not something a child "will grow out of." Warshak points out how easy it is to manipulate the behaviors of toddlers and preschoolers and how small children will act the way the alienating parent has told them to.

7) Alienated adolescents' stated preferences should dominate court decisions.

Warshak gives two separate sets of reasons judges are apt to act this way. First, the governing assumption is that a teenager has the cognitive capacity to form mature judgments that are independent of the favored parent's influence; that's not true for numerous reasons, not the least of which is that the human brain doesn't reach maturity until between the ages of 25 and 30. Second, while the courts may think that the adolescent shouldn't sever ties, they may think that the order will be impossible to enforce. (Enforcement is a whole other issue, which we will discuss further.)

8) Children who emotionally reject a parent but thrive in other respects need no intervention.

He rightly argues that it's not impossible that a child's apparent thriving—please note the word "apparent" in this context—in other areas may coexist with significant prosocial problems. (We've seen this with other kinds of parental verbal abuse as well.) Second, being alienated from a loving parent is a problem in its own right and never a stand-alone impairment. I believe he is 100 percent correct.

9) Severely alienated children are best treated with traditional therapy techniques while living with their favored parent.

This misses the point entirely; whatever the child is feeling hasn't been internally generated but has been inculcated through the actions and words of that favored parent. Additionally, as Warshak writes, "A therapist's facilitation of a child's complaints about a parent and rehashing conflicting accounts of the parent's past behavior may be counterproductive and prevent the parent and child from having experiences that move the relationship in a positive direction." It goes without saying that if the favored parent sabotages treatment, there's basically no point.

10) Separating children from an alienating parent is traumatic.

According to Warshak, this is a prevalent assumption but based on no peer-reviewed studies and a mash-up of attachment theory.

In another study published in 2020 and titled "When Evaluators Get It Wrong: False Positive IDs and Parental Alienation," Warshak discusses at length how oversimplification and misunderstanding of what parental alienation and alienating behaviors are and aren't, as well as critical biases, lead to false positive identifications by evaluators. He also argues that there's a continuum of behaviors that could be considered "alienating," but they differ in kind and degree. He writes that "mild alienating behaviors" are those that occur occasionally, such as "incidental bad-mouthing and criticisms of the other parent with no consistent attempt to undermine the child's overall positive relationship with the parent who is the target." I am willing to bet that there isn't a single divorced parent in the world who hasn't done this at least once. (Yes, while I happen to like the father of my daughter and we did not have a fractious divorce, I have certainly done this.) But the next two steps up in the continuum are different in kind because these behaviors actively seek to undermine the relationship of the child to the targeted parent. "Moderate" alienating behaviors do that, but "severe" ones take it a step further, "taking on the complexion of a hostile campaign against a parent, fueled by recurring harsh unmitigated behavior." Here the intention is to actually destroy the child's relationship to the parent, and it is deliberate. In some cases, the alienating parent's behavior is explicit, requiring that the child choose between the parents and pledge allegiance to one, with the threat to punish him or her if he or she wishes to see the other parent.

This is bad stuff and very abusive. That said, though, parental alienation isn't easy to prove in a court of law, and as I've said, since it involves loss of parental contact, it probably shouldn't be unless it is crystalline in all respects. What follows is a story of one such case, which, to use a highly technical term, is a doozy.

A Cautionary Tale: J. F. v. V. F.

There are a number of interesting things about this case, which played out in New York's Supreme Court and was decided in 2018. First, it underscores the role a judge plays—and the effect of his or her sensibility and attitude on the outcome—since two judges reached different conclusions about whether or not parental alienation had taken place.

The judge who originally presided over the case died, so a new judge, the Honorable Richard A. Dollinger, reviewed all the evidence presented at trial; Judge Dollinger happens also to be a fine writer with a dry wit and a kind of clarity that is admirable, which sets this judgment apart. Second, the parent alleging alienation was the father, and his team of experts included Dr. Amy J. L. Baker (whose peer-reviewed articles I have cited), Dr. Robert Evans, and Linda Gottlieb, LSCW, all of whom are in this field. Both parents were highly educated—she an attorney and he a college professor—and hugely litigious and angry, and each wanted to win. They also had relatively deep pockets, so court was the preferred venue over talking it through, as the judge noted.

While the couple had signed a custodial agreement and then a property settlement in 2013, the father (who was the custodial parent, but the three children rotated between the two households) filed for and obtained an order of protection against the mother just one month after the papers were signed. Then the court intervened to resolve a series of visitation and scheduling issues within the first year after the agreement was reached and, in 2015, had to intervene to deal with competing affidavits. Then, in the judge's words, "Within two years, the parties began another litigation war of attrition." The mother sued for sole custody, claiming the father refused to take the daughters to activities, thus limiting their growth; the father sued for sole custody, claiming that the mother scheduled activities that cut into his parenting and, more important, had alienated the children from him.

The court also scheduled a Lincoln hearing, which is a session with minor children with only an attorney present and no parents; the three daughters were 15, 13, and 7 at the time. That judge found evidence of "mild alienation" but stated that both parents were guilty of it; that said, she did modify the visitation schedule and gave each parent final authority in certain areas—the mother, medical and religious decisions, the father, on education and extracurricular activities—as joint custody continued. Unfortunately, after signing this temporary order, the judge died, and Judge Dollinger was given the task of reviewing all the transcripts, the admitted exhibits, prior orders, and the transcript of the Lincoln hearing, which he did; in my opinion, he did so with vigor and consummate skill.

Do keep the behavior of both parties, who chose litigation as a way of resolving differences, in mind as you read Judge Dollinger's stated position: "The parental alienation doctrine has become a basis for contentious parents to undercut parenting agreements; agreements that were based, at their inception, on a parental concurrence of the best interests of the children." There it is in a nutshell from a judicial point of view: a tool to game the court system. He expands on that with a review of case law pertaining to parental alienation, which, as mentioned, hasn't fared well in the courts. Over the course of 61 pages (including footnotes), Judge Dollinger walks us through the maze of contradictory claims, of the he said/she said aspects of both parents' testimony, along with that of the experts called. In a side note, we learn that the father's girlfriend is, indeed, the children's former nanny (!!!), which may explain some of the animosity between the two parties. (Ya think?) Judge Dollinger's handling of this is particularly deft when he cites Baker's assertion that "the mother's use of the daughters to spy on the father was evidence of an alienation against him." The judge acknowledges that "the proof establishes that the daughters did talk about their father and his girlfriend" and then writes, "But, it is inconceivable that three young girls who spend substantial time with their father and knew that their father's girlfriend was their former nanny, would not talk to their mother about this relationship." As to the 17 identifications offered up by Parker (which we covered in the previous chapter, pages 184-185), the judge ticks them off one by one and finds little evidence of alienation.

The second expert, Linda Gottlieb, fares way worse, and I must say I was on Team Judge for this one, too. He writes: "For this court, the expert's comment, at times, reached almost the apex of foolishness; she testified that a mother who tells her children that she misses them when they are gone is guilty of alienating conduct and manipulation. If so, every mother in the world needs reprogramming." The bottom line for the judge is that not one of the three experts actually interviewed either the children or the mother; they were applying theory to the "facts" as supplied by the father. It is, indeed, a cautionary tale.

In his decision, the judge rightly noted that both parents had behaved badly and that there were indeed tensions between the children and their father, which could just as easily be laid at the feet of different rules of behavior in his household and kids pushing back. The judge found that there'd been no alienation of the children and thus he rejected the idea that the residency requirements be changed to favor the father. Similarly, even though the children had asked to live with their mother full-time during the Lincoln hearing, he rejected that, too. because he didn't see any hardship in their hewing to the agreed-upon schedule. Instead, he left open the possibility that the parents could, if they wished, renegotiate residential arrangements on their own without appealing to the court; basically, he wanted the court to get out of the business of playing umpire for these two litigious parties. That said, he did cite the mother for what he saw as clear violations of the custody agreement.

This case makes it clear that, while parental alienation does, in fact, happen, proving it is another matter entirely, and Judge Dollinger's view that claiming parental alienation can easily be used as a tool to punish and to undo agreed-to terms is one that should be kept in mind, especially if you find yourself either considering a charge or are fighting off parental alienation.

Verbal Abuse and the Justice System

Throughout this book, we've talked about how physical abuse is the gold standard against which what the culture calls "emotional" or "psychological" abuse—what we are calling verbal abuse—is measured, and how the culture assumes that, of the two, physical abuse is more damaging. In that light, it's sobering to realize that, even when the abused shows bruises and evidence of physical violence, those in authority cannot be relied upon to take action. A monthlong study of domestic violence and sexual assault conducted by the American Civil Liberties Union in 2015 with more than 900 respondents revealed that 88 percent reported that police "often" or "sometimes" do not believe survivors or blame survivors for the violence. Eighty-three percent noted that police "often" or "sometimes" don't take allegations of sexual assault and domestic violence seriously. If this is the gold standard, what will the response be when there are no bruises? Keep in mind, as the ACLU study notes, that physical violence is underreported to begin with; it cites The National Crime Victimization Survey, which stated that 65 percent of rapes and sexual assaults aren't reported to police, and so-called "simple assault"—shoving, pushing, slapping—was only reported 56 percent of the time, which testifies to the complexity of the problem. There's no single or standard reason why women don't report. Twenty-eight percent said they were afraid of reprisal or getting their abuser in trouble.

They also cite other studies' findings that the primary reasons for nonreporting were embarrassment, fear of reprisal, fear that police won't believe them, and the belief that police are likely to be ineffective. This study looked at reporting to the police; what happens to physical abuse, much less verbal abuse, in the court system?

One answer is supplied by a 2019 article written for the *University of Pennsylvania Law Review* by Deborah Epstein, who has been the director of the Georgetown University School of Law Center's Domestic Violence Clinic for 25 years and has represented hundreds of women in civil protection order cases, and Lisa A. Goodman, a professor of psychology at Boston College who is also an expert on domestic violence. The title of their article pretty much says it all: "Discounting Women: Doubting Domestic Violence Survivors' Credibility and Dismissing Their Experiences." While written from a decidedly feminist perspective, it is abundantly footnoted and carefully documented. It is, not surprisingly, a disheartening look at the sexism of a largely male judiciary and women survivors, often representing themselves *pro se* in civil proceedings, but perhaps the most salient examples are those of what judges believe domestic abuse "should" look like in the telling and what female survivors *actually* say in court. Epstein and Goodman point out that, since physical harm is prioritized over psychological harm in the written law, judges believe that physical violence is far worse than psychological abuse. So, they write, "A common judicial expectation is that a 'real' victim will lead with physical violence in telling her story on the witness stand. But, in fact, many survivors tell their stories quite differently." So there's the judicial script—which expects the witness to lead with physical violence—and the inner script of the witness who, according to the authors, will lead with what she considers the most salient aspect of her abuse, which may well be, as they point out, "the constant derogatory name-calling, the way he made her feel that everything was her fault, the way he always checked her phone to see who she was talking to." They note that, in the victim's telling, physical violence—especially if it is sporadic or nonexistent—may take a backseat or might not even be mentioned unless she is asked.

We already know that the problem here is not with the survivor's script but that it runs counter to the one the judiciary expects and the script the written law presents. (We'll be discussing how advocates have sought to deal with both scripts with the introduction of the concept of coercive control next.)

Not surprisingly, when the scripts diverge, female survivors are often wrongly denied lifelines and help because judges believe they lack credulity. When a survivor leads with or emphasizes her stories of verbal abuse or only mentions physical abuse when questioned about it, Epstein and Goodman write, "because so many judges do not understand survivors' frames for their experiences, they may suspect that women's too little, too late testimony about physical violence is either exaggerated or fabricated out of whole cloth; that they add it only after belatedly realizing the law demands such facts." If you consider the culture's general dismissal of verbal abuse, this is a scenario that is easy to imagine. On a more depressing note, the authors write that "recent studies of family court decisions reveal that mothers who allege intimate partner violence are actually *more* likely to lose custody than those who do not allege those assertions." That, alas, is not the full extent of the bad news, which echoes other findings we've already discussed: "Judges tend to corroborate, typically with no other evidence than the perpetrator-father's uncorroborated assertions, that women are fabricating abuse allegations as part of a strategic effort to alienate children from their father."

Once again, the fact that the culture still adheres to the "sticks and stones" theory remains an enormous problem. Next, we'll look at efforts to fix that by criminalizing what's called "coercive control" and see whether it's a panacea in the making or just another way of muddying the waters.

Should We Add in "Coercive Control"?

Our American problem with prosecuting domestic abuse is echoed elsewhere, and other parts of the English-speaking world took action, most particularly England; Scotland; and Queensland, Australia, by criminalizing behaviors that fall under the term "coercive control." In the United States, two states—California and Hawaii—have made coercive control illegal, and there is ongoing discussion about doing so in other states as well. But whether this is actually a good idea is the subject of much serious debate.

The term is an American export; while it wasn't invented by Evan Stark, a sociologist, he was in the forefront of the movement to protect women from abusive men that culminated in his very scholarly and footnoted book, *Coercive Control: How Men Entrap Women in Personal Life.* The title makes it clear that, while the author is male, the point of view is that of an ardent feminist. Since he is highly sought after as a consultant, expert witness, and speaker, his influence has been enormous, even though the jury is still out on whether coercive control should be criminalized and prosecuted.

That said, Stark's book illuminates the history of domestic violence, which many readers—and I include myself in that number—may not be aware of. It is stunning to realize that, until the passage of the Violence Against Women Act in 1994, men faced little or no sanctions for beating the hell out of "their" women. Astonishingly, according to Stark, by the end of 1976—when I was 26 and reasonably informed but did not know about this—there were only two dozen emergency services for women in the entire country; most of the early shelters were homegrown affairs, financed by donations and determination. The term "coercive control" is an effort to move past the legal definitions, which hinge on whether physical violence has occurred, and to focus instead on incidents or a pattern of controlling, coercive, or threatening behavior. He defined controlling behavior as efforts to make a person dependent or subordinate through isolation, depriving them of the means to be independent, and regulating their everyday lives. Coercion encompasses psychological, physical, sexual, financial, and emotional abuse. Threatening behaviors are understood broadly and not just limited to the threat of physical violence. In his book—which is voluminous at just under 500 pages—Stark adduces dozens and dozens of stories of how coercive control works in the lives of

women who have experienced it: monitoring phone calls and movements, rules and regulations whose breach will be punished, and more.
He lays out in detail how a woman's sense of self and agency is un-
dermined on the daily, effectively imprisoning her in the relationship.

But proving that coercive control has taken place isn't that easy,
especially if no one has died or been grievously injured; it may be a
story best told in retrospect if there is a dire ending. A story written by
the reporter Marie Solis and published in 2021 contained an anecdote
that has stuck with me. Solis was interviewing Maya Raghu, senior
counsel at the National Law Center, about the challenges of prosecuting domestic abuse cases. Raghu told the story of how one woman's
abuser would leave flowers and gifts on her car while she was at work.
While coworkers were charmed by his thoughtfulness and generosity,
the woman knew better: The gifts were a message that, no matter
where she was, he would always be able to get to her. While the story
is bone chilling, there's a basic problem, too—convincing others that
gifts and flowers are part of coercive control. In his book, Stark uses
another example of an abusive partner bringing his woman a sweatshirt when she'd performed well in her sport; while, on the surface, this
looks like a kind gesture, in context this was code for her to cover up,
since she was violating his rule not to make him jealous by appearing
attractive to other men.

But the proof of the pudding, as they say, is in the tasting, so let's
look at places where coercive control has been criminalized. So far,
what has happened isn't what proponents had hoped for. An article by
Julia R. Tolmie, a professor of law in New Zealand, lays out some of
the difficulties. She makes it clear that it's not the first time that efforts
have been made to identify patterns of harm—such as stalking—in
contrast to the one-time events that tend to define intimate partner
violence (IPV). But, Tolmie points out, prosecuting coercive control
requires a nuanced factual analysis—remember the examples of the
gifts left on the car and the sweatshirt—that may be elusive in a court
setting. As Tolmie writes, "Appreciating the harms of coercive control requires a focus not only on what the abusive partner has done,
but what the victim has been prevented from doing." Still, since the

context of the relationship is so important, the reliance on personal testimony to prosecute becomes even more so. She rightly points out that, while we all agree that physical violence is unacceptable, "it is not automatically unacceptable for the male partner to control a couple's finances, to hold joint property in their name, to make major life decisions on behalf of both, and to dislike and want to minimize contact with their in-laws." It obviously depends on many factors, all of them subtle in nature. With two sides arguing different points of view, how *do* you determine why the flowers and gifts were left on the car? A review by Evan Stark and Marianne Hester of laws in England, Wales, and Scotland also notes the problems of implementation.

I turned to Leigh Goodmark, Marjorie Cook Professor of Law and co-director of the Clinical Law Program at the University of Maryland Frances King Carey School of Law, for her thoughts on whether or not criminalizing coercive control was a good idea; her answer was straightforward and illuminating: "Because we have no reason to believe that criminalization decreases or deters intimate partner violence, adding any additional crime provides lawmakers with the illusion that they're 'doing something' about intimate partner violence without actually accomplishing anything. As to coercive control specifically, police are regularly failing to respond productively when there is clear physical violence; expecting them to do the kind of nuanced analysis necessary to determine that coercive control is happening is ridiculous. And there is good reason to fear that such laws would be used against survivors of violence, particularly because they include so many nonphysical forms of harm." Take a moment to appreciate that last sentence, too.

Given what we know about the court system and nonphysical abuse, I asked her how hard it would be to prove that coercive control had occurred. Once again, there is much to learn from her response: "Proving that coercive control is happening isn't hard so long as judges are willing to find survivors credible. Survivors can describe the various tactics that their partners have used to isolate and control them and limit their liberty and autonomy. But it's much harder to present physical evidence (photographs, etc.) of these kinds of tactics. And so these trials are likely to become 'he said/she said' affairs where judges throw up their hands and say they don't know whose testimony to credit. And proving that someone intended to coercively control their partner is much more difficult."

Once again, I'd argue that if the culture would acknowledge that verbal abuse isn't benign and is always about control, which is coercive in nature and highly damaging, there'd be greater clarity.

What's to Be Learned from the Tragic Case of Gabby Petito?

In the summer of 2021, both mainstream media and social media closely followed the case of a 22-year-old woman gone missing named Gabby Petito until the grisly unearthing of her remains in mid-September, when the focus shifted to locating her fiancé, who had apparently vanished. The mystery was deepened by the players themselves: the blond, pretty, and photogenic slip of a girl whose Instagram testified both to her ambitions and her joyfulness, and the taciturn fiancé, Brian Laundrie, who remained " a person of interest" for weeks after her disappearance and who refused to talk to police. The mystery and the speculation that accompanied the case came to an abrupt and shocking end with the 23-year old Laundrie's suicide (and confession), but that, too, contributed to the staying power of the story. The widely disparate behaviors of the parents of these two young adults drove interest as well: The Laundries, with whom the couple had lived, stonewalled police investigators and immediately lawyered up, in contrast to Gabby's divorced and both remarried father and mother, who stood solid together and tearfully pleaded for the public to help find their daughter.

What makes this story pertinent to our narrative is that the couple's life together, while ostensibly being conducted on a public stage, was also highly curated, most probably to shield a dark secret. Additionally, a run-in with police in Moab, Utah, on August 12, 2021—just 15 days before Gabby would call her mother, Nichole Schmidt, for the last time—illuminates many of the assumptions made about verbal abuse and domestic violence by police officers and ordinary people, as well as the continuing cultural struggle to deal with both.

An aspiring "influencer" in the world of van life—you might not know it, but there are many dozens of blogs on the joys of travel and nomadic life in a van—Gabby set off with Laundrie on July 2, 2021, to visit the national parks for what was supposed to be a monthslong trip and the launch of the vlog that she hoped would make her name. The first photos she posted to Instagram were idyllic, and she waxed poetic about the tiny camper that they shared but she owned. A scant six weeks later, a stranger's call to 911 in Moab and a statement by another witness brought the police into contact with the two. One important thing to know is that laws pertaining to domestic violence in Utah are highly specific and dictated by legislative action; one governing assumption is that the person who initiated and perpetrated the physical violence is considered the aggressor, regardless of gender or stature. That assumption—and unarticulated assumptions about relationships between young adults and the relative mental health of each member of the couple made by officers on the spot—made it unlikely the abusive pattern in the relationship would be revealed.

We cannot know whether Gabby would have been spared being another domestic violence statistic if things had played out differently, but a detailed investigation was released in January of 2022 by the Moab Police Department, written by Captain Brandon Ratcliffe, which made an effort to answer the question. I have drawn details from this more than 100-page document, along with released police bodycam videos and news reports.

The police got involved when they received a 911 call describing a man slapping a woman on the street, in broad daylight, outside a café. The caller described how the two people ran up and down the sidewalk and then hopped into a white van; he was able to identify both the make of the van and the license plate number. A second witness described an altercation between a man and a woman that involved the man grabbing a phone from the woman, locking her out of the van, some mutual shoving and pushing. and then the woman climbing through the driver's window, over the man and into the passenger seat. The witness heard Gabby say, "Why do you have to be so mean?" He was unsure of what was going on—was it some kind of trafficking situation, he wondered—but as he put it in his statement, "from my point of view, something did not seem quite right." A call went out over the police radio, and police located and then pulled up behind the van with their lights and sirens on; with Laundrie at the wheel, the van swerved from one lane to another and ended up hitting the curb. What happened next is both bewildering and understandable at once.

As the investigator noted, despite the 911 call and witness statement, the officers seemed to forget that Laundrie was the man a 911 caller described as slapping a woman and were focused on the van crossing lanes and hitting the curb; they wanted to know if the driver was drunk. He wasn't, but their questioning led Gabby to admit that Laundrie hit the curb because she hit him in the shoulder. That, under Utah law—once the reported incidents about the guy hitting the girl were somehow forgotten—made Gabby the instigator of violence, and if anyone was going to jail, it would be she. And then, as Captain Brandon Ratcliffe pointed out, the "confirmation bias" kicked in. I find it interesting that he uses a psychological term—referring to the bias in human thinking to tailor facts and information to fit what we already know and think—to describe their responses from this point forward.

And that is precisely what happened; everything they did and didn't do pertained to the narrative of Laundrie as the victim and Gabby as the aggressor. They photographed Brian's "injuries," but despite the visible mark on Gabby's face, which was the result of Brian's grabbing it, they took none of her. They passed judgment on Gabby's weeping and difficulty speaking because of how upset she was but made no note of the cool-as-a-cucumber demeanor of the young man who was comfortable enough to make jokes. She sat alone in an air-conditioned police car so that she could "calm down," talking to her mother as she was being questioned, while Brian was outside in the sun, chatting.

The way in which this incident derailed tells us a great deal about how police officers aren't, on the one hand, trained to "read" interpersonal dynamics but believe that they are doing it with skill, on the other. The report reveals what triggered this fight, which was Brian's telling Gabby that she was going to fail at the vlog, but none of that registered. Between their take on the two (she's got "mental" issues, and he doesn't) and their problem with the specificity of the Utah law as written (the girl was tiny and didn't seem to pose a physical threat to the guy, who seemed older and more mature, and besides, the guy didn't want her to go to jail), the officers scrambled for some way of dealing that didn't include jailing Gabby and forcing the two through the system. They called around for advice on the law (and read the statute the way they want it to read, which is another good example of the confirmation bias at work), all the while guided by their "take" on the situation. Ultimately, they decided to separate the two for the night and find Brian lodging, cited her for disorderly conduct, and that was that. There was no follow-up, no mental health recommendation, no nothing.

What we know now is that, five days later, Laundrie flew back to Florida "to deal with things" on August 17, as his parents' lawyer revealed, and left Gabby in Utah. He returned on August 23, and three days later, she spoke to her mother for the last time. On September 1, Laundrie pulled into his parents' driveway in the white van without Gabby. He went camping with his parents the following week. Gabby's parents reported her missing on September 11, and her body was found ten days later. Laundrie disappeared September 17, prompting a search that would only end with the discovery of remains identified as his on October 20. The mystery was over.

Domestic violence, as well as the verbal abuse that precedes it, is often only confirmed in 20/20 hindsight, as it was in this case, and the investigative report does its very best to make that point when the Utah police stop became a focal point. In the conclusion to his report, Captain Ratcliffe states that it was very likely that Gabby "was a long-term victim of domestic violence, whether that be physically, mentally and/or emotionally." He rightly points out Laundrie's denigration of her efforts to make a success of herself, how he tried to control her physically and emotionally by mocking her, grabbing her phone, locking her out of the van, insisting that she "calm down." (He basically gaslights her when he talks to the officers about her "crazy" behavior, so it's likely he did that regularly.) In her book *No Visible Bruises*, Rachel

Louise Snyder points out that strangulation is the method of choice for abusers who wish to subdue; the area around the throat also often doesn't display "visible bruises" and is known to be a key predictor of more violence to come. It is not an accident that Gabby died of strangulation.

But the narrative isn't over because Gabby's parents sued the Laundries on March 11, 2022, in the state of Florida, seeking damages in excess of $30,000. The lawsuit filed reads like a public airing of how despicably the Laundries behaved and is clearly meant as a form of redress, since the murderer took his own life. In it, Joseph Petito and Nichole Schmidt assert that Brian confessed to his parents that he'd killed Gabby on August 28 and that they then hired an attorney. They detail how Brian used Gabby's cell phone to text her mother to convince Nichole that Gabby was alive when she wasn't. Even though the two sets of parents had had a cordial relationship, they note that, on September 10, Roberta Laundrie blocked Nichole Schmidt on her cell phone and Facebook so that direct communication was impossible; the Laundries only issued statements through their attorney. The text of the complaint makes it clear that Gabby's parents are on a moral mission and perhaps not a legal one; they accuse the Laundries of being unwilling to alleviate their suffering, since they knew not only that Gabby was dead but also where her remains were. In the same vein, they accused the Laundries of acting "beyond the bounds of common decency" and, through their "willfulness and maliciousness" caused the plaintiffs to experience "pain and suffering, mental anguish, inconvenience, loss of capacity for the enjoyment of life experienced in the past and to be experienced in the future." As this book went into production, Circuit Court Judge Hunter Caroll cleared the way for the lawsuit to proceed. Additionally, on August 9, 2022, her parents filed a notice of claim against the Moab. Utah Police Department over its handling of the incident.

I'm not a lawyer but I don't blame them one bit.

In the end, the case of Gabby Petito illuminated many things, including the deficiencies in our system and culture. And while the Utah laws are politically correct—yes, men can be victims of domestic violence, too—they oversimplify and ignore the fact that long-term victims may, in the moment, become aggressive, but that doesn't change the underlying pattern. It is always a matter of who has the upper hand and the power.

Verbal Abuse in the Workplace: What's HR Gonna Do About It?

Since workplaces tend to be organized by hierarchy, and the distribution of power is, by definition, unequal, it's not precisely surprising, given our inquiry, that verbal abuse finds fertile ground there—whether it's high in an office tower, in the aisles of a supermarket, in a restaurant, or on the floors of a hospital or school. Often, the tone is set by the "boss"—that is how corporate or work cultures evolve—and it's up to the individual worker to draw a line in the sand when it comes to verbal abuse, or not. I know what you're thinking: Wait, it's someone's livelihood, and it's not easy to draw that line, and there are repercussions like bad references, and maybe the person in question won't find a job that's any better, or maybe he or she just can't afford financially to take the risk. Of course, the verbal abuser knows all of that, and it gives him or her an edge.

That said, just as those who grew up with verbal abuse and normalized it are more likely to find themselves in other verbally abusive intimate relationships as adults, these people are also more likely to normalize verbal abuse in the workplace. That became clear to me some years ago when I was interviewing people for my book *Mastering the Art of Quitting*; Carolyn's story is one that still stands out. Raised in the Midwest, where she also attended college, Carolyn came to New York City with high hopes of becoming a professional photographer. She landed a job as the receptionist in the studio of a very famous and well-regarded female photographer and was thrilled when, two years later, she was promoted to become her assistant. Mind you, this photographer was also renowned for how she dressed people down for every mishap and for the high turnover of employees. The photographer was brilliant but also hot-tempered and nasty. It didn't take long for her to put Carolyn in a no-win situation: While she would berate Carolyn for being lazy and not taking enough initiative, she'd also complain that Carolyn was being "territorial" or "not respecting boundaries" when she did take initiative. Carolyn felt emotionally beaten up, and everyone, from her friends to her colleagues, counseled her to quit. But she kept thinking that if she hung on and learned more about her craft—the photographer had much to teach her, she said, over and over, despite her abuse— she'd be in better shape, so another year passed, some 300 days of misery and upset. It was her sister's visit to the studio that fourth year that finally proved to be the tipping point. The photographer screamed at Carolyn for setting up the lights incorrectly, even though she had dictated their placement; Carolyn dissolved into a puddle of apologies as her boss railed and called her worthless. After they left the studio, her sister, Lydia, commented that the photographer reminded her of their father and his rants and how Carolyn used to apologize and placate him just so he'd stop belittling her. That was the turning point for Carolyn. She prioritized getting the word out that she was available, and a few months later, another photographer—a longtime competitor of the boss—offered her a job, and she went for it.

How Common Is Verbal Abuse in the Workplace?

It's very common, which hardly ranks as the surprise of the century. One study, published in 2007, by Pamela Lutgen-Sandvik, Sarah J. Tracy, and Jess K. Alberts looked specifically at workplace bullying. With 469 participants and using a very tight definition of bullying ("at least two negative acts, weekly or more often, for six or more months in situations where targets find it difficult to defend against and stop abuse"), the researchers set out to establish a prevalence for bullying in the United States and to compare that to the prevalence discovered by researchers in Scandinavian countries. The 22 situations participants identified as having experienced ranged from "had information withheld that affected your performance," "reminded repeatedly of your errors and mistakes," "had insulting/offensive remarks made about you," "subject to excessive teasing and sarcasm," and the like. In fact, 48.6 percent of the Americans surveyed reported one negative act per week over the previous six months, compared with 15.8 percent of Danish workers and 24.1 percent of Finnish workers. Twenty-eight percent reported two negative acts per week for the previous six months, which the researchers identified as evidence of being bullied. One thing that the researchers flagged as surprising—which won't be surprising to my readers, since we've seen this pattern in other studies—was that only one-third of those whom the researchers identified as being bullied actually identified as having been targets; as the authors write, "This suggests that although U.S. workers in this study reported persistent negativity in the workplace, they did not always equate that negativity with the concept of *bullying*." This is a function of what we have called "normalizing" verbal abuse; in the authors' words: ". . . it could be that respondents have naturalized bullying as a normal part of the job . . ."

While precise statistics on what I am calling verbal abuse in the workplace vary, there's consensus that it is remarkably widespread and that, while it is more systemic in certain professions such as nursing, there's also no industry or workplace that is exempt. Part of the problem is terminology because, as we've seen with the terms "emotional abuse," "coercive control," and "parental alienation," how toxic or unacceptable workplace behavior is defined matters enormously. And there's no agreed-upon definition when it comes to the workplace. While some, such as Pamela Lutgen-Sandvik, have argued for a universal term (in her case, she advocated for "employee emotional abuse"), it is variously called bullying, mobbing (in the United Kingdom and elsewhere), and emotional harassment, among other terms. Unlike the term "sexual harassment," which has acquired a tight legal definition and which organizations have learned to respond to and deal with, there is no agreed-upon term or definition when it comes to the complex of behaviors I have called "verbal abuse" in these pages.

This isn't a new problem; the rise of verbal abuse and incivility in the workplace began to ring bells in the research community in the 1990s, and the cultural developments since—especially technological changes—have certainly amped up the volume. (Not answering someone's phone calls in the 1990s was really aggressive and out there; ghosting someone on email doesn't work up a sweat.) In one study, published in 2005, Christine M. Pearson and Christine L. Porath looked at the cost to organizations (high in terms of employee turnover, productivity, and performance plus a decline in job satisfaction and loyalty) and found that, unsurprisingly, people with greater power "have more ways to be uncivil and get away with it." They found significant gender differences in how men and women responded to incivility. They discovered that male targets were more likely to go mano-a-mano with instigators and give back tit for tat, whereas a female target would more likely try to avoid the instigator and put distance between them. Women were also more likely to confide in those outside of the organization about the situation—friends and family—than in those within it. But none of this meant that women played the role of the sacrificial lamb; they noted that, "although women do not tend to respond with overt, immediate payback, the incident does not necessarily go unrequited. Instead, we found that female targets will tend to reinforce their support, regain their balance, and recoup their strength so that they are ready to take recourse when the best opportunity arises." It's noteworthy that, of those workers targeted, only a quarter of them were satisfied with how the organization responded.

Another study conducted in 2010 by William Martin and Helen LaVan looked at litigated cases of workplace bullying in the United States; their method was to pull a random sample of 45 cases to see if they could find discernible patterns. What they found is, on one level, unsurprising but also sobering. Again, they, too, noted the lack of cultural and legal agreement on what precisely constitutes workplace bullying—the same problem we've seen on both a personal level and a social/cultural one. Drawing from various theorists, they used a combination of defining characteristics, including an imbalance of power and frequency and persistence of mistreatment. Their inquiry yielded some pertinent observations. First, of the cases, close to 74 percent were won by the employer, who was the defendant! Second, bullying often dovetailed with other legal issues, such as race, gender, and country of origin discrimination, which are actually covered by law; that's not surprising but still of interest. Close to two out of three cases occurred in the public sector, and of those, 60 percent were in the service sector (and just under 28 percent of them in schools). Men were more likely to be both the bully instigator (73.3 percent) and the victim (55.5 percent). Of interest, too, were what the researchers detailed as the "enabling structures" that facilitated workplace bullying; the highest ranking were perceived status incongruence/power imbalance (84 percent), low perceived costs to the perpetrator (64.4 percent), lack of policy against bullying (64.4 percent), and lack of punishment (53.3 percent). In contrast, bullying as a rite of passage was not seen as enabling (2.2 percent).

What their study brought home to me—these were court cases, and almost 74 percent of them were at the district level—is how the cultural and social blurriness about verbal abuse amplifies personal hesitation to label mistreatment and incentivizes normalizing on the part of victims. And the blurriness puts the organization in the catbird's seat, just as it does the controller and abuser in a personal relationship, especially in both a court of law and that of public opinion.

When Verbal Abuse Is Endemic in a Profession

In researching this book, nothing was as surprising as discovering that nursing is, hands down, the winner of the prize given to the profession most beset by verbal abuse. The amount of scholarly research is voluminous and has been conducted in countries as various as the United States, Korea, the United Kingdom, Greece, Norway, and Iran, to name a few. I found the research deeply ironic, since, having grown up at a time when books about female heroes were few and far between, I devoured the series Cherry Ames, Student Nurse and read everything I could about Florence Nightingale. For a profession devoted to caretaking, the contemporary portrait of how nurses treat one another is nothing like what I imagined in my girlhood. Cole Edmonson and Caroline Zelonka's first sentence in a 2019 article entitled "Our Own Worst Enemies: The Nurse Bullying Epidemic" is this: "Nurses in the profession call it 'eating our young.'" Think about that for a moment. What's amazing is that the findings are so robust and consistent everywhere in the world.

Edmunson and Zelonka's recitation of the facts, all drawn from research, is profoundly distressing. A study showed that 78 percent of students experienced bullying in nursing school. In their first clinical rotations, over half of nursing students witnessed or experienced nurse-on-nurse bullying. Sixty percent of nurses leave their first jobs within six months because of coworkers' behavior. And, it turns out, being high up on the totem pole doesn't exempt you from bullying if you are a nurse; a 2018 study of managers, directors, and executives found that 60 percent of them had experienced bullying (and 26 percent of those called it "severe"). All the forms of what we have called verbal abuse—both overt and covert, such as exclusion and gossip—are duly noted by the authors as being prevalent. If you believe that, as someone who's not in the medical field, this doesn't affect all of us, think again. Consider yourself or a loved one as a patient and then read what the authors, both nurses, have to say: "Bullying sacrifices an organization's ability to achieve consistent, high-quality outcomes with high-reliability science. It is not possible to achieve the goal of high reliability in health care in [an] environment that permits or promotes bullying."

That pretty much says it all.

A Forward Glance

While neither complete nor encyclopedic, this chapter does give you a sense of the hidden cost of verbal abuse to individuals, society, and the culture at large and how both our tolerance of verbal abuse and our inability to define it with meaningful precision cause all manner of damage.

It is time for a wake-up call.

Chapter Seven

Looking Forward:
Boundaries and Understanding

I don't think there's any question that verbal abuse has permeated the culture in ways that are regrettable and that influence all of us in both subtle and not-so-subtle ways. Culturally, a significant percentage of us have mislabeled types of verbal abuse—calling someone derogatory names, shaming them, mocking someone with disabilities—as being "brash" or "contrarian" or "not pulling any punches" or "direct and forthright" when uttered in the political arena by powerful politicians, and yes, the currents flow down from the top in every setting. Celebrities have had to turn off comments so as to self-protect themselves from a firestorm of verbal abuse bouncing around social media. More mundanely, PsychologyToday.com, for which I have written for a decade, used to have a comments section on posts, which often yielded vibrant dialogue and insight and it was shut down in 2021 because of abuse and spam. The trolls who used to live under bridges in fairytales have been reinvented in the age of social media, half-hidden by anonymity or a fake name, and as a society we have indulged them personally while the technology companies who have the power to shut them down have ignored them for reasons both valiant (free speech) and spurious (see below).

Take the slander websites, for example, which have flourished over the years; these websites solicit unverified information about supposed cheaters, sexual predators, scammers, and deadbeats along with those people's names. Yes, the tips are all anonymous, which is a perfect set-up for the abuser. Google the name of the subject of that supposed tip or reveal and, indeed, this information floats to the very top of a Google search. For years, Google considered its search engine algorithm inviolate—it took the position that the results were the results and they yielded what they yielded—so the hapless victim of the anonymous smear would have no way of getting rid of the slander other than by paying the website off or hiring a firm that dealt with reputation defense. As it turns out, an investigative report in *The New York Times* by Aaron Krolik and Kashmir Hill in April of 2021 revealed that the slander industry was the Internet's version of the three-card monte scam; some of the slander websites and the reputation-cleaner-uppers were actually owned and operated by the same people, so the victim would be enriching the perpetrator in his or her role as the "fixer." And it cost very serious money—thousands and thousands of dollars! How did Krolik discover this? He slandered himself by posting a comment—"Adam Krolik New York is an unqualified loser" and a selfie that was less than flattering—and then watched the information proliferate on the Internet like an algae bloom. Finally, in June 2021, *The New York Times* reported that Google was springing into action to suppress that content.

But incivility and verbal abuse aren't just limited to cyberspace, of course. Sports "fans" have been banned from arenas for verbally abusing players, apparently thinking that the price of entry entitles them to say whatever they want. None of this is new, but the uptick in incidents in 2021—after the pandemic effectively shut down sports in 2020—was widely reported. Of course, the pandemic wasn't the cause of the behavior; it just added some fuel to an already burning fire of indulgence.

It is time we each take a stand—in our personal, professional, and civic lives—to stop the indulgence. If we do so collectively, on all fronts, it will reform the cultural confusion about what verbal abuse looks like. Finally, we will be able to see the face of verbal abuse.

There are two absolute truths to keep in mind. The first is that verbal abuse is *never* okay. The operative word in that sentence is "never." It doesn't matter whether the person saying the words is wearing Chanel or a bespoke suit or sweats or a ratty old tee shirt. How powerful that person is in your life changes absolutely nothing about this truth; knowing the truth, it's incumbent on you to figure out how to get out of that person's orbit. It also doesn't matter whether that person is highly educated or never finished high school; having facility with words or lacking it changes nothing. Verbal abuse permeates every social class, is as prevalent in a trailer park as it is on Park Avenue, and can be experienced in a steel-and-glass corporate aerie, in the aisles of a grocery store or bodega, or on the floor of a manufacturing plant. Incivility—believing that you have the right to denigrate someone or try to shame them by calling them names—is an engraved invitation to have the very worst version of yourself show up. And playing tit-for-tat when it comes to verbal abuse doesn't excuse you either because there are other and better ways to defend yourself. One of them is heading for the exit.

The second truth is that verbal abuse is meant to damage, and it does. How much damage it does depends on a number of factors, including your age at the time the abuse is rained upon you and the importance of the abuser to you, your life, and your world. Childhood is clearly the most vulnerable time, and as we've seen, it sets up the child's adult self for a variety of complex responses—none of them good—to verbal abuse in the future. But this doesn't render anyone who has been the target of verbal abuse as a child helpless or without recourse; there is much that can be done once one realizes that normalizing abuse or placating one's abuser only empowers him or her and disempowers the target. That is true of intimate relationships as well as those that play out in the workplace and outer world. Since this is a controller's power game, your strategy must be to regain your power.

In these final pages, let's nail the Jell-o to the wall on the "sticks and stones" thing. Believing that words don't hurt or matter makes it clear that anyone who thinks so is both on the side of bullies *and* is also a dope, since this book is packed with enough science to sink a battleship full of deniers. Keep that in mind when you confront an abuser because your efforts to educate will likely fail on both fronts. And if you're thinking about fighting back in kind, ask yourself whether you want to be a dope. Really.

The high road is the best road when it comes to verbal abuse. It's a club you don't want to join.

Setting Boundaries and Being Linguistically Aware

I am putting my ballet flats on my soapbox here, so get ready. Setting boundaries is the best defense against verbal abuse, along with a policy of zero tolerance. Having zero tolerance means being absolutely positive about one thing: You are worthy of having your boundaries and integrity as a human being respected.

Think about the word "worthy" for a moment. It means being of value, and my position is that worthiness is bestowed upon you at the moment of birth. It isn't earned or paid for, nor is it bestowed upon you by another person; it is yours the second you take your first breath. If you actually believe that—and recognize it as an inalienable truth—then you will not need to be convinced that *no one* has the right to marginalize, denigrate, ignore, stonewall, belittle, or scapegoat you. Yes, the operative words are "no one." "No one" includes close relatives, spouses and partners, people with whom you are close and people with whom you're not, employers, and passersby. But embracing the idea of "worthy" as a birthright and "worthiness" as automatic is more of a social contract than not. If I know that I am worthy of being treated respectfully simply because I am a human being—again, this is neither earned nor conveyed by someone else—then I have to embrace and accept that everyone else is worthy of decent and civil treatment and that verbal abuse is *never* okay. That means that all the justifications for verbal abuse we've seen in this book—including discipline, supposedly "helpful" criticism, a way of making sure someone doesn't get too headstrong or full of him- or herself, tough love, and the like—are off the table.

Part of setting boundaries and believing that you are worthy entails committing to the worthiness of others, too, and that, in turn, means a commitment to using language selectively and sensitively and becoming a good steward of your own words. Taking responsibility for the words you use, especially if you are speaking to someone who depends on you in one way or another, is paramount.

Understanding Metamessages

Words are weaponized when they are deliberately hurtful or insulting. Sometimes they are transparent; when someone calls you "an ugly, stupid pig," we don't need to dispute meaning or intention. But a great deal of verbal manipulation is more subtle than this example, and this is where metamessages come in. It's not the literal words themselves that aim to hurt, as Deborah Tannen explains in her book *You're Wearing THAT?* but the message they deliver. Say the title without emphasizing "that" and then say it again, giving the last word a nasty spin, as intended. That's a metamessage as delivered by a mother to her daughter in Tannen's example. It's how and why words are uttered that matter; motive and intention push them beyond their literal meaning. Our emotional histories with the speaker shape the metamessages we hear; those same emotional histories inform the speaker's words as well. Take Tannen's title and add a few words—"You're wearing that? I thought we'd decided to go casual"—and the question loses its toxic spin. Metamessages are conveyed through facial and body language, emphasis, and tone and are informed by the nature of the relationship between the speaker and the listener. In a healthy relationship between a mother and daughter, the question that is Tannen's title, without its italics, is nothing more than an unremarkable question said in the moment.

Words become weapons for both linguistic and psychological reasons. Many years ago, I had a professor at Columbia University who was so gifted at taking students down verbally that it was said his wit was rapier swift and you didn't even know what happened until you saw the blood. But it wasn't "wit," of course, but verbal abuse, and why a world-renowned authority and bestselling author needed to humiliate his students is a psychological matter and about the maintenance of control, as we've discussed in these pages. But this guy—and other women and men like him—who like flaunting their power aren't everyone. There are those who are linguistically sloppy and thoughtless, and they may convey messages and metamessages they don't intend and sometimes pay the price. These folks are essentially well-meaning and are appropriately contrite when they're called out. There are also the linguistic slobs who let words tumble out of their mouths with nary a consideration, filter, censor, or brakes; it's up to the listener to determine their intent. Sometimes they just like hearing themselves talk, but sometimes, their intent is malignant.

So, think about metamessages and pony up to some honesty and ask yourself the following questions. Think of this as an exercise, not a test or a judgment, because you'll assess your skills more honestly.

- How skilled do you think you are at using your words the way you intend?

- When you've decided to make an important statement—it might be to a child, a spouse or partner, or an employee or colleague— have you checked your own vitals first? Are you calm or reactive or vindictive?

- When you speak out, do you have a goal, or are you simply reacting and claiming territory?

- Are you thinking about the other person and his or her responses? Again, what is your goal?

- Do you sometimes use physical gestures or a specific tone of voice to make your points? Do you think of this as sending a metamessage?

- How conscious are you of the effect of your words? Do you ever see that you need to put on the brakes or simply stop? Again, be honest with yourself.

Metamessages (and Subtexts) in Action

Becoming consciously aware of how you use words and getting used to taking responsibility may take a bit of practice. Again, while most of us aren't verbally abusive as a rule, we may cross the line at moments, either unwittingly or deliberately when we're piqued or angry. The goal here is to be consciously aware of your linguistic behavior so that you're in control of the words you use.

Take a look at these examples I've assembled—offered up in a thoroughly unscientific way—and ask yourself: Have I ever said this or something like it? If so, why was I saying it? Have I been the javelin thrower or on the receiving end?

- "I'm finally done with the project. I'm thrilled."
"At least you got something done for once."
A withering put-down that turns the speaker's joy into an opportunity to hurt and criticize. It's even worse if uttered by a parent to a child.

- "I have something I want to show you/tell you that I'm happy about."
"Not now. Can't you see I'm busy? Whatever it is, it'll keep."
This dialogue is often reported by the adult children of detached parents or by spouses or partners. Yes, it's true enough that parents and even partners can't be available 24/7 and that sometimes they are busy, but here the intention is to marginalize the speaker and make him or her feel insignificant. Better answer? "Sure, give me ten minutes so I can finish what I am doing."

- "Let me do that for you."
"No, I'll do it. That way, it'll be done right."
Yes, no good offer of help goes unpunished. This type of dialogue appears with frequency in relationships that are very distressed, especially in marriages where the level of dissatisfaction is very high. It's a war of words associated with gatekeeping and territoriality, wherein one part of the dyad is intent on highlighting the other's deficiencies. If that person attempts a comeback of sorts, it's likely the conversation will devolve into what John Gottman has called "kitchen sinking"—a free-for-all catalogue of the speaker's every flaw.

- "I'm happy I got a B on that exam. I was terrified to take it."
"Your brother/sister/cousin/friend aced it, you know."

An example of the "let's rain on your parade" response. No, children do not find it inspirational, nor does it help them try harder the next time. They get the message, and it hurts.

- "We really need to talk about this."
"Again? I am so sick and tired of talking."
This is the demand/withdraw pattern in action—where one partner makes a request, even a reasonable one, and the other partner withdraws. In this case, the withdrawal is laced with aggression and contempt and marginalizes the speaker's intention. It is utterly defeating and highly damaging, and, as we have seen, one of the most destructive patterns in a relationship.

- "Should I wear the blue dress?"
"That? It makes you look even fatter."
No comment needed here. This is not flat-footed but intentionally abusive, and the kind of comment that needs to be singled out as deliberately cruel and completely unacceptable.

- "You hurt my feelings by saying that."
"You're just too sensitive. It meant nothing."
This is the classic blame-shift. Own up to your behavior if you want to be worthy. Note the use of "it" rather than "I," which further deflects the responsibility away from the person doing the talking, The toxicity of this response is impossible to understate.

- "I've decided on my science project."
"Talk to your dad. He'll know what you should do."
Alas, this response may not be intentionally marginalizing, but it does the work anyway. The metamessage or subtext is: "Your decision is most likely wrong, and you'll need guidance to make the right one." Even if offered "helpfully" by an overly involved or helicopter parent, it conveys the message that the child isn't capable of making a good choice. If this happens often enough, the child comes away thinking that he or she is deficient and incapable of succeeding on his or her own. That information becomes internalized and can be a self-fulfilling prophesy.

- "How are you?"

"Not good. Things have been really hard. I've been stressed and sleeping badly."

"Did I tell you what happened to me last week?"

This dialogue or one like it is the hallmark of the "Me! Me! Me!" person in your life, who's utterly self-involved and whose actual participation in what appears to be a conversation is limited to getting his or her own words heard. People like this are quite literally not interested in what you have to say, and their responses make that crystal clear. This pattern is merely annoying or par for the course if the person is an acquaintance or less; if the person is someone you actually feel close to or want to share intimacies with, it can be devastating. Coming from a parent or someone who you think cares about you and your welfare, it's beyond painful.

- "I'm so upset about what's been going on at home."

"Tell me about it. But you know, things could always be worse."

This is the standard response of someone lacking in empathy, who knows it's considered polite to listen but has no real emotional connection to you, the words you're saying, or the situation you're describing. The reference to even more dire circumstances sends the message that you are overreacting and that you and your travails aren't important. Additionally, there's a subtext that you should probably stop whining and deal. The irony here is that the respondent often mistakenly believes that what he or she is saying is for the benefit of the speaker. Actually, not. Simply listening without commentary is the worthy response.

Check your own sensitivity to these exchanges and ask yourself whether you've actually been in either position. Be a good steward of words because words matter.

How to Critique Helpfully and Not Hurtfully

Keep in mind that marital expert John Gottman makes the distinction between a "criticism" and a "complaint," and it's one worth keeping in mind. While the dictionary definition of "criticize" means to consider both the merits and demerits of someone or something,

its secondary meaning—to find fault with—has become the primary meaning colloquially, and that is what Gottman is focused on. As
we've already discussed (see page 56), a complaint is about a specific
behavior or action, while a criticism tends to sweep in the behavior as
indicative of the person's character.

It's true enough that, sometimes, critiquing someone constructively is both necessary and called for, but there's confusion about what
constructive criticism is and how to do it right. Let's address what is
and isn't. Criticism isn't punishment, payback, or retribution; if that's
in your mind, whether you are talking about a child, an intimate, or an
employee, you will certainly cross the line into abuse. But how to critique well? There's lots of lousy advice out there, one bit of which was
highly touted as a management tool and was familiarly called "the criticism sandwich." The idea here is that criticism, when "sandwiched"
between two statements of praise, would be more easily digested and
listened to by the person being criticized than a straightforward criticism without padding. Remember how the brain works in terms of
negative commentary—the whole "bad is stronger than good" thing?
Well, it's not exactly a surprise that when researchers Paul E. Madlock
and Carrie Kennedy-Lightsey actually compared the effects of positive mentoring in the workplace to negative communications, they
found that the influence of verbal aggression far outweighed the effects of positive mentoring. That is, of course, the problem with the
"criticism sandwich" because the brain is so busy decoding the negative ("Possible threat!" "You're going to get fired!") and putting it into
long memory that there's literally not enough cognitive power left to
register or store the positive. Once again, "bad is stronger than good."

So how to work around that? Well, the first thing is to make sure
that your best self is present when you deliver a complaint or critique,
not an angry or punitive self who wants to get someone to toe the line,
or an irritated self who is annoyed that this issue is coming up again.
Cool down and collect yourself before you venture out. Second, you
should know what you're going to say and, more important, how you
are going to say it. Remember that a constructive critique never hinges
on the personal; you are not addressing the person's character but his

or her actions or behaviors. (If you aim to criticize the person's character and you believe that he or she is unworthy of your attention, you should be delivering an exit speech, not a critique. And it should be short.) Don't just criticize someone's actions or behaviors and leave it at that, but offer alternatives that would have led to better outcomes for him or her and you. Remind the person that there were better ways of handling whatever it was and that the outcome would have been significantly improved if he or she had done X instead. Again, do pay attention to the response of the person you are critiquing, especially his or her body language; if the person is beginning to assume a defensive crouch, you should regroup.

Understanding Words and Power: What We All Can Do

I don't believe we can rid the world of verbal abuse—or incivility, for that matter—but when we bring our knowledge of how the imbalance of power underlies all forms of verbal abuse, we can take action in meaningful ways. More important, we can become good stewards of our own words and make sure that we spread the message and educate others.

We can each set boundaries on what we permit to be said to us and what we allow ourselves to say to others. We can pledge to call out verbal abuse in our workplaces, no matter what we do for a living, whether we are managers, bosses, or workers, no matter the setting. If we are parents, we can make sure that we model good behaviors for our children and that we call them out for being verbally abusive when it happens. We can pay attention to the techniques used by teachers, trainers, and other mentors in our children's lives and make sure that their methods do not include verbal abuse disguised as "inspiration" or "discipline."

Shall I say it again? Verbal abuse is *never* okay. Yes, the operative word is "never."

Acknowledgments

It's true enough that books get written in isolation, with a writer hunched over a computer and, in this case, surrounded by piles of research papers, books, and filled-out questionnaires from volunteers. Those male and female volunteers, each protected by a pseudonym, contributed their stories in answer to a callout on verbal abuse and to subsequent callouts on the various sub-topics in the book. I literally could not have written this book without you, so a huge thank-you to all! Then, too, there are my readers who contribute to a vibrant dialogue on my author Facebook page, which keeps me thinking new thoughts and, more important, finding new questions to answer. A huge *merci beaucoup* to all of you.

Two men, both psychologists and fellow bloggers at *Psychology Today* and now friends, are really the big players who read not only my first self-published book, *Daughter Detox*, but also this one. In alphabetical order, they are Dr. Joseph Burgo and Dr. Craig Malkin. They read my manuscript and they advised me to make changes, either because I didn't have it right or because I hadn't done it well enough. What can I say? I went to grad school in English Literature, and I bow in thanks to my mentors. Many, many *mercis*, my friends. That said, every mistake remaining in these pages is mine. Thanks, too, to fellow blogger Alli Spotts-De Lazzer for our conversations. Thank you to Professor Leigh Goodmark for her time and expertise.

I must say that this book took forever to write, although I admit that I have *never* been anywhere close to actually getting a book done in the time I originally allotted to it, and I want to thank friends who cheered me along the way: Joanne Almvig; Joseph Fournier (for giving me Long Beach and then Far Rockaway); Ray Healey, pal for half a century; Rich Kelley; Mary Kirkpatrick; Leslie Garisto Pfaff (a great friend of more than three decades, a terrific writer, and a superb co-pyeditor); Patti Pitcher, the mother I deserved; Warren Rej, for being half of The Children and for general advice on media and branding;

Claudia Karabaic Sargent, for being you, a great consigliere, and for a long history of fruitful collaboration; and Lori Stein, although the pandemic robbed me of the best omelets anywhere. A special thank-you to Callie Beaulieu, actress and narrator.

Thanks to the editors at *Psychology Today*—Kaja Perina, Lybi Ma, Gary Drevitch, and Tyler Woods—for the perch on their website and the company of bloggers; many parts of this book were first test-driven as blog posts. Thank you to the team of people who took a big pile of manuscript and turned it into a book, including Leslie Garisto Pfaff, Chris Berge at Berge Design, and Maria Fairchild.

Index of Key Words and Topics

The page numbers in **bold** indicate a primary definition or discussion.

References

Introduction

Baumeister, Roy, Ellen Bratslavsky, Catrin Finkenauer, and Kathleen D. Vohs. Bad Is Stronger than Good. *Review of General Psychology*, 2001, vol. 5(4), pp. 323-370.

Polcari, Ann, Karen Rabi, Elizabeth Bolger, and Martin H. Teicher. Parental Verbal Affection and Verbal Aggression in Childhood Differentially Influence Psychiatric Symptoms and Wellbeing in Young Adulthood. *Child Abuse & Neglect*, 2014, vol. 38(1), pp. 91-102.

Chapter One: The Face of Abuse: Myths and Facts

Barry, Robin A., and Erika Lawrence. "Don't Stand So Close to Me": An Attachment Perspective of Disengagement and Avoidance in Marriage. *Journal of Family Psychology*, 2013, vol. 27(3), pp. 564-494.

Casas, Juan F., Stephanie M. Weigel, Nikki R. Crick, Jamie M. Ostrov, et al. Early Parenting and Children's Relational and Physical Aggression in the Preschool and Home Contexts. *Journal of Applied Developmental Psychology*, 2006, vol. 27(3), pp. 209-227.

Caspi, Jonathan. *Sibling Aggression: Assessment and Treatment*. New York: Springer Publishing Company, 2012.

Crick, Nicki R., and Jennifer K. Grotpeter. Relational Aggression, Gender, and Social - Psychological Adjustment. *Child Development*, 1995, vol. 66, pp. 710-722.

Dickson, Daniel J., Brett Laursen, Olvia Valdes, and Häkan Stattin. Derisive Parenting Fosters Dysregulated Anger in Adolescent Children and Subsequent Difficulties with Peers. *Journal of Youth and Adolescence*, 2019, vol. 48, pp. 1567-1578.

Dunn, Judy, and Robert Plomin. *Separate Lives: Why Siblings Are So Different*. New York: Basic Books, 1990.

Finzi-Dottan, Ricky and Toby Karu. From Emotional Abuse in Childhood to Psychopathology in Adulthood: A Path Mediated by Immature Defense Mechanisms and Self-Esteem. *The Journal of Nervous and Mental Disease*, 2006, vol. 194, pp. 616-621.

Fischer, Agneta H., and Ira J. Roseman. Beat Them or Ban Them: The Characteristics and Social Functions of Anger and Contempt. *Journal of Personality and Social Psychology*, 2007, vol. 93(1), pp. 103-115.

Flanders, Joseph, Vanessa Leo, Daniel Paquette, Robert Pihl, and Jean Séguin. Rough-and-Tumble Play and the Regulation of Aggression: An Observational Study of Father-Child Play Dyads. *Aggressive Behavior*, 2009, vol. 35, pp. 285-295.

Gemmill, Gary. The Dynamics of Scapegoating in Small Groups, *Small Group Research*, 1989, vol. 20(4), pp. 406-418.

Gottman, John, and Julie Schwarz Gottman. Emotional Abuse Questionnaire. https://accesscm.org/wp-content/uploads/2013/03/Gottman-Emotional-Abuse-Questionare.pdf

Jacobson, Neil, and John Gottman. Gottman Emotional Abuse Questionnaire. https://www.fjcsafe.org/wp-content/uploads/2016/11/Emotional-Abuse-Questionnaire.pdf

Jensen, Alexander C., Shawn D. Whiteman, Karen L. Fingerman, and Kira S. Birditt. "Life Still Isn't Fair: Parental Differential Treatment of Young Adult Siblings. *Journal of Marriage and Family*, 2013, vol. 75(2), pp. 438-452.

Kawabata, Yoshito, Lenneke R. A. Alink, Wan-Ling Tseng, Marinus H. van Ijzendoorn, and Nicki R. Crick. Maternal and Paternal Parenting Styles Associated with Relational Aggression in Children and Adolescents: A Conceptual Analysis and Meta-Analytic Review. *Developmental Review*, 2011, vol. 32, pp. 240-278.

Malkin, Craig. *Rethinking Narcissism: The Secret to Recognizing and Coping with Narcissists*. New York: Harper Perennial, 2016.

Nelson, David A., Craig H. Hart, and Clyde C. Robinson. Relational and Physical Aggression of Preschool-Age Children: Peer Status Linkages Across Informants. *Early Education and Development*, 2006, vol. 16, pp. 115-130.

Papp. Lauren M., Chrystyna D. Kouros, and E. Mark Cummings. Demand-Withdraw Patterns in Marital Conflict in the Home. *Personal Relationships*, 2009, vol.16(2), pp. 285-300.

Pollack, William. *Real Boys: Rescuing Our Sons from the Myths of Boyhood*. New York: Henry Holt, 1998.

RAINN statistics: https://www.rainn.org/articles/child-sexual-abuse

Richmond, Melissa K., Clare M. Stocker, and Shauna L. Rienks. Longitudinal Associations Between Sibling Relationship Quality, Parental Differential Treatment, and Children's Adjustment. *Journal of Family Psychology*, 2005, vol. 19(4), pp. 550-559.

Rothschild, Zachary K., Mark J. Landau, Daniel Sullivan, and Lucas A Keefer. A Dual-Motive Model of Scapegoating: Displacing Blame to Reduce Guilt or Increase Control. *Journal of Personality and Social Psychology*, 2012, vol. 102(6), pp. 1148–1163.

Schrodt, Paul, Paul L. Witt, and Jenna R. Shimkowski. A Meta-Analytical Review of the Demand/Withdraw Pattern of Interaction and Its Associations with Individual, Relational, and Communicative Outcomes. *Communication Monographs*, 2014, vol. 81(1), pp. 27-58.

Simmons, Rachels. *Odd Girl Out: The Hidden Culture of Aggression in Girls*. Orlando: Harvest/Harcourt, Inc., 2002.

Snyder, Rachel Louise. *No Visible Bruises: What We Don't Know About Domestic Violence Can Kill Us*. New York: Bloomsbury Publishing, 2019.

Tippet, Neil, and Dieter Wolke. Aggression Between Siblings: Associations with the Home Environment and Peer Bullying. *Aggressive Behavior*, 2015, vol. 41(1), pp. 14-24.

Tronick, Edward Z. Emotions and Emotional Communication in Infants. *American Psychologist*, 1989, vol. 44, pp. 112-126.

Tronick, Edward, Heidelise Als, Lauren Adamson, Susan Wise, and T. Berry Brazelton. The Infant's Response to Entrapment Between Contradictory Messages in Face-to-Face Interaction. *Pediatrics*, 1978, vol. 17(1), pp. 1-13.

Whiteman, Shawn D., Susan M. McHale, and Anna Soli. Theoretical Perspectives on Sibling Relationships. *Journal of Family Theory & Review*, 2011, vol. 3(2), pp. 124-139.

Wiseman, Rosalind. *Queen Bees & Wannabees: Helping Your Daughter Survive Cliques, Gossip, Boyfriends, and Other Realities of Adolescence*. New York: Three Rivers Press, 2002.

Wolke, Dieter, and Alexandra J. Skew. Bullying Among Siblings. *International Journal of Adolescent Medicine and Health*, 2012, vol. 24(1), pp. 17-25.

Chapter Two: What Science Knows

Adolphs, Ralph, Simon Baron-Cohen, and Daniel Tranel. Impaired Recognition of Social Emotions Following Amygdala Damage. *Journal of Cognitive Neuroscience*, 2002, vol. 14(8), pp. 1274-1284.

Ainsworth, Mary D. Salter, Mary C. Blehar, Everett Waters, and Sally N. Wall. *Patterns of Attachment: A Psychological Study of the Strange Situation*. Hillsdale, N.J.: Lawrence Erlbaum Associates, 1978.

Badawy, Rebecca L., Brooke A. Gazdag, Jeffrey R. Bentley, and Robyn L. Brouer. Are All Imposters Created Equal? Exploring Gender Differences in the Imposter Phenomenon-Performance Link. *Personality and Individual Differences*, 2018, vol. 131, pp. 156-163.

Bartholomew, Kim, and Leonard M. Horowitz. Attachment Styles Among Young Adults: A Test of a Four-Category Model. *Journal of Personality and Social Psychology*, 1991, vol. 61(2), pp. 226-244.

Bowlby, John. *Attachment and Loss, Volume 1*. New York: Basic Books, 1969.

Bowlby, John, *Attachment and Loss, Volume 2: Separation, Anxiety and Anger*. New York: Basic Books, 1973.

Cassidy, Jude, and Phillip R. Shaver, eds. *Handbook of Attachment: Theory, Research, and Clinical Applications*. Second edition. New York: Guilford Press, 2008.

Choi, Jeewook, Bumseok Jeong, Michael L. Rohan, Ann M. Polcari, and Martin H. Teicher. Preliminary Evidence for White Matter Tract Abnormalities in Young Adults Exposed to Parental Verbal Abuse. *Biological Psychiatry*, 2009, vol. 65(3), pp. 227-34.

Clance, Pauline Rose, and Suzanne Imes. The Imposter Phenomenon in High Achieving Women: Dynamics and Therapeutic Intervention. *Psychotherapy: Theory, Research & Practice*, 1978, vol. 15(3), pp. 241-247

Derntl, Birgit, Ute Habel, Christian Windischberger, et al. General and Specific Responsiveness of the Amygdala During Explicit Emotion Recognition in Females and Males. *BMC Neuroscience*, 2009, 10:91 DOI: 10.1186/1471-2202-10-91.

Irving, Shalon M., and Kenneth F. Ferraro. Reports of Abusive Experiences During Childhood and Adult Health Ratings: Personal Control as a Pathway? *Journal of Aging and Health*, 2006, vol. 18(3), pp. 458-485.

Komori, Kaori, Masahiro Komori, Masamitsu Eitoku, et al. Verbal Abuse During Pregnancy Increases Frequency of Newborn Hearing Screening Referral: The Japan Environment and Children's Study. *Child Abuse & Neglect*, 2019, vol. 90, pp. 193-201.

Langford, Joe, and Pauline Rose Clance. The Imposter Phenomenon: Recent Research Findings Regarding Dynamics, Personality and Family Patterns and Their Implications for Treatment. *Psychotherapy*, 1993, vol. 30(3), pp. 495-501.

LeDoux, Joseph. The Emotional Brain, Fear, and the Amygdala. *Cellular and Molecular Neurobiology*, 2003, vol. 23(4/5), pp. 727-738.

Lee, Sang Won, Jeewook Choi, Jong-Sun Lee, Jae Hyun Yoo, Ko Woon Kim, Dongchan Kim, HyunWook Park, and Bumseok Jeong. Altered Function of Ventrolateral Prefrontal Cortex in Adolescents with Peer Verbal Abuse History. *Psychiatry Investigation*, 2017, vol. 14(4), pp. 441-451.

Lee, Sang Won, Jae Hyun Yoo, Ko Woon Kim, Dongchan Kim, HyunWook Park, Jeewook Choi, Martin H Teicher, and Bumseok Jeong, Hippocampal Subfields Volume Reduction in High Schoolers with Previous Verbal Abuse Experiences. *Clinical Psychopharmacology and Neuroscience*, 2018, vol. 16(1), pp. 46-56.

Nelson, Charles A.. Incidental Findings in Magnetic Resonance (MRI) Research. *Journal of Law, Medicine, and Ethics*, 2008, vol. 36(2), pp. 315-319.

Pechtel, Pia, Karlen Lyons-Ruth, Carl M. Anderson, and Martin H. Teicher. Sensitive Periods of Amygdala Development: The Role of Maltreatment in Preadolescence. *Neuroimage*, 2014, vol. 97, pp. 236-244.

Polcari, Ann, Keren Rabi, Elizabeth Bolger, and Martin H. Teicher. Parental Verbal Affection and Verbal Aggression in Childhood Differentially Influence Psychiatric Symptoms and Wellbeing in Young Adulthood. *Childhood Abuse and Neglect*, 2014, vol. 38(1), pp. 99-102.

Rohrmann, Sonja, Myriam N. Bechtoldt, and Mona Leonhardt. Validation of the Imposter Phenomenon Among Managers., *Frontiers in Psychology*, 2016, vol. 7, p. 821. http://doi.org/10.3389/fpsyg.2016.00821

Schore, Allan N. Attachment and the Regulation of the Right Brain. *Attachment and Human Development*, 2000, vol. 2(1), pp. 23-47.

Schore, Allan N. Relational Trauma and the Developing Right Brain: An Interface of Psychoanalytic Self Psychology and Neuroscience. *Annals of the New York Academy of Science*, 2009, pp. 1-15.

Schore, Judith R., and Allan N. Schore. Modern Attachment Theory: The Central Role of Affect Regulation in Development and Treatment. *Clinical Social Work Journal*, 2008, vol. 36, pp. 9-20.

Syme, Kristen L., and Edward H. Hagen. Mental Health Is Biological Health: Why Tackling "Diseases of the Mind" Is an Imperative for Biological Anthropology in the 21st Century. *American Journal of Physical Anthropology*, 2019, vol. 171, pp. 87–117.

Teicher, Martin H., Carl M. Anderson, Jacqueline A. Samson, and Kyoko Ohashi. The Effects of Childhood Maltreatment on Brain Structure, Function and Connectivity. *Nature Reviews Neuroscience*, 2016, vol. 16, pp. 652-666.

Teicher, Martin H., and Jacqueline A. Samson. Annual Research Review: Enduring Neurobiological Effects of Childhood Abuse and Neglect. *Journal of Child Psychology and Psychiatry*, 2016, vol. 57(3), pp. 241-266.

Tomoda, Akimi, et. al. Exposure to Parental Verbal Abuse Is Associated with Increased Gray Matter Volume in Superior Temporal Gyrus. *Neuroimage*, 2011, vol. 54, pp. 5280-5286.

Van der Kolk, Bessel. *The Body Keeps the Score: Brain, Mind, and Body in the Healing of Trauma.* New York: Penguin Books, 2014.

Warnell, Katherine Rice, Meredith Pecukonis, and Elizabeth Redcay. Developmental Relations Between Amygdala Volume and Anxiety Traits: Effects of Informant, Sex, and Age. *Development and Psychopathology*, 2017, vol. 30(4), pp. 1503-1515.

Chapter Three: How (And Why) We Normalize Abusive Behavior

Carr, Kristen, Amanda J. Holman, Jenna Abetz, Jody Koenig Kellas, and Elizabeth Vagnoni. Giving Voice to the Silence of Family Estrangement: Comparing Reasons of Estranged Parents and Adult Children in a Non-matched Sample. *Journal of Family Communication*, 2015, vol. 15(2), pp. 130-140.

Fincham, Frank D. The Kiss of the Porcupines: From Attributing Responsibility to Forgiving. *Personal Relationships*, 2000, vol. 7(1), pp. 1-23.

Goldsmith, Rachel E., and Jennifer J. Freyd. Awareness for Emotional Abuse. *Journal of Emotional Abuse*, 2005, vol. 5(1), pp. 95-123.

Goldsmith, Rachel E., Jennifer J. Freyd, and Anne P. DePrince. To Add Insight to Injury: Childhood Abuse, Abuse Perceptions, and the Emotional and Physical Health of Young Adults. *Journal of Aggression, Maltreatment, & Trauma*, 2009, vol. 18, pp. 350-366.

Gray, Kurt, and Daniel M. Wegner. The Sting of Intentional Pain. *Psychological Science*, 2008, vol. 19(12), pp. 1260-1262.

Luchies, Laura B., Eli J. Finkel, James K. McNulty, and Madoka Kumashiro. The Doormat Effect: When Forgiving Erodes Self-Respect and Self-Concept Clarity. *Journal of Personality and Social Psychology*, 2010, vol. 98, pp. 734-749.

Mehus, Christopher J., and Megan E. Patrick. Prevalence of Spanking in US National Samples of 35-Year-Old Parents From 1993 to 2017. *JAMA Pediatrics*, 2021, vol. 175(1), pp. 92–94.

Scharp, Kristina M., and Elizabeth Dorrance Hall. Family Marginalization, Alienation, and Estrangement: Questioning the Nonvoluntary Status of Family Relationships. *Annals of the International Communication Association*, 2017, vol. 41 (1), pp. 28-45.

Scharp, Kristina M. "You're Not Welcome Here": A Grounded Theory of Family Distancing. *Communication Research*, 2017, vol. 46, pp. 427-255.

Chapter Four: Effects and Affect: How Verbal Abuse Changes Us

Butler, Lisa D., and Susan Nolen-Hoeksema. Gender Differences in Response to Depressed Mood in a College Sample. *Sex Roles*, 1984, vol. 30(5/6), pp. 331-346.

Chaplin, Tara M., and Amelia Aldao. Gender Differences in Emotion Expression in Children: A Meta-Analytic Review. *Psychological Bulletin*, 2013, vol. 139(40), pp. 735-765.

Coates, Erica E., Tara Dinger, Matthew Donovan, and Vicky Phares. Adult Psychological Distress and Self-Worth Following Child Verbal Abuse. *Journal of Aggression, Maltreatment, & Trauma*, 2013, vol. 22(4), pp. 394-407.

Elliot, Andrew J., and Harry T. Reis. Attachment and Exploration in Adulthood. *Journal of Personality and Social Psychology*, 2003, vol. 85(2), pp. 317-331.

Elliot, Andrew J., and Todd M. Thrash. Approach-Avoidance Motivation in Personality: Approach and Avoidance Temperaments and Goals. *Journal of Personality and Social Psychology*, 2002, vol. 82(5), pp. 804-818.

Elliot, Andrew J., and Todd M. Thrash. The Intergenerational Transmission of Fear of Failure. *Personal and Social Psychology Bulletin*, 2004, vol. 30(8), pp. 957-971.

Fivush, Robyn. Exploring Sex Differences in the Emotional Content of Mother-Child Conversations About the Past. *Sex Roles*, 1989, vol. 20(11/12), pp. 675-691.

Freyd, Jennifer J. *Betrayal Trauma: The Logic of Forgetting Childhood Abuse*. Cambridge, Mass.: Harvard University Press, 1996.

Gemmill, Gary. The Dynamics of Scapegoating in Small Groups. *Small Group Research*, 1989, vol. 20(4), pp. 406-41.

Hagborg, Johan Melander, Inge Tidefors, and Claudia Fahlke. Gender differences in the Association Between Emotional Maltreatment with Mental, Emotional, and Behavioral Problems in Swedish Adolescents. *Child Abuse & Neglect*, 2017, vol. 67, pp. 249-259.

Johnson, Jeffrey G., Patricia Cohen, Elizabeth M. Smailes, Andrew E. Skodol, Jocelyn Brown, and John M. Oldham. Childhood Verbal Abuse and Risk for Personality Disorders During Adolescence and Early Adulthood. *Comprehensive Psychiatry*, 2001, vol. 42(1), pp. 16-23.

Malkin, Craig. *Rethinking Narcissism: The Secret to Recognizing and Coping with Narcissists*. New York: Harper Perennial, 2016.

Mehus, Christopher J., and Megan E. Patrick. Prevalence of Spanking in US National Samples of 35-Year-Old Parents From 1993 to 2017. *JAMA Pediatrics*, published online July 27, 2020. doi:10.1001/jamapediatrics.2020.2197

Nolen-Hoeksema, Susan. and Bonita Jackson. Mediators of the Gender Difference in Rumination. *Psychology of Women Quarterly*, 2001, vol. 25, pp. 37-47.

Orth, Ulrich, and Richard W. Robins. The Development of Self-Esteem. *Current Directions in Psychological Science*, 2014, vol. 23(5), pp. 381-387.

Riggs, Shelley A., and Patricia Kaminski. Childhood Emotional Abuse, Adult Attachment, and Depression as Predictors of Relational Adjustment and Psychological Aggression. *Journal of Aggression, Maltreatment & Trauma*, 2010. vol. 19 (1), pp. 75-104.

Rothschild, Zachary K., Mark J. Landau, et al. A Dual Motive Model of Scapegoating: Displacing Blame to Reduce Guilt or Increase Control. *Journal of Personality and Social Psychology*, 2012, vol. 102(6), pp. 1148-1161.

Sachs-Ericsson, Natalie, Edelyn Verona, Thomas Joiner and Kristopher J. Preacher. Parental Verbal Abuse and the Mediating Role of Self-Criticism in Adult Internalizing Disorders. *Journal of Affective Disorders*, 2006, vol. 93(1-3), pp. 71-78.

Straus, Murray A., and Carolyn J. Field. Psychological Aggression by American Parents: National Data on Prevalence, Chronicity, and Severity. *Journal of Marriage and Family*, 2003, vol. 65, pp. 795-808.

Taillieu, Tamara L., Douglas A. Brownridge, Jitender Sareen, and Tracie O. Afifi. Childhood Emotional Maltreatment and Mental Disorders: Results from a Nationally Representative Adult Sample from the United States. 2016, *Child Abuse & Neglect*, 2016, vol. 59, pp.1-12.

Tronick, Edward, Heidelise Als, Lauren Adamson, Susan Wise, and T. Berry Brazelton. The Infant's Response to Entrapment Between Contradictory Messages in Face-to-face Interaction. *Pediatrics*, 1978, vol. 17(1), pp. 1-13.

Vissing, Yvonne M., Murray A. Straus, Richard J. Gelles, and John W. Harrop. Verbal Aggression by Parents and Psychosocial Problems of Children. *Child Abuse & Neglect*, 1991, vol. 15, pp. 223-238.

Wang, Ming-Te, and Sarah Kenny. Longitudinal Links Between Fathers' and Mothers' Harsh Verbal Discipline and Adolescents' Conduct Problem and Depressive Symptoms. *Child Development*, 2014, vol. 85(3), pp. 908-923.

Weinberg, M. Katherine, Edward Z. Tronick, Jeffrey F. Cohn, and Karen L. Olson, Gender Differences in Emotional Expressivity and Self-Regulation During Early Infancy. *Developmental Psychology*, 1999, vol. 35(1), pp. 175-188.

Chapter Five: Breaking Free: Dynamics and Strategies

Baker, Amy J. L. Reliability and Validity of the Four-Factor Model of Parental Alienation. *Journal of Family Therapy*, 2020, vol. 42, pp. 100-118.

Baker, Amy J. L. The Long-Term Effects of Parental Alienation on Adult Children: A Qualitative Research Study. *The American Journal of Family Therapy*, 2005, vol. 33, pp. 289-302.

Bentley, Caitlin, and Mandy Matthewson. The Not-Forgotten Child: Alienated Adult Children's Experience of Parental Alienation. *American Journal of Family Therapy*, 2020, vol. 48(5), pp. 509-529.

Blake, Lucy. Hidden Voices: Family Estrangement in Adulthood. *University of Cambridge Centre for Family Research/Stand Alone.* http://standalone.org.uk/wp content/uploads/2015/12/HiddenVoices.Final Report.pdf

Bushman, Brad J. Does Venting Anger Feed or Extinguish the Flame? Catharsis, Rumination, Distraction, Anger, and Aggressive Responding. *Personality and Social Psychology Bulletin*, 2002, vol. 28(6), pp. 724-731.

Carver, Charles S., and Eddie Harmon-Jones. Anger Is an Approach-Related Affect: Evidence and Implications. *Psychological Bulletin*, 2009, vol. 135(2), pp. 183-204.

Coleman, Joshua. *Rules of Estrangement: Why Adult Children Cut Ties and How to Heal the Conflict.* New York: Harmony Books, 2020.

Conti, Richard P. Family Estrangement: Establishing a Prevalence Rate. *Journal of Psychology and Behavioral Science*, 2015, vol. 3(2), pp. 28-35.

Evans, Patricia. *The Verbally Abusive Relationship: How to Recognize It and How to Respond.* Adams Media: Adams, Massachusetts, 2010.

Fischer, Agneta, and Catherine Evers. The Social Costs and Benefits of Anger as a Function of Gender and Relationship Context. *Sex Roles*, 2011, vol. 65, pp. 23-34.

Gardner, Richard. *The Parental Alienation Syndrome: A Guide for Mental Health and Legal Professionals.* Cresskill, N.J.: Creative Therapeutics, 1987.

Garfinkel, Sarah N., Emma Zorab, et al. Anger in Brain and Body: The Neural and Physiological Perturbation of Decision-Making by Emotion. *Social Cognitive and Affective Neuroscience*, 2016, vol. 11(1), pp. 150-158.

Gilligan, Megan, Jill Suitor, and Karl Pillemer. Estrangement Between Mothers and Adult Children: The Role of Norms and Values. *Journal of Marriage and Family*, 2015, vol. 77(4), pp. 908-920.

Gilovich, Thomas, and Victoria Husted Medvec. The Experience of Regret: What, When, and Why. *Psychological Review*, 1995, vol. 102(2), pp. 379-395.

Harman, Jennifer J., Edward Kruk, and Denise A. Hines. Parental Alienating Behaviors: An Unacknowledged Form of Family Violence. *Psychological Bulletin*, 2018, vol. 144(12), pp. 1275-1299.

Harman, Jennifer J., Sadie Leder-Elder, and Zeynep Biringen. Prevalence of Adults Who Are the Targets of Parental Alienating Behaviors and Their Impact. *Children and Youth Services Review*, 2019, vol. 106, pp. 1-13.

Houchin, Timothy M., John Ranseen, Phillip A. K. Hash, and Daniel J. Bartnicki. The Parental Alienation Debate Belongs in the Courtroom, Not in DSM-5. *Journal of the American Academy of Psychiatry and the Law*, 2012, vol. 40, pp. 127-131.

Lerner, Harriet. *The Dance of Anger: A Woman's Guide to Changing the Patterns of Intimate Relationships*. New York: William Morrow, 2014.

Meier, Joan S. A Historical Perspective on Parental Alienation Syndrome and Parental Alienation. *Journal of Child Custody*, 2009, vol. 6, pp. 232-257.

Pollack, William. *Real Boys: Rescuing Our Sons from the Myths of Boyhood*. New York: Henry Holt and Company, 1998.

Rittenour, Christine, Stephen Kromka, Sara Pitts. et. al. Communication Surrounding Estrangement: Stereotypes, Attitudes, and (Non)Accommodation Strategies. *Behavioral Sciences*, 2018, vol. 8(10), doi:10.3390/bs8100096

Salerno, Jessica M., and Liana C. Peter-Hagene. One Angry Woman: Anger Expression Increases Influence for Men, but Decreases Influence for Women, During Group Deliberation. *Law and Human Behavior*, 2015, vol. 39(6), pp. 581-592.

Sarkis, Stephanie Moulton. *Gaslighting: Recognize Manipulative and Emotionally Abusive People—and Break Free*. New York: Da Capo Press, 2018.

Scharp, Kristina M., and Elizabeth Dorrance Hall. Family Marginalization, Alienation, and Estrangement: Questioning the Nonvoluntary Status of Family Relationships. *Annals of the International Communication Association*, 2017, vol. 41(1), pp. 28-45.

Scharp, Kristina M., Lindsay J. Thomas, and Christina G. Paxman. "It Was the Straw that Broke the Camel's Back": Exploring the Distancing Processes Communicatively Constructed in Parent - Child Estrangement Backstories. *Journal of Family Communication*, 2015, vol. 15(4), pp. 330-348.

Snyder, Rachel Louise. *No Visible Bruises: What We Don't Know About Domestic Violence Can Kill Us*. New York: Bloomsbury Publishing, 2019.

Chapter Six: Who's to Judge: The Culture and Verbal Abuse

ACLU. Responses from the Field: Sexual Assault, Domestic Violence, and Policing. October, 2015. https://www.aclu.org/sites/default/files/field_document/2015.10.20_report_responses_from_the field.pdf

Beard, Alison, and Bela Karolyi. *Harvard Business Review*, July/August, 2012. https://hbr.org/2012/08/bela-karolyi-on-gold-medal-tea

Clark, Claire D. Tough Love: A Brief Cultural History of the Addiction Intervention. *History of Psychology*, 2012, vol. 15(3), pp. 233-246

Cohen, Bonni, and Jon Shenk, *Athlete A: A Documentary*. A Netflix original.

Dollinger, Judge Richard A., *J.F. v D.F.* 2018 NY Slip Op 51829(U) Decided on December 6, 2018 Supreme Court, Monroe County. Published by New York State Law Reporting Bureau pursuant to Judiciary Law § 431. This opinion is uncorrected and will not be published in the printed Official Reports.

Edmonson, Cole, and Caroline Zelonka. Our Own Worst Enemies: The Nurse Bullying Epidemic. *Nursing Administration Quarterly*, 2019, vol. 43(3), pp. 274-279.

Epstein, Deborah, and Lisa Goodman. Discounting Women: Doubting Domestic Violence Survivors' Credibility and Dismissing Their Experiences. *University of Pennsylvania Law Review*, 2019, vol. 167, pp. 399-462.

Ford, Bonnie D., and Alyssa Roenick. The Gymnastics Factory: The Rise and Fall of the Károlyi Ranch. https://www.espn.com/espn/feature/story/_/id/29235446/the karolyi-ranch-where-us-women-gymnastics-gold-was-forged-price

Green, Lauren. The Medals Keep Piling Up. But at What Cost? *Sports Illustrated*, July/August 2021. https://www.si.com/olympics/2021/07/30/can-usa-gymnastics-be-saved-daily-cover

Lutgen-Sandvik, Pamela, Sarah J. Tracey, and Jess Alberts. Burned by Bullying in the American Workplace: Prevalence, Perception, Degree and Impact. *Journal of Management Studies*, 2007, vol. 44(6), pp. 837-861.

Lutgen-Sandvik, Pamela. The Communicative Cycle of Employee Emotional Abuse: Generation and Regeneration of Workplace Mistreatment. *Management Communication Quarterly*, 2003, vol. 16(4), pp. 471-503.

Macur, Juliet. Olympic Gymnast Recalls Emotional Abuse "So Twisted That I Thought It Couldn't Be Real." https://www.nytimes.com/2020/05/01/sports/maggie-haney-gymnastics-abuse.html

Macur, Juliet. A Gymnastics Coach Accused of Emotional Abuse Speaks Out: "I Cared Too Much." https://www.nytimes.com/2020/11/30/sports/olympics/gymnastics-abuse-laurie hernandez-haney.html

Macur, Juliet. Suspension Reduced for Coach Accused of Emotional and Physical Abuse. https://www.nytimes.com/2020/12/09/sports/olympics/maggie-haney-gymnastics abuse.html?action=click&module=Well&pgtype=Homepage&section=Sports

Martin, William, and Helen LaVan. Workplace Bullying: A Review of Litigated Cases. *Employee Responsibilities and Rights Journal*, 2009, vol. 22, pp. 175-194.

Milliken, Bill, with Char Meredith. *Tough Love*. Old Tappan, New Jersey: Fleming H. Revell Company, 1968.

Moab City Investigative Report. https://moabcity.org/DocumentCenter/View/3432/Combined-Statement-and-Investigative-Report---Petito-Laundrie-Incident

Pearson, Christine M., and Christine L. Porath. On the Nature, Consequences and Remedies of Workplace Incivility: No Time for "Nice"? Think again. *Academy of Management Executive*, 2005, vol. 19(1), pp. 7-18.

Pesta, Abigail. *The Girls: An All-American Town, a Predatory Doctor, and the Untold Story of the Gymnasts Who Brought Him Down*. New York: Seal Press, 2019.

Joseph Petito and Nichole Schmidt v. Christopher and Roberta Laundrie, Court Filing. https://nbc-2.com/wp-content/uploads/2022/03/PETITO-VS-LAUNDRIE.pdf

Katelnn Ohashi: "I Wanted to Bring the Joy Back to Gymnastics." https://www.espn.com/olympics/story/_/id/27498992/katelyn-ohashi-wanted-bring-joy-back gymnastics-body-issue-2019

Solis, Marie. Do "Coercive Control" Laws Really Help Victims? https://www.thecut.com/2021/02/coercive-control-laws-domestic-abuse.html

Stark, Evan. *Coercive Control: How Men Entrap Women in Personal Life*. Oxford University Press: Oxford and New York, 2009.

Stark, Evan, and Marianne Hester. Coercive Control: Update and Review. *Violence Against Women*, 2019, vol. 25(1), pp. 81-104.

Tolmie, Julia R. Coercive Control: To Criminalize or Not to Criminalize? *Criminology & Criminal Justice*, 2017, vol. 18(1), pp. 50-66.

Warshak, Richard A. Ten Parental Alienation Fallacies that Compromise Decisions in Court and in Therapy. *Professional Psychology: Research and Practice*, 2015, vol. 46(4), pp. 235–249.

Warshak, Richard A. When Evaluators Get It Wrong: False Positive IDs and Parental Alienation. *Psychology, Public Policy, and Law*, 2020, vol. 26(1), pp. 54-68.

Williams, Alison. Rates of Depression and Emotional Abuse in Elite United States Synchronized Swimmers. 2019, 10.13140/RG.2.2.25197.92641.

Chapter Seven: Looking Forward: Boundaries and Understanding

Gottman, John. *Why Marriages Succeed or Fail: And How You Can Make Yours Last.* New York: Fireside, 1994.

Madlock, Paul E., and Carrie Kennedy-Lightsey. The Effects of Supervisors' Verbal Aggressiveness and Mentoring on Their Subordinates. *Journal of Business Communication*, 2010, vol. 47(1), pp. 42-62.

Tannen, Deborah. *You're Wearing THAT?: Understanding Mothers and Daughters in Conversation.* New York: Ballantine Books, 2006.

Printed in Great Britain
by Amazon

35769639R00159